Accounts and Audit of Limited Liability Partnerships

Accounts and Audit of Limited Liability Partnerships

Fourth edition

Steve Collings FMAAT FCCA

Bloomsbury Professional

Published by
**Bloomsbury Professional Ltd, Maxwelton House, 41–43 Boltro Road,
Haywards Heath, West Sussex, RH16 1BJ**

© Bloomsbury Professional Ltd 2014

Bloomsbury Professional is an imprint of Bloomsbury Publishing Plc

British Library Cataloguing-in-Publication Data.
A catalogue record for this book is available from the British Library.

ISBN 978 1 84766 991 9

Typeset by Phoenix Photosetting, Chatham, Kent
Printed and bound in Great Britain by CPI Group (UK) Ltd, Croydon, CR0 4YY

Preface

The number of Limited Liability Partnerships (LLPs) that have emerged since the Limited Liability Partnerships Act 2000 came into force in 2001 has increased significantly over the years. This is testament to the flexibility which is offered by the structure of LLPs by maintaining a traditional partnership existence in the ways that profits are shared among members but also offering members the concept of *Limited Liability* which is traditionally afforded to Limited companies; the price to be paid, of course, for such a privilege is the requirement to file, on public record, the LLPs financial statements at Companies House.

Accounting in the United Kingdom and Republic of Ireland is changing extensively – in fact the most significant change in a generation is set to affect the ways in which LLPs will report financial information. The changes come in the form of FRS 102 *The Financial Reporting Standard applicable in the UK and Republic of Ireland* which is mandatory for accounting periods commencing on or after 1 January 2015, although earlier adoption of the standard is permissible.

As a direct consequence of the introduction of FRS 102, the Statement of Recommended Practice (SORP) relating to LLPs *Accounting for Limited Liability Partnerships* had to be revised and this was issued on 15 July 2014. The impact of FRS 102 on all companies and LLPs that fall under its scope can, in certain situations, be fairly significant, affecting many accounting policies and recognition and measurement issues for the financial statements.

It was not surprising that the UK and Republic of Ireland were to experience such a wholesale change in Generally Accepted Accounting Practice (GAAP) – such a project was initiated by the previously known Accounting Standards Board (ASB) several years ago with the intention that the UK and Republic of Ireland would always report under an international-based financial reporting framework. This was evidenced by the ASB's constant efforts to converge UK GAAP to international equivalents and the LLP SORP was amended in May 2006 to reflect changes in GAAP in respect of financial instruments.

In this fourth edition, I have incorporated the specific accounting issues brought about by FRS 102 and included practical examples where considered appropriate to 'bring to life' the theory inherent in accounting standards. FRS 102 essentially modernises the way in which all entities under its scope will account for items, although many of the 'traditional' accounting practices which have been established in the UK and Republic of Ireland for several years have also been carried over into the new UK GAAP (for example valuation of assets under the revaluation model and the option to capitalise borrowing costs). This fourth edition also incorporates new 'Signposts' at the start of each chapter so as to direct users to the relevant sections of the chapter that they need for easier navigation.

Special thanks go to Sarah Laing CTA and David Whiscombe who wrote the chapter on taxation.

I sincerely hope that this book will prove to be a useful reference guide to those dealing with the accounting and auditing issues relating to LLPs and feedback is welcomed via the publishers for future editions of this book.

Steve Collings, FMAAT FCCA
Audit and Technical Director
Leavitt Walmsley Associates Ltd

August 2014

Contents

Contents

Contents

Abbreviations and definitions

ASB	=	Accounting Standards Board
CA 06	=	Companies Act 2006
CCAB	=	Consultative Committee of Accountancy Bodies
EEA	=	European Economic Area
EU	=	European Union
FRC	=	Financial Reporting Council
FRS	=	Financial Reporting Standard (issued by the ASB)
FRSSE	=	Financial Reporting Standard for Smaller Entities
HMRC	=	HM Revenue & Customs
IFRS	=	International Financial Reporting Standard
IGU	=	Income-generating unit
LLP	=	Limited liability partnership
LLPA	=	Limited Liability Partnerships Act 2000
LLPAAR 2008	=	Limited Liability Partnerships (Accounts and Audit) (Application of Companies Act 2006) Regulations 2008
LLP 2001	=	Limited Liability Partnerships Regulations 2001
LMLLPR 2008	=	Large and Medium-sized Limited Liability Partnerships (Accounts) Regulations 2008
SLLPR 2008	=	Small Limited Liability Partnerships (Accounts) Regulations 2008
SORP	=	Statement of Recommended Practice Accounting by Limited Liability Partnerships
SSAP	=	Statement of Standard Accounting Practice (issued by the predecessor body to the ASB)
STRGL	=	Statement of total recognised gains and losses
UITF	=	Urgent Issues Task Force (assists the ASB in providing guidance on specific accounting areas; produces UITF Abstracts)

Table of Statutes

Table of Statutory Instruments

[All references are to paragraph numbers and appendices]

Table of Examples

Chapter 1

The law and practice of limited liability partnerships

SIGNPOSTS

- The Limited Liability Partnerships Act 2000 (LLPA) created the first new major form of legal vehicle available under UK law since the establishment of joint stock companies in 1844 (see **1.1**).

- A limited liability partnership (LLP) is an independent legal entity; it is a body corporate which provides the benefits of a partnership but has a separate legal personality and unlimited capacity to contract (see **1.1**).

- Professional advice should always be sought before transferring an existing entity into an LLP (see **1.1**).

- The LLPA is a short Act of 19 sections but cannot be read in isolation from the regulations which implement the LLPA including the Limited Liability Partnership Regulations 2001 and the Limited Liability Partnerships (Application of the Companies Act 2006) Regulations 2009 (see **1.2**).

- Before an LLP can be incorporated, two or more persons associated with carrying on a lawful business with a view to profit must have subscribed their names to an incorporation document (see **1.3**).

- LLP status is not applicable for certain activities (for example non-profit making activities) (see **1.3**).

- Unlike limited companies, an LLP has no share capital and there is no requirement to file a memorandum and articles of association on incorporation (see **1.3**).

- Form LL IN01 needs to be completed in order to form an LLP (see **1.4**).

- When a new member is appointed to the LLP, form LL AP01 has to be submitted which gives the new member's details and has to be submitted to the Registrar of Companies within 14 days of their appointment (see **1.4**).

- A members' agreement should be drawn up on formation of an LLP which is a private document and does not have to be filed with the Registrar of Companies (see **1.5**).

- The drawing up of the members' agreement should be considered carefully and the importance of seeking professional advice in this respect cannot be over-emphasised (see **1.5**).

- LLPs must have at least two designated members which will have a number of defined responsibilities and duties including the signing of the accounts and filing of those accounts, appointing the auditors and determining their remuneration, making statutory declaration of solvency on a members' voluntary winding up and filing the various statutory returns (see **1.6**).

- Each member is an agent of the LLP and not of each other and an LLP is not bound by anything done by a member dealing with another person if that member has no authority for that act (see **1.7**).

- If a member is liable to a third party (other than another member) as a result of his own wrongful act or omission in the course of business, the LLP is also liable to that person to the same extent as the member (see **1.7**).

- The Supreme Court has recently heard a case and held that members of an LLP are to be classed as 'workers' for the purpose of employment legislation and will receive the same levels of protection as employees if they 'blow the whistle' at work (see **1.8**).

1 INTRODUCTION

1.1 The Limited Liability Partnerships Act 2000 (LLPA) created the first new major form of legal vehicle available under UK law since the establishment of joint stock companies in 1844. The law came into force on 6 April 2001 and the number of LLPs in existence some 13 years later has seen a significant increase, mainly due to the flexibility the LLP structure offers. LLPs were introduced in Northern Ireland in November 2004, with the Limited Liability Partnerships Regulations (Northern Ireland) 2004 implementing the Limited Liability Partnerships Act (Northern Ireland) 2002. The most important feature of the LLP is that it is an independent legal entity – similar to a Limited Liability company which is distinct from its shareholders and is an entity in its own right. An LLP is a body corporate and not a partnership. An LLP, however, provides the benefits of a partnership in that members (who are referred to as 'members' and not 'partners' in the legislation) are free to organise their own internal affairs through a private members' agreement. However, unlike a partnership, an LLP has separate legal personality and unlimited capacity to contract. Members are the agents of the LLP and not of each other. The concept of mutual agency between partners, which results in innocent partners being bound by the acts of fellow partners to the full extent of their personal assets, does not apply to LLPs.

The limitation of members' personal liability will be central to those considering either setting up or transferring their business to an LLP. Its limitations should, however, also be clearly understood and professional advice should always be sought before transferring to an LLP in order to ensure that (a) the requirements are understood, and (b) transferring the partnership to an LLP is appropriate in the business' and partners' interests. Although a member's personal assets should be protected in the event of a catastrophic or 'Armageddon' claim against the LLP to the extent it exceeds the firm's professional indemnity insurance cover and assets, there will still be the need to adopt strict risk management procedures. Professional practices should maintain their indemnity insurance levels and all members will continue (in much the same way as directors in companies) to be personally liable for their own negligent acts and defaults where they have assumed a personal responsibility to a client which has subsequently been relied upon. Where the LLP has client relationships and where it is permitted, terms of engagement should seek to limit personal liability. This is, however, a complex area and legal advice should always be sought.

As a consequence of what was referred to in the House of Lords' debates during the passage of the LLP legislation, as the 'great privilege' of limited liability status, an LLP is required to file accounts with the Registrar of Companies (Companies House) as the price to pay for the affordability of limited liability. Most of the provisions of the Companies Acts in respect of the preparation and filing of accounts are therefore applied to LLPs (see Chapter 2). An LLP can, as a body corporate, also grant charges over its undertakings. In addition, most of the provisions of the Insolvency Act 1986 are also applicable to an LLP.

2   THE LEGISLATION

1.2   The LLPA is a short Act of 19 sections, the longest of which concerns taxation and ensuring that the position in respect of LLPs and taxation is the same as for general law partnerships, as well as providing that there is (subject to various conditions being met) tax neutrality on the transfer of a partnership's business to an LLP.

However, the LLPA cannot be read in isolation from the regulations which implement the LLPA, consisting primarily of the Limited Liability Partnership Regulations 2001 (the 2001 Regulations) and the Limited Liability Partnerships (Application of the Companies Act 2006) Regulations 2009 (the 2009 Regulations).

Parts II to IV of the 2001 Regulations make applicable to LLPs the relevant parts of the Companies Act 2006 (CA 2006) and the 2009 Regulations, the Company Directors Disqualification Act 1986, and the Insolvency Act 1986. Part V of the 2001 Regulations applies provisions of the Financial Services and Markets Act 2000 to LLPs. Part VI sets out a set of default rules which will apply to an LLP in the absence of a members' agreement. For the reasons set out later in this chapter, those forming an LLP would generally be ill-advised to allow themselves to be governed by these default rules.

The 2009 Regulations apply certain provisions of the CA 2006 to LLPs, and seek to harmonise some aspects of the operation of LLPs and companies. Consequently, parts of the CA 2006 governing the formalities of doing business, names and trading disclosures, arrangements and reconstructions, registration of charges, as well as registration and disclosure of members' details, have been applied to LLPs. Some of these, including the disclosure requirements, have imposed new obligations on LLPs and their members.

The provisions of the 2001 Regulations have to be read together with the Schedules attached to them, which set out the modifications to the relevant statutes they apply. Publications are available which incorporate these modifications into the actual body of the legislation, which makes it much easier to understand the necessary detail. The 2009 Regulations, however, consist of consolidated text which can be read with limited reference to the CA 2006.

3   INCORPORATION

1.3   As a result of its corporate status, the incorporation of an LLP follows much the same procedure as the incorporation of a company. The LLPA states that, before an LLP can be incorporated, 'two or more persons associated for carrying on a lawful business with a view to profit' must have subscribed their names to an incorporation document. This is a wider definition than under the Partnership Act 1890, s 1, which defines the relationship between partners as 'persons carrying on business in common with a view of profit'. 'Persons' includes not only individuals but also corporate entities such as another LLP or company. LLPs are not limited to regulated professions, as had originally been the government's intention, and their uses can be extremely varied and are only likely to be prohibited by illegality. However, LLPs are not applicable for certain activities – for example non-profit making activities.

An LLP has no share capital, and there is no requirement to file a memorandum and articles of association on incorporation. There is no LLP equivalent to the model articles of association that can be adopted by a company.

4   FORMING AN LLP

1.4   With the increase in use of technology, an LLP can be formed electronically through appropriate software systems. This has become more popular over recent years and many formation agents (or 'incorporation agents') and software providers have produced their own software which, in certain cases, allows their customers to form their own LLP via the formation agent's website. Information relating to software filing and a list of providers can be found on the Companies House website at www.companieshouse.gov.uk.

To incorporate an LLP via paper, Form LL IN01 has to be completed and delivered to Companies House with a registration fee (currently £40, or £100 for a 'same day' incorporation). The forms can be obtained from the Companies House website at www.companieshouse.gov.uk, and various guidance notes are available. Form LL IN01 requires the name of the LLP which is to be registered, the names and addresses of the members, and specification of which members are to be designated members. The duties and obligations of the designated members, which are much like those of a company secretary, are dealt with later in this chapter.

An LLP cannot have the same name as a registered company or another LLP, and vice versa. It is, however, inadvisable to use a shelf LLP to protect a name, in the way in which shelf companies are used, if the LLP business will be transferred to it by a partnership. This is because the stamp duty and stamp duty land tax rules on the transfer of a partnership's business to an LLP (LLPA, s 12 and Finance Act 2003, s 65) provide an exemption from stamp duty and stamp duty land tax where there is identical membership in the predecessor partnership immediately prior to incorporation of the LLP and in the LLP immediately after transfer to it of the partnership's business. The exemption is, however, only available for a period of 12 months from the date of incorporation of the LLP. In such circumstances, the appropriate route for name protection continues to be the use of a shelf company.

In respect of the members' details which need to be provided to Companies House, a new disclosure regime came into force for LLPs on 1 October 2009. Each member is required to provide a service address to appear on the public record, and a usual residential address which will be kept confidential (although the Registrar of Companies may disclose it to specified bodies in certain circumstances). Both the service address and the residential address may be the same. There is an ongoing duty to notify the Registrar each time the membership of an LLP changes or the personal details of a member change.

Where any new member is appointed to the LLP, Form LL AP01, providing that member's details, has to be submitted to Companies House within 14 days of their appointment. The same applies to the termination of the appointment of a member, the relevant form being LL TM01.

An LLP must also keep a publicly disclosable list of members at its registered office, but this only has to show a service address. A separate register of residential addresses must also be maintained, which is not disclosable to the public.

Form LL IN01 also carries a formal statement of compliance, to be completed either by a member or the solicitor engaged in the formation of the LLP, to the effect that the persons named on the form as members are associated for carrying on a lawful business with a view to profit. The nature of the business does not have to be stated.

The Registrar of Companies will issue a certificate of incorporation to the LLP with its own registered number which begins with the prefix OC3. The detailed rules in respect of the display of a registered company's name and details on business stationery and at its premises apply to LLPs and as a consequence it will be important to register the LLP well in advance of the actual transfer of the business to an LLP so that the necessary details are available for the LLP's stationery and signage.

5   THE MEMBERS' AGREEMENT

1.5   The default rules set out in the 2001 Regulations are unlikely to be suitable for the majority of LLPs. They draw heavily on the Partnership Act 1890, although the LLPA specifically disapplies partnership law to LLPs. The default rules provide, for example, that each member is entitled to share equally in the capital and profits of the LLP, that every member can take part in the management of the LLP, and that the consent of all existing members is necessary before a new member can be admitted. In addition, differences between members concerning ordinary matters connected with the business may be decided by a majority of the members.

For a business of any size or sophistication, these rules will be inappropriate and incapable of providing a workable management structure. Furthermore, the legislation clearly contemplates LLPs regulating their own internal structure and management, and there are various central issues (for example, the application to LLPs of CA 2006, s 994 regarding the protection of minorities from unfairly prejudicial conduct) which are not addressed in the default rules.

The members' agreement is a private document and does not have to be filed at Companies House. As well as dealing with the usual matters found in a partnership agreement, such as management structure, sharing of profits (and losses), admission of members, contribution of capital, the conduct of members and their departure, there are issues unique to LLPs that must be addressed.

These include the powers and duties of the designated members, the preparation, approval and audit of the statutory accounts, the ability and authority to create fixed and floating charges, and the position of any salaried members. One other major issue is the effect of the company insolvency regime being applicable to LLPs. The members' agreement must deal with the effect of a dissolution, either by acts of the members or by virtue of insolvency. Furthermore, unlike in a partnership, it is possible to have a members' voluntary liquidation of an LLP, and the powers of reconstruction set out in the Insolvency Act 1986 apply to LLPs. The legal opinion set out in Appendix 5 of the 2014 version of the LLP SORP in respect of the difference between distribution and allocation of profits (see Chapter 5), means that the profit-sharing mechanism will need to be carefully worded and it is advisable to seek professional advice on this. Whilst the LLP SORP classifies amounts owing to members as either debt or equity, the general principles regarding the distinction between the allocation and division of profits remain unchanged.

Whilst a partnership agreement will often provide the basic structure for a members' agreement, the new, often corporate concepts are technical, and it is fundamentally important to have them correctly drafted and hence the importance of seeking professional input where this is concerned cannot be over-emphasised. The drawing-up of the members' agreement is not a job for the amateur, and the expense of getting it right will stand any LLP in good stead for its commercial future. It will also provide an opportunity for existing partnerships to conduct an extensive review of their current internal arrangements.

6 DESIGNATED MEMBERS

1.6   LLPs have to have at least two designated members, who have a number of defined responsibilities and duties. On incorporation, the LLP will have to state whether all the members are to be designated, or name those who are. This position can be subsequently changed. Companies House must be notified of any changes to the designated members within 14 days of the change, using Form LL CH01. Designated members automatically cease to be designated when they cease to be members. In larger organisations, there will probably be a small group of designated members (ie those who are involved in management and compliance issues) whilst, in the smaller organisation, it may be that each member should assume the role.

The key duties of designated members include the signing (on behalf of members) and filing of the annual accounts, the appointment of the auditors and determining their remuneration, making a statutory declaration of solvency on a members' voluntary winding up, and filing the various statutory returns (for example, the LLP's annual return and the notification to the Registrar of Companies regarding a change in membership in the LLP). There are penalties for breaches of the filing requirements in the form of fines. In most cases, the legislation provides protection for designated members who were not knowingly and wilfully involved in the offence in question, or where they took reasonable steps to avoid an offence occurring.

7 DUTIES AND RESPONSIBILITIES OF MEMBERS

1.7   The relationship between members should be regulated by the members' agreement. As already explained, by virtue of LLPA, s 6(1) each member is the agent of the LLP and not of each other. This is the basis for the protection of members from personal liability in respect of another member's negligence.

Section 6 further provides that an LLP is not bound by anything done by a member dealing with another person if that member has no authority for that act, and that person either knows the member has no authority or does not know or believe the member to be a member of the LLP.

Where a member is liable to a third party (other than another member) as a result of his own wrongful act or omission in the course of the business, then the LLP will be liable to that person to the same extent as the member.

The possibility of a member still being liable for his own wrongful acts and omissions is discussed above. Such remaining personal liability may possibly be excluded by clear terms of engagement between the LLP and its clients and, again, this is an area where those considering converting to LLP status would be well advised to take professional advice.

8 WHISTLEBLOWING PROTECTION

1.8 In a landmark ruling by the UK Supreme Court in 2014, accountants and other professionals who are partners within an LLP and who speak out publicly about wrongdoings within the LLP receive legal protection on the basis that they are classed as 'workers' for the purposes of employment legislation.

Prior to the ruling, partners in LLPs were excluded from legal protection on the grounds that they were not considered to be employees. The ruling follows a three-year legal battle involving a partner at a law firm who was expelled from the partnership after the ex-partner blew the whistle on the managing partner of an associated firm after the managing partner admitted he had paid bribes to secure cases and to secure the outcome of the cases. The firm had tried to prevent a claim by the ex-partner on the grounds that she was not classed as an employee as she had partner status and hence had no protection when she was dismissed for whistleblowing.

The Supreme Court held that members of an LLP are to be classed as 'workers' for the purposes of employment legislation and will receive the same levels of protection as employees if they 'blow the whistle' at work.

The impact of this ruling is likely to be far-reaching and accountants, lawyers and other professionals who are connected with LLPs will have to consider this ruling – particularly where they come across acts of wrongdoing within the LLP.

Chapter 2

General accounting requirements and the LLP SORP

SIGNPOSTS

- Parts 1 to 9 of the Limited Liability Partnerships Accounts and Audit Regulations 2008 deal with the general accounting requirements of LLPs (see **2.1**).

- The size and complexity of the business the LLP undertakes will essentially dictate the level of sophistication of the accounting records maintained by the LLP (see **2.2**).

- Failure to maintain adequate accounting records is an offence and is also a matter which will be referred to in the audit report (see **2.2**).

- Regulations say that accounting records should be maintained for three years from the date on which they are prepared, although tax legislation requires that records be retained for a longer period (see **2.2**).

- For the first period after incorporation, the accounting reference date is the last day of the month in which the anniversary of its incorporation falls (see **2.3**).

- The first accounting period cannot be shorter than six months or longer than 18 months and it is possible to change the accounting reference date (see **2.3**).

- LLPs with subsidiaries should ensure that each subsidiary has a uniform year to that of the parent (see **2.3**).

- The members are responsible for preparing financial statements at the end of each financial year which give a true and fair view of the state of the affairs of the LLP and hence will have to comply with applicable accounting standards (see **2.4**).

- The 2014 SORP identifies certain information which must be included within the members' report (see **2.5**).

- The 2014 SORP was issued on 15 July 2014 and was revised due to the introduction of new UK GAAP (see **2.6**).

- An LLP which is the parent of a group may have to prepare consolidated financial statements in addition to its own separate financial statements (see **2.7**).

- There are certain exemptions from preparing consolidated financial statements (see **2.7** and **2.9**).

- Financial statements must be approved by the members of the LLP and signed on their behalf by a designated member (see **2.8**).

- The designated members are responsible for ensuring that the financial statements are delivered to the Registrar of Companies within nine months of the period-end (different deadlines may apply to an LLP's first accounting period) (see **2.8**).

- There are special provisions which apply to small, eligible LLPs (see **2.9**).

- There are choices available for small LLPs as to what financial information is filed with the Registrar of Companies (see **2.9**).

- In practice there are few differences between the requirements for medium-sized LLPs and those which are large where the abbreviated financial statements are concerned (see **2.10**).

- FRS 102 *The Financial Reporting Standard applicable in the UK and Republic of Ireland* was issued by the Financial Reporting Council (FRC) in March 2013 and replaces all extant FRSs, SSAPs and UITF Abstracts with effect for accounting periods commencing on or after 1 January 2015. FRS 102 will have a significant impact and hence the revised 2014 SORP was issued in July 2014 (see **2.11**).

- There are notable differences between FRS 102 and previous UK GAAP which are likely to affect the way that amounts are recognised and measured (see **2.12**).

1   STATUTORY PROVISIONS

2.1   The general accounting requirements for LLPs are set out in the Limited Liability Partnerships Accounts and Audit Regulations 2008, Parts 1 to 9. These provisions take the Companies Act 2006 (CA 2006), Part 15 (accounts and reports), which deals with the requirements to prepare accounts, and make such modifications as are necessary to deal with the particular circumstances of LLPs. The requirements in relation to the form and content of an LLP's financial statements are contained in the Small Limited Liability Partnerships (Accounts) Regulations 2008 for small LLPs (see below) and Large and Medium-sized Limited Liability Partnerships (Accounts) Regulations 2008 for all other LLPs. With the exception of the rules with respect to filing of accounts considered in **2.8** below, all of the provisions are applicable to accounting periods that began on or after 1 October 2008.

2   REQUIREMENTS TO KEEP ACCOUNTING RECORDS

2.2   The level of sophistication of the accounting records maintained by an LLP will vary dependent on its size and the complexity of the business it undertakes. The legal requirements are that the accounting records must be sufficient to record and explain the LLP's transactions and disclose with reasonable accuracy, at any time, the financial position of the LLP. They must also contain sufficient information to enable accounts to be prepared in accordance with the legislation. Additional requirements may be imposed where an LLP is subject to further regulation, such as LLPs that are authorised by the Financial Conduct Authority. Failure to maintain adequate records is an offence and is also a matter which is required to be referred to in the audit report (see **3.8**). The accounting records are required to be kept at the registered office unless the members consider it appropriate to keep them elsewhere. The members of the LLP have the right to inspect the records at any time. To the extent that the records are held outside the United Kingdom, accounts and returns with respect to those records must be sent to, and retained in, the United Kingdom.

Whilst the regulations require that accounting records be retained for three years from the date on which they are prepared, tax legislation requires that the records be retained for five years and 10 months from the end of the tax year in which the accounting period ends. For example, records relating to accounts prepared for the year ended 30 April 2010 (which falls in the tax year ending 5 April 2011) would need to be retained until 31 January 2017. There may also be other requirements specific to the nature of the business of the LLP (for example, where it has long-term contracts) which would result in a longer period of retention being necessary.

3   ACCOUNTING REFERENCE DATES AND ACCOUNTING PERIODS

2.3   For the first period after incorporation, the accounting reference date of an LLP (ie the date to which the accounts are prepared) is the last day of the month in which the anniversary of its incorporation falls. In the absence of any application to shorten or lengthen the accounting period (see below), the first accounting period will start on the date of incorporation and end on that accounting reference date. The first accounting period cannot be shorter than six months or longer than 18 months. Subsequent accounting periods will then cover a year from the date of the end of the previous accounting period, unless an application is made to amend the accounting reference date.

To make provision for those LLPs who want to prepare their accounts for a 52- (or 53-) week period, accounts may be prepared to a date which is no more than seven days either side of the accounting reference date.

Where an LLP has subsidiary undertakings, the members should ensure that the financial year of each subsidiary coincides with that of the LLP, unless there is a good reason for it not to. For example, where the regulations of an overseas jurisdiction require a different date.

LLPs are able to change their accounting reference dates, subject to certain restrictions. It is possible to change either:

- the current accounting reference period (and subsequent periods); or

- after the end of the immediately preceding accounting period, for that immediately preceding accounting reference period (and subsequent periods), provided that the period for filing accounts (see **2.8**) has not expired.

An accounting reference period cannot be extended beyond 18 months. In addition, an LLP cannot usually extend its accounting period more than once in any five-year period. The exception is where the LLP becomes a subsidiary or parent of another EEA undertaking, and the change is necessary in order to align accounting reference dates across a group.

4 FORM AND CONTENT OF ACCOUNTS

2.4 The members are responsible for preparing, at the end of each financial year, a profit and loss account (income statement/statement of comprehensive income) and a balance sheet (statement of financial position) which give a true and fair view of the state of affairs of the LLP at the end of the financial period and of the profit or loss for that financial period. A report to the members (members' report) is also required. The form and content of the balance sheet, profit and loss account and notes to the accounts are set out in the Small Limited Liability Partnerships (Accounts) Regulations 2008 for small LLPs and Large and Medium-sized Limited Liability Partnerships (Accounts) Regulations 2008 for all other LLPs.

The fact that the accounts of an LLP are required to give a true and fair view means that they also have to comply with all sections of FRS 102 *The Financial Reporting Standard applicable in the UK and Republic of Ireland*. Therefore, where required, they will also need to include a cash flow statement (statement of cash flows) and a statement of changes in equity. Small LLPs may continue using the Financial Reporting Standard for Smaller Entities (FRSSE). However, at the time of writing there was some uncertainty surrounding the future of the FRSSE and so readers are encouraged to review the Financial Reporting Council's website frequently to keep up to date on these developments.

As discussed in more detail in Chapter 5, the SORP also requires disclosure of total members' interests on the face of the balance sheet, as a memorandum item. The LLP SORP has been updated to comply with the provisions in FRS 102 and the revised LLP SORP is effective for periods commencing on or after 1 January 2015 and for any earlier periods in which an entity chooses to adopt FRS 102 and the Financial Reporting Standard for Smaller Entities (FRSSE (effective January 2015)).

Illustrative accounts for large and small LLPs are set out in Appendices 1 and 2 in this book.

5   THE MEMBERS' REPORT

2.5   Whilst the requirements of the Companies Act 2006 (CA 2006) relating to the form and content of the financial statements are largely reflected in the regulations, the requirements with respect to preparing a directors' report and the content thereof are not. However, the SORP does require that a members' report is prepared. The reason for including this requirement within the SORP is that it is considered that the financial statements and notes alone cannot provide all the information about the financial performance of the LLP. Some narrative reporting is required in order to provide complete communication with the users of the LLP's annual report.

The SORP requires that the following are included within the members' report:

- the principal activities of the LLP and its subsidiary undertakings, indicating any significant changes during the year;

- an indication of the existence of any branches outside the UK;

- the identity of anyone who was a designated member during the year; and

- the policy of the LLP regarding members' drawings and the subscription and repayment of amounts subscribed or otherwise contributed by members.

LLPs are not, therefore, required to prepare a Strategic Report or detailed business review required of limited companies, nor make the disclosures in respect of corporate governance required of listed companies. There is, however, an increasing trend, particularly amongst larger LLPs, to provide further information about their businesses, resulting in disclosures that are in practice not dissimilar to those of limited companies. The objective of such disclosures is to make the financial statements more understandable and to aid transparency.

Narrative reporting can provide a good opportunity for the members to further explain matters affecting their financial performance, which are either not adequately dealt with within the disclosure requirements of accounting standards or which cannot be included because they are subjective and incapable of verification by the auditors.

In preparing any additional narrative reporting, members of an LLP need to be mindful that they should not prepare anything that could be construed as misleading by users of the accounts or include any additional information which is unnecessary (ie to reduce 'clutter' within the financial statements). Matters to consider include:

- Ensuring that the report is a reasonably balanced reflection of the LLP's financial performance. It is human nature to focus on what has gone well and to not want to discuss what has not gone quite so well. It is unlikely that a balanced view can be given without giving some consideration to both.

- When discussing the future, this needs to be done in a realistic way in order to avoid users placing undue reliance on what may turn out to be over-optimism.

- Anything that is said in the narrative reporting about the financial position and performance of the LLP must be consistent with what is shown in the financial statements. Any inconsistencies will render the financial statements to be misleading.

- Any numbers that are quoted should be capable of reconciliation to the financial statements.

Auditors are not required to give an opinion on information that is presented with the financial statements, such as the members' report, but they are required to draw attention to any matters referred to that are inconsistent with the financial statements. As a consequence, the auditors will request to see all information that will accompany the financial statements before they sign their audit report.

6   STATEMENT OF RECOMMENDED PRACTICE – ACCOUNTING BY LIMITED LIABILITY PARTNERSHIPS

2.6   The current version of the SORP was issued by the CCAB (the five major accountancy institutes in UK and Ireland) on 15 July 2014 and was revised due to the introduction of a new UK GAAP which saw all extant SSAPs, FRSs and UITF Abstracts being withdrawn and replaced with FRS 102 *The Financial Reporting Standard applicable in the UK and Republic of Ireland*. Development of the SORP is overseen by a steering committee whose membership is drawn from industries and professions whose members are, or are expected to become, LLPs. An exposure draft of a revision to the SORP was issued in October 2013, with a final version issued in July 2014.

Whilst there is no legal requirement to comply with the SORP, non-compliance would need to be reported in the accounts, and it is likely that the non-compliance would result in the accounts not giving a true and fair view. Where the LLP is subject to audit this would result in the audit report being qualified as a result of the non-compliance if the non-compliance is material.

The SORP does not provide details of all of the reporting requirements which are applicable to LLPs, but it does provide interpretation of those accounting standards where there are specific issues regarding their application to the circumstances of an LLP. There is a requirement within the SORP (specifically paragraph 132 *Compliance Statement*) that the note to the financial statements which deals with accounting policies should refer to the LLP's compliance with the SORP, together with any non-compliance and the reasons.

Areas of the financial statements dealt with within the SORP, together with the specific paragraphs which deal with those areas, are as follows:

	Paragraphs
The contents of the annual report and financial statements	25–31
Members' remuneration and interests	32–74B
Retirement benefits	75–94
Taxation	95–99
Inventories	100–101
Business combinations and group accounts	102–119
Provisions and other implications of section 21 of FRS 102	120–127
Related parties	128–131

7   GROUPS

2.7   Where, at the end of the financial period, an LLP is a parent undertaking, both individual and group (consolidated) accounts are required. The LLP is not required to present its own profit and loss account (income statement) as part of those group accounts, but must state that it has taken advantage of the exemption contained in Companies Act 2006 (CA 2006), s 408 (as applied to LLPs), and the profit or loss of the LLP must be disclosed in the notes to the accounts. The profit and loss account is, however, still required to be prepared and approved by the members.

Exemption from the preparation of group accounts is available where the LLP is itself a wholly or majority (greater than 50%) owned subsidiary, and notice has not been served on the LLP by members holding either, in aggregate, more than half of the remaining interest in the LLP, or 5% in total of the interest in the LLP, that they require group accounts to be prepared. The exemption is also conditional on the following:

- The LLP must be included in consolidated accounts prepared by the parent of a larger group and those accounts are either at the same date as the LLP's own accounts or an earlier date in the same financial year.

- Where the parent is established under the law of an EEA State, the accounts of the parent must be prepared either in accordance with the provisions of the Seventh Directive 83/349/EEC or in accordance with EU-endorsed International Financial Reporting Standards.

- Where the parent is not established under the law of an EEA State, the accounts of the parent must be prepared either in accordance with the Seventh Directive or an 'equivalent manner'.

- The parent company's accounts must be audited.

- The LLP must disclose that it is exempt from the requirement to prepare group accounts, together with the name of the parent within whose accounts the LLP is included and, if that parent is incorporated outside the United Kingdom, the country in which it is incorporated.

- Copies of the parent's group accounts have to be filed with the Registrar of Companies (ie Companies House). If they are not in English, a certified translation must be attached.

Exemption from the requirement to prepare group accounts is also available to small groups (see **2.9**).

Subsidiaries may be excluded from consolidation in the following circumstances:

- The amounts are immaterial and, where there is more than one such subsidiary, also immaterial in aggregate.

- Severe long-term restrictions exist which hinder the LLP from exercising its rights over the subsidiary.

- Control by the LLP is only temporary (ie the interest in the subsidiary is held exclusively with a view to resale).

The Limited Liability Partnership Accounts and Audit Regulations 2008 also allows a subsidiary to be excluded from consolidation in circumstances where the information necessary for the preparation of group accounts cannot be obtained without disproportionate expense or delay. This exemption is not, however, permitted by accounting standards, and cannot therefore be used by an LLP if the financial statements are to give a true and fair view.

Chapter 11 discusses some of the practical aspects of preparing group accounts.

8   APPROVAL, PUBLICATION AND FILING OF ACCOUNTS

2.8   The accounts are required to be approved by the members and signed on their behalf by a designated member. This signature must be on the balance sheet. Obtaining the approval of all members can pose potential practical problems because of the large numbers that could be involved. However, use of electronic communication (email, websites, intranets, etc) should considerably simplify the process.

A copy of the accounts together with the audit report (see Chapter 3) is required to be sent to every member no later than the end of the period for filing the accounts with the registrar or, where earlier, the actual date of filing the accounts. The designated members are responsible for delivering the accounts to the Registrar of Companies – in practice, this will most probably be delegated to one person. Delivery to the Registrar has to be within nine months of the period end. Where it is the first accounting period and it covers more than 12 months, the period allowed is nine months from the first anniversary of the date of incorporation, or three months from the end of the accounting reference period, whichever expires last.

9   SPECIAL PROVISIONS APPLICABLE TO SMALL LLPs

2.9   Qualification as a small LLP is based on the requirements in CA 2006. The qualifying conditions, of which two or more have to be met, are as follows:

Turnover	Not more than £6.5 million
Balance sheet total	Not more than £3.26 million
Number of employees	Not more than 50

At the time of writing it had been intimated that the above levels, which also apply to audit exemption, are likely to increase significantly due to changes made in the EU Accounting Directive which was introduced in 2013. Turnover limits are likely to increase to £10 million or more and gross assets is likely to rise up to somewhere in the region of £5 million or more. These amendments are expected to occur in 2016 following a consultation by the Department of Business, Innovation and Skills which was published in August 2014.

Balance sheet total is total assets (fixed and current) before taking into account any of the LLP's liabilities.

Where the period covered by the financial statements is not a year, the turnover limit should be pro-rated.

An LLP qualifies as small in the following circumstances:

- If, in respect of the first financial period, it meets the criteria for that period.

- For subsequent financial years, it may qualify if it meets the criteria in both that year and the previous year, and it met the qualifying criteria in the preceding year.

The provisions do not apply if the LLP was, at any time within the financial period, authorised to undertake insurance business, an e-money issuer, a MiFID investment firm or a UCITS management company, carried on insurance business or it was a member of an ineligible group. An ineligible group is one where any of its members is:

- a public company or body corporate whose shares are admitted to trading on a regulated exchange in an EEA state;

- a banking company;

- an authorised insurance business;

- an e-money issuer;

- a MiFID investment firm or a UCITS management company;

- a person who carries on insurance market activity; or

- an authorised person (other than a small company or small LLP) under the Financial Services and Markets Act 2000.

Where an LLP qualifies as small, it is permitted to prepare its accounts using the requirements set out in the Small Limited Liability Partnerships (Accounts) Regulations 2008 (SLLPR 2008), which reduces the amount of disclosure required within the accounts compared to medium-sized and large LLPs. This is referred to as the 'small LLPs regime'. Where financial statements are prepared in accordance with the small LLPs regime, this fact must be disclosed on the balance sheet above the signature.

A small LLP can choose, however, to comply with the requirements of Large and Medium-sized Limited Liability Partnerships (Accounts) Regulations 2008 (LMLLPR 2008) and make the additional disclosure requirements required under those regulations – although in reality few small LLPs apply the LMLLPR 2008, choosing to take advantage of the reduced disclosures required under the small LLPs regime.

Small LLPs are also able to apply the Financial Reporting Standard for Smaller Entities (FRSSE), should the members consider this to be appropriate. To the extent that there is a conflict between requirements in the FRSSE and those in the SORP, the FRSSE should have precedence. At the time of writing, the future of the FRSSE (effective April 2008) and (effective January 2015) was uncertain in light of the EU Accounting Directive and this will have an impact on the way that small LLPs eventually report if the FRSSE is withdrawn and no decision at the time of writing had been made as to the future of the FRSSE.

A small LLP has a choice as to what financial information is filed with the Registrar of Companies:

- the full financial statements; or

- the balance sheet, the notes thereto, and a copy of the audit report (where one is prepared). Where this option is taken, there must be a statement to this effect on the balance sheet, and the auditors may wish to include a preface to their report explaining that it was issued on the full accounts, all of which have not been filed; or

- abbreviated accounts, the contents of which are specified in SLLPR 2008 and upon which a special auditor's report must be issued if the full accounts (which must also be prepared for members) are subject to audit.

A parent LLP need not prepare group accounts for a financial period if it qualifies as a small group and is not an ineligible group as defined above. The qualification criteria for being a small group are similar to those for individual companies, in that the criteria have to be met:

- in the first financial period, in respect of that period;

- in subsequent periods, in both that period and the preceding period; or

- the group needs to have met the qualifying criteria in the preceding period.

The qualifying conditions are as follows:

Turnover	Not more than £6.5 million net (or £7.8 million gross)
Balance sheet total	Not more than £3.26 million net (or £3.9 million gross)
Number of employees	Not more than 50

Gross figures are the aggregated amounts for the group before eliminating group transactions and balances. Again, it is to be noted at the time of writing that these thresholds are likely to increase in 2016.

10 PROVISIONS APPLICABLE TO MEDIUM-SIZED LLPs

2.10   At the time of writing, qualification as a medium-sized LLP is based on the requirements in CA 2006. The qualifying conditions, of which two or more have to be met, are as follows:

Turnover	Not more than £25.9 million
Balance sheet total	Not more than £12.9 million
Number of employees	Not more than 250

Other qualifying conditions are the same as those for small LLPs.

There are, in practice, very few differences between the requirements for medium-sized LLPs and for those which are large. Whilst medium-sized LLPs may file abbreviated accounts, the exemptions are very limited. Whilst the previous regulations, derived from CA 1985, allowed the profit and loss account to start with the line 'gross profit' and did not require the disclosure of turnover, LMLLPR 2008 permits only the combination of certain expense headings but requires disclosure of turnover, thus removing what was probably one of the main advantages of filing abbreviated accounts.

11 INTERNATIONAL FINANCIAL REPORTING STANDARDS AND INTERACTION WITH NEW UK GAAP

2.11   The Large and Medium-sized Limited Liability Partnerships Regulations 2008 permit the use by LLPs of EU-endorsed International Financial Reporting Standards (IFRS). The SORP does not deal with the application of EU-endorsed IFRS to LLPs and, to date, whilst some large LLPs have chosen to prepare their accounts in accordance with EU-endorsed IFRS, the majority remain with UK GAAP. In September 2012, the Department for Business, Innovation and Skills published the Companies and Limited Liability Partnership (Accounts and Audit Exemptions and Change of Accounting Framework) Regulations 2012 ('the Regulations'). The impact of these changes created a number of new exemptions and widened certain existing exemptions in relation to requirements to prepare, file and audit annual accounts under the Companies Act 2006. Specifically, the Regulations were relaxed for LLPs which prepare accounts under EU-endorsed IFRS and they now allow LLPs to prepare non-IFRS accounts. If the entity preparing IFRS accounts has not, at any time, during the five years before the first day of the relevant financial year, prepared Companies Act/non-IFRS accounts it will be free to switch. Any change during the preceding five years due to a relevant change of circumstance is to be ignored.

The 2012 Regulations came into force on 1 October 2012.

The Financial Reporting Council (FRC) issued FRS 102 *The Financial Reporting Standard applicable in the UK and Republic of Ireland* in March 2013 which replaces all extant FRSs, SSAPs and UITFs with effect for accounting periods commencing on or after 1 January 2015 and the LLP SORP was revised and re-issued in July 2014 for the consequential effects of FRS 102.

FRS 102 is essentially based on the *IFRS For SMEs* which was issued by the International Accounting Standards Board and followed a long consultation by the (now defunct) Accounting Standards Board to overhaul UK GAAP. It had been the intention by the UK and Republic of Ireland standard-setters that the UK would always report under an international-based framework which is what FRS 102 effectively is. FRS 102 overhauls UK GAAP and is regarded as the most significant change in accounting in a generation. Previous UK GAAP had become overly complex in a lot of areas and was considered to be far too voluminous. In contrast to old UK GAAP (at just over 3,500 pages), FRS 102 is 360 pages long and brings with it a modernised way of accounting for many companies and LLPs whilst retaining some of the more established values enshrined in previous UK GAAP (eg use of the revaluation model for fixed assets and the adoption of the 'merger method' of accounting for group reconstructions).

The *Basis for Conclusions* at paragraph BC41 acknowledges that the FRC considers there to be space for supplementary guidance, where relevant, in the form of SORPs. As a consequence, the LLP SORP (as well as many of the other SORPs) had to be updated to bring them in line with FRS 102.

Paragraph BC42 to the LLP SORP acknowledges that whilst many of the changes to the SORP are straightforward and will not affect existing practice, paragraph BC42 does highlight more substantive changes to the SORP following the publication of FRS 102, including:

● Updating the guidance on business combinations and group accounts (paragraphs 102-119) to reflect the fact that FRS 102 only allows merger accounting to be used for group reconstructions and some public benefit entity combinations.

● Updating the guidance on contractual or constructive obligations (paragraph 76) and annuities (paragraph 80) to reflect the fact that FRS 102's requirements relating to financial liabilities differ from previous UK GAAP requirements.

- Updating references throughout to reflect the introduction of the option to produce a single statement of comprehensive income, including an additional exhibit in Appendix 1.

12 THE MAIN DIFFERENCES BETWEEN PREVIOUS UK GAAP AND FRS 102

2.12 Notwithstanding the similarities between the previous UK GAAP and FRS 102, there are some notable differences which are likely to affect the way that amounts are recognised and measured in LLP financial statements and which may need consideration during the transition from UK GAAP to FRS 102 for LLPs.

The notable changes relate to the following issues:

- Accounting policies.
- Defined benefit pension schemes.
- Employee benefits.
- Fixed assets.
- Investment properties.
- Leases.
- Prior period adjustments.
- Revenue recognition.
- Stock valuations.

Accounting policies

2.13 Accounting policies, estimates and errors are covered in Section 10 of FRS 102. Paragraph 10.4 tells financial statement preparers that if FRS 102 does not specifically address a transaction, or other event or condition, an entity's management must develop and apply an accounting policy which is:

- **Relevant** – information is relevant to aid the decision-making process of the users; and

- **Reliable** – will result in the financial statements faithfully representing the financial position, performance and cash flows. In addition, the policy must also reflect the economic substance of the transaction(s)/event(s)/ condition(s) rather than reflecting the legal form. To achieve reliability, the policy adopted must also be neutral, prudent and complete in all material respects.

FRS 18 *Accounting Policies* was very similar, but in some cases the end result and impact on profit or loss would not necessarily have been the same.

Defined benefit pension schemes

2.14 Section 28 *Employee Benefits* at paragraph 28.18 provides a number of simplifications where the valuation basis (the Projected Union Credit Method) would require undue cost or effort. Section 28 does not require the use of an independent actuary to provide a valuation as previous FRS 17 *Retirement Benefits* did. However, the entity must be able to measure its obligation and cost under defined benefit pension plans without undue cost or effort. Therefore, in reality, the vast majority of LLPs will have to use the services of an actuary to arrive at the valuations required to include the defined benefit pension plan within the financial statements.

The SORP acknowledges that the accounting and disclosures will differ depending on whether an LLP's obligation for defined benefit pension obligations falls within the scope of FRS 102 or FRS 103 *Insurance Contracts* and, if the former, depending on whether the obligation falls within the scope of Section 11 *Basic Financial Instruments* or Section 12 *Other Financial Instruments Issues* or Section 21 *Provisions and Contingencies*. Paragraph 76B includes a flowchart which summarises how to determine which guidance applies to a particular obligation.

Employee benefits

2.15 The main issue surrounding this area is the fact that under Section 28 *Employee Benefits*, accruals for short-term employee benefits (eg holiday pay) will have to be made. There was no specific requirement in previous UK GAAP to make such accruals and the difficulty is potentially in the calculation of holiday pay that is to be carried over for future use and pulling this information together for the very first time. This is likely to be time-consuming and cumbersome, particularly for large organisations where there is no central record of this information.

Fixed assets

2.16 Previous FRS 15 *Tangible Fixed Assets* went into a lot of detail about the capitalisation criteria for 'subsequent expenditure'. As a general rule, FRS 15 required subsequent expenditure to be written off to profit or loss unless the expenditure:

- Provided an enhancement of the economic benefits of the asset in excess of the previously assessed standard of performance.

- Related to a component of a tangible asset that had been treated separately for depreciation purposes which was replaced or restored.

- Related to a major inspection or overhaul of the tangible fixed asset that restored the economic benefits of the asset(s) that had been used up by the entity and which had already been reflected in the depreciation charge.

There were several paragraphs dealing with subsequent expenditure in FRS 15. However, FRS 102 does not specifically cover 'subsequent expenditure', but merely states at paragraph 17.15 that day-to-day servicing of property, plant and equipment must be recognised in profit or loss in the periods during which the costs are incurred. Users would therefore be directed to the *Concepts and Pervasive Principles* in Section 2 to FRS 102 to determine whether any subsequent expenditure does, in fact, meet the definition and recognition criteria of an asset outlined at paragraphs 2.15(a) and 2.27(a) and (b).

Paragraph 17.5 deals with 'spare parts and servicing equipment'. Under previous UK GAAP, these were normally carried in the financial statements as stock with recognition taking place as and when such parts/equipment were used in the business. FRS 102 at paragraph 17.5 requires 'major' spare parts and stand-by equipment to be included within the cost of the fixed asset(s) to which it relates when the business is expected to use them for more than one accounting period. The main difference is that FRS 15 did not make reference to 'major spare parts/servicing equipment' and hence the treatment under FRS 102 would essentially mean that the cost of major spare parts/servicing equipment would be recognised within the depreciation charge as opposed to consumption of stock (cost of sales).

Where fixed assets are acquired under deferred payment arrangements (in other words deferred beyond normal credit term), the cost of the asset under FRS 102 must be the present value of all future payments in accordance with paragraph 17.13 of FRS 102. Such issues were not specifically covered in FRS 15 and would mean that under previous GAAP the value of assets would have been under-stated, giving rise to a lower depreciation charge. FRS 102 addresses this issue so that the book value of fixed assets under new UK GAAP will be higher, but this would also have a consequential increase in depreciation charges, thus reducing profitability or increasing losses in an LLP where appropriate.

Investment properties

2.17   SSAP 19 *Accounting for Investment Properties* required such proper-ties to be measured in the balance sheet at their market value, with any changes in this market value going through the revaluation reserve account (ie reported through the statement of total recognised gains and losses).

Paragraph 16.7 to FRS 102 effectively extinguishes the user of the revaluation reserve account and requires all changes in fair value to be recognised in profit or loss. The upshot of this treatment is that reported profit or loss would be different than would otherwise have been the case under previous GAAP.

It is also worth noting that FRS 102 requires fair values to be obtained when obtaining such values can be done without 'undue cost or effort', whereas SSAP 19 did not make this exemption. In FRS 102, if obtaining fair values would result in undue cost or effort, then the entity would account for such properties in accordance with Section 17 *Property, Plant and Equipment* until such time as a reliable fair value of the property becomes available. In reality, the entity would commission a surveyor to undertake the valuation and it is therefore quite difficult to see how obtaining such values for investment property would cause undue cost or effort.

Leases

2.18   Previous SSAP 21 *Accounting for Leases and Hire Purchase Contracts* set out a specific numeric benchmark when determining whether a lease is a finance lease or an operating lease. This benchmark was where the minimum lease payments equated to 90% or more of the fair value of the asset subjected to the lease.

The classification under Section 20 *Leases* does not refer to a 90% benchmark, but instead offers examples of the various situations that individually, or in combination, would give rise to a lease being classified as a finance lease. The classification criteria are found in paragraphs 20.5 and 20.6 and are based upon the risks and rewards of ownership of the associated asset and which party retains those risks and rewards. There are a number of factors which can determine whether risks and rewards of ownership have, or have not, been transferred from lessor to lessee and therefore paragraph 20.7 to FRS 102 acknowledges that the examples in paragraphs 20.5 and 20.6 are not conclusive in every respect and consideration must therefore be given to other indicators that risks and rewards may (or may not) have transferred from lessor to lessee and hence there is more judgement required under FRS 102.

Prior period adjustments

2.19   The difference in this area relates to error correction. Error correction is dealt with in Section 10 *Accounting Policies, Estimates and Errors* (paragraphs 10.19–10.23). Paragraph 10.21 requires an entity to correct an error by way of a prior period adjustment if the error is 'material'. In contrast, FRS 3 *Reporting Financial Performance* required an entity to correct an error by way of a prior year adjustment if the error was 'fundamental'. Fundamental errors were deemed to be those which essentially destroyed the truth and fairness of the financial statements as well as the validity of those financial statements.

The terms 'material' and 'fundamental' could be interpreted differently amongst preparers of financial statements. It is likely, however, that more errors will be corrected by way of a prior period adjustment under FRS 102.

Revenue recognition

2.20   There are some slight variations to the wording relating to the measurement of revenue in Section 23 *Revenue*. For example, in paragraph 23.3, FRS 102 refers to revenue being the fair valuation of the consideration 'received or receivable'. Application Note G to FRS 5 *Reporting the Substance of Transactions* said that a seller would recognise revenue under an exchange transaction with a customer when, and to the extent that, it obtained the 'right to consideration' in exchange for its performance.

This subtle difference in wording could *potentially* allow for later recognition of profit. It is possible that the Financial Reporting Council could issue an Abstract to clarify this point.

Paragraph 23.15 to FRS 102 refers to a 'specific act' and a 'significant act'. The paragraph says that when a specific act is much more significant than any other act, the entity postpones revenue recognition until the significant act is executed. UITF 40 was more prohibitive in that it required revenue to be recognised in line with performance (passing a 'milestone' or the occurrence of a 'critical event') and earning the right to consideration, hence there is more judgement needed in FRS 102.

Paragraph 23.16 of FRS 102 says that if a client cannot estimate the outcome of a service contract then the entity should only recognise revenue to the extent of the costs incurred. In contrast, paragraph 10 to SSAP 9 *Stocks and Long-Term Contracts* said that where the outcome of a long-term contract could not be assessed with reasonable certainty, no profit should be reflected in profit or loss and suggested showing as turnover a proportion of the total contract value using a zero estimate of profit.

Stock valuations

2.21   SSAP 9 *Stocks and Long-Term Contracts* allowed stock to be valued using the 'last-in first-out' (LIFO) method. Whilst this methodology was permissible in SSAP 9, the standard itself acknowledged that there must have been justifiable reasons for its use.

Paragraph 13.18 of FRS 102 follows the same stance as *IFRS for SMEs* which outlaws the use of the LIFO method as a basis of inventory valuation.

Chapter 3

The LLP and auditor relationship

SIGNPOSTS

- Unless covered by exemption, all LLPs are required to appoint auditors and have their accounts audited (see **3.1**).

- Exemption from audit is available for an LLP that qualifies as a small LLP (see **3.2**).

- ⸳ LLPs which do not have an audit are still required to file their financial statements with the Registrar of Companies (see **3.2**).

- It is the members' responsibility to prepare financial statements which give a true and fair view (see **3.3**).

- There are a range of matters which the auditors are required to communicate with the members of the LLP throughout the entire audit process (see **3.4**).

- An engagement letter should be in place between the LLP and the audit firm which sets out the terms on which the auditor will act and explains the respective responsibilities of the members and the auditor (see **3.5**).

- The 'preconditions' for an audit must be present before the auditor can accept engagement or reappointment as auditor (see **3.5**).

- The auditor may seek representations from the members during the course of the audit, which is usually in written form, and there are certain specific representations which the auditor must obtain to comply with the International Standards on Auditing (UK and Ireland) (see **3.6**).

- Any deficiencies in internal control should be brought to the attention of the members (see **3.7**).

- At the end of the audit process, the auditor will produce an audit report on the financial statements which contains the auditor's opinion as to whether the financial statements give a true and fair view and have been properly prepared in accordance with the financial reporting framework and legislation. There are certain elements that the audit report must contain (see **3.8**).

- Auditors also have to report on certain matters by exception (see **3.8**).

- There may be additional reports needed covering an LLP's compliance with certain regulations which is required to be supplied to regulators and the format is usually specified by relevant legislation (see **3.9**).

- If a third party is required to be provided with reports on certain aspects of the LLP's financial information, the auditor may require the third party to be included in the engagement letter before it will report to them (see **3.10**).

- Legislation and certain protocol have to be complied with if an LLP wishes to remove or change its auditors, or if the auditor wishes to vacate office (see **3.11**).

- Regulatory bodies (such as the auditor's professional body) may also have to be notified when the auditor vacates office (see **3.11**).

- A statement of circumstances must be lodged with Companies House within 14 days of the auditor vacating office (see **3.11**).

1 GENERAL REQUIREMENT TO APPOINT AUDITORS

3.1 The requirements with respect to audit are set out in Parts 10 to 14 of the Limited Liability Partnerships Accounts and Audit Regulations 2008.

Unless entitled to the exemptions set out below, all LLPs are required to appoint auditors and have their accounts audited. For the first accounting period, auditors must be appointed no later than 28 days from the time allowed for sending out copies of the LLP's accounts to members (see **2.8**). Thereafter, the regulations require appointment or reappointment for the subsequent year's audit to be made no later than 28 days after the date upon which the financial statements are required to be filed with the Registrar of Companies (Companies House) or, if earlier, the date on which the previous year's financial statements are sent to members. However, where it is intended that the auditors for the previous financial year should stay in office, no action is required, as the regulations permit the auditors to be deemed as reappointed, unless:

- the members' agreement requires actual reappointment; or

- members representing at least 5% of total voting rights in the LLP give notice that the auditor should not be reappointed; or

- the members have determined the auditor should not be reappointed; or

- the designated members have determined that no auditor should be appointed for the financial year in question.

2 EXEMPTION FROM AUDIT

3.2 Exemption from audit is available for an LLP that both qualifies as a small LLP in respect of a particular financial year (see **2.9**) and which has turnover of less than £6.5 million and a balance sheet total (total assets before taking account of liabilities) that does not exceed £3.26 million (note – at the time of writing, these limits were set to be increased to around £10 million for turnover and around £5 million total assets potentially in 2016). Audit exemption, however, is not available where the LLP:

- has securities admitted for trading on a regulated market in an EEA state;

- is an authorised insurance company, a banking LLP, an e-money issuer, a MiFID investment firm or UCITS management company;

- is carrying on insurance market business;

- is an employers' association as defined in section 122 of the Trade Union and Labour Relations (Consolidation) Act 1992; or

- is a parent or a subsidiary unless:

  - throughout the financial period in which it was a subsidiary, it was dormant; or

  - it is a parent or subsidiary in a small group (see **2.9**) for the definition of a small group). In addition, the group's aggregate turnover should not be more than £6.5 million net (or £7.8 million gross) and the group's aggregate balance sheet total should be no more than £3.26 million net (or £3.9 million gross). It should be noted that the rules with respect to groups require all worldwide interests to be taken into account and not just the UK position. (Note – at the time of writing these limits were being reviewed with a view to them being increased in 2016.)

An LLP which is exempt from audit is still required to file accounts with the Registrar of Companies and must also circulate a full set of the accounts to each member.

Entitlement to the exemption is dependent on inclusion on the balance sheet of the statement set out below, which must be inserted immediately above the signature of the designated member(s):

'For the financial year ended [insert year-end date], the LLP was entitled to exemption from audit under section 477 Companies Act 2006 (as applied to LLPs). The members acknowledge their responsibilities for ensuring that the LLP keeps accounting records which comply with section 386 of the Act (as applied to LLPs) and for preparing accounts which give a true and fair view of the state of affairs of the LLP as at the end of the financial year and of its profit or loss for the financial year in accordance with the requirements of section 394 and 395 (as applied to LLPs) and which otherwise comply with the requirements of the Companies Act 2006 (as applied to LLPs) relating to accounts, so far as applicable to the LLP.'

3   RESPONSIBILITIES OF MEMBERS AND AUDITORS

3.3   As noted at **1.6** the members of the LLP have ultimate responsibility for preparing accounts that give a true and fair view. This responsibility remains the same, even in circumstances where the audit firm may have been engaged to assist in the preparation of those accounts.

4   COMMUNICATION BETWEEN THE AUDITOR AND THE LLP

3.4   UK and Ireland International Standards on Auditing require auditors to communicate with the members of the LLP on a range of matters throughout the audit process, including:

●   the terms under which the auditor will act for the LLP, including the respective responsibilities of the auditors and the LLP (see below);

●   any relationships between the LLP and the audit firm that may affect, or be perceived to affect, the audit firm's independence;

●   the nature and scope of the audit work to be performed;

●   the findings from the audit, including:

—   the auditor's views about the qualitative aspects of the LLP's accounting practices;

—   the written representations the auditor will be requesting from management and, where applicable, those charged with governance, in respect of the audit (see **3.6**);

—   the extent of uncorrected misstatements found during the course of the audit;

—   any expected modifications to the audit report; and

—   material weaknesses in internal controls identified during the audit.

5   TERMS OF ENGAGEMENT

3.5   ISA (UK and Ireland) 210 *Agreeing the terms of audit engagements* sets out the requirements for the auditor and the LLP to agree the terms on which the auditor will act. Ordinarily the terms will be agreed in the form of an engagement letter which will be signed by both parties. The auditor must review the terms of the engagement letter at the commencement of each audit (ie annually) and determine whether the engagement letter should be updated or the LLP reminded of the engagement terms. Appendix 1 to this chapter provides an illustrative letter of engagement in respect of an audit assignment (note – this illustrative engagement letter is not definitive).

The engagement letter issued by the auditor sets out the terms on which the auditor will act and also establishes, in writing, the respective responsibilities of auditors and members. Where the audit firm is to provide other services in addition to the audit (for example, taxation advice), to the extent that these services are also of a recurring nature, they may be included in the same letter or may be the subject of a separate letter dependent on the procedures of the audit firm – in practice many firms issue separate letters to cover such circumstances so that the audit engagement is clearly separate. It is not unusual for the same firm in addition to provide services to individual members (for example the completion of a member's self-assessment income tax return). Such services will be covered by separate letters of engagement between the audit firm and the individual member.

As well as detailing the services being provided, the engagement letter will also set out the limitations in the audit process and it is essential that the members understand the scope of the services being provided. The audit firm will ask that a designated member sign a copy of the letter confirming, on behalf of all members, that they understand and agree with the terms.

ISA (UK and Ireland) 210 requires the auditor to ensure that the 'preconditions' for the audit are present before acceptance of the audit engagement. To ensure that the preconditions are present, the auditor shall:

- establish if the financial reporting framework used in preparation of the LLP's financial statements is acceptable; and

- obtain the members' agreement that they acknowledge and understand their responsibility:

  — to prepare the financial statements in accordance with the applicable financial reporting framework including, where relevant, their fair presentation;

  — for such internal control as the members' deem necessary to enable the LLP's financial statements to be prepared free from material misstatement, whether such misstatement is due to fraud or error; and

  — to provide the auditor with:

    1. access to all the information of which the members are aware which is relevant to the preparation of the financial statements;

    2. any additional information which the auditor may request from management for the purposes of the audit; and

    3. unrestricted access to persons within the entity from whom the auditor determines it is necessary to obtain audit evidence.

Example – preconditions not present

An audit firm has been approached by ABC Partnership LLP to audit the LLP's financial statements for the year-ended 31 December 2014. Discussions with the members and the auditor have taken place and during that discussion the designated members refused permission for the auditor to have unrestricted access to anyone within the entity (other than the designated members) to obtain audit evidence as the designated members did not want any other individuals within the LLP discussing financial issues with the auditors.

In this scenario the preconditions for an audit are not fully present because unrestricted access to persons within the entity from whom the auditor determines it is necessary to obtain audit evidence has been refused.

In such cases paragraph 8 to ISA (UK and Ireland) 210 says that the auditor has to discuss the matter with management (ie obtain reasons why access is restricted). Once discussions have been entered into and the preconditions are still not present, the auditor must not accept the proposed audit engagement.

The recurring nature of the audit appointment means that it may not be necessary to reissue the letter of engagement every year. However, as part of their annual planning process, the auditors will reconsider the content of the letter and decide whether it is necessary to reissue it. This may be required where there is a significant change of management, a significant change in the membership of the LLP, or a change in any relevant legal or professional requirements. An important point to emphasise is that regulatory bodies which inspect the audit quality of audit firms must be satisfied that the letter of engagement is up-to-date – many audit firms are criticised for failing to have an up-to-date letter of engagement and in some rarer cases firms are criticised for failing to have a letter of engagement on file at all.

6   WRITTEN REPRESENTATIONS

3.6   Some of the evidence obtained by the auditors will come in the form of oral representations from the management of the LLP. In order to clarify understanding of these representations and to enable the auditors to fully document the evidence upon which their opinion is based, the auditors will request written confirmation prior to the audit report being signed. The written representation most usually takes the form of a representation letter to the auditors signed on behalf of the LLP by a designated member or members. However, on occasions it may be a letter from the auditors outlining their understanding of the representations received, which is then acknowledged and confirmed in writing by the members.

ISA (UK and Ireland) 580 *Written representations* deals with the auditor's responsibilities to obtain written representations from the LLP. This UK and Ireland ISA requires the auditor to ask for a written representation from the appropriate members that they acknowledge their responsibility for the financial statements and that the members have discharged their responsibility for the preparation of the financial statements in accordance with the applicable financial reporting framework including, where relevant, their fair presentation.

3.6 *The LLP and auditor relationship*

In addition, ISA (UK and Ireland) 580 requires written confirmation from the members of the LLP regarding the following:

- That the members have provided the auditor with all relevant information and access as agreed in the terms of the audit engagement.

- That all transactions have been recorded and are reflected within the LLP's financial statements.

- That the members acknowledge their responsibility for the design and implementation of controls to prevent and detect fraud and that they have disclosed to the auditors their knowledge of fraud or suspected fraud.

- That the members have disclosed to the auditors any events that involve possible non-compliance with the laws or regulations, providing the legal framework within which the LLP conducts its business and which are central to the LLP's ability to conduct its business.

- That information provided regarding the related party and control disclosures in the financial statements is complete. (See **9.37–9.42** for a further discussion of related parties.)

- An explanation of the reasons for not adjusting any misstatements brought to the attention of the members by the auditors.

- The members' assessment of whether the LLP is a going concern (see Chapter 10).

- These confirmations would usually be included in the written representation.

Appendix 1 to ISA (UK and Ireland) 580 contains a list of paragraphs within other UK and Ireland ISAs which the auditor should obtain specific representations, including:

- ISA (UK and Ireland) 240 *The Auditor's Responsibilities Relating to Fraud in an Audit of Financial Statements* – paragraph 39.

- ISA (UK and Ireland) 250 *Consideration of Laws and Regulations in an Audit of Financial Statements* – paragraph 16.

- ISA (UK and Ireland) 450 *Evaluation of Misstatements Identified During the Audit* – paragraph 14.

- ISA (UK and Ireland) 501 *Audit Evidence – Specific Considerations for Selected Items* – paragraph 12.

- ISA (UK and Ireland) 540 *Auditing Accounting Estimates, Including Fair Value Accounting Estimates, and Related Disclosures* – paragraph 22.

- ISA (UK and Ireland) 550 *Related Parties* – paragraph 26.

- ISA (UK and Ireland) 560 *Subsequent Events* – paragraph 29.

- ISA (UK and Ireland) 570 *Going Concern* – paragraph 16(3).

- ISA (UK and Ireland) 710 *Comparative Information – Corresponding Figures and Comparative Financial Statements* – paragraph 9.

An example written representation letter is shown in Appendix 2 to this chapter.

7   MATERIAL WEAKNESSES IN INTERNAL CONTROL

3.7   The communication of material weaknesses is usually in the form of a letter of recommendation (often referred to as a management letter or letter of comment) to the LLP. The LLP will usually be requested to include the extent of any action they intend to take as a consequence of the letter of recommendation.

The communication from the auditor will also explain that it is restricted to those matters that come to the attention of the audit firm during the course of their work, and that the audit is not designed to identify all matters that may be of relevance to the members of the LLP.

ISA (UK and Ireland) 265 *Communicating deficiencies in internal control to those charged with governance and management* is appropriate where the auditor has discovered deficiencies within internal control and considers it appropriate that such deficiencies warrant the attention of management and those charged with governance of the entity. 'Significant deficiencies' in internal control must be communicated to those charged with governance and paragraph 6(b) to ISA (UK and Ireland) 265 says that a deficiency is significant when, in the auditor's professional judgement, such a deficiency is of sufficient importance that it warrants the attention of those charged with governance.

A deficiency in internal control exists when the control(s) present will not prevent, detect or correct misstatements arising in the financial statements on a timely basis. This can also be the case when a misstatement(s) arises in the financial statements and necessary controls are missing.

Example – missing internal controls

A firm of accountants operates as an LLP and the financial statements for the year-ended 31 March 2015 are currently being audited. Analytical review procedures have been adopted by the auditor and these have highlighted a disproportionate increase in payroll costs for the accountancy firm which was not expected. The payroll charge has been disaggregated into each respective month and it was noted that for the last six months of the financial year the payroll costs have increased significantly, but staff numbers have remained consistent.

Additional audit procedures have been undertaken which has revealed that two audit teams have claimed overtime payments each month. Examination of the time sheets for each audit team member have been scrutinised and these reveal no additional overtime has been undertaken. A discussion with the payroll supervisor indicates that the audit team merely emails their overtime each month and this is included in the payroll by the payroll supervisor. There are no checks undertaken by the partners of the accountancy firm on either the payroll or the overtime worked by the audit teams.

The controls that should be present (ie authorisation of overtime and authorisation of the payroll by a senior official) are not present. Such overtime claims by the audit teams in this example could be indicative of a fraud risk factor and such matters should be brought to the attention of those charged with governance of the LLP.

---

8   THE AUDIT REPORT

3.8   The audit report is generally the only output of an external statutory audit which the members receive. ISA (UK and Ireland) 700 *The independent auditor's report on financial statements (Revised June 2013)* establishes the form and content of the auditor's report on the LLP financial statements. The report itself will contain certain elements as follows:

- **Title:** It will have an appropriate title to distinguish the audit report from other reports in the LLP's financial statements.

- **Addressee:** It will be appropriately addressed to the members' of the LLP.

- **Introductory paragraph:** The report will identify the financial statements of the LLP which have been audited, including the date of, and period covered by, the financial statements.

- **Respective responsibilities of members and auditors:** This will make reference to the fact that the members are responsible for the preparation of the financial statements and reference that it is the auditor's responsibility to audit and express an opinion on the LLP's financial statements in accordance with applicable legal requirements and UK and Ireland ISAs. The auditor's report must also make reference to the requirement for the auditor to comply with ethical standards.

- **Scope of the audit:** The auditor's report should include a description of the scope of the audit by either cross-referencing to the appropriate version of a *Statement of the Scope of an Audit* maintained on the FRC's website or cross-referencing to a statement contained elsewhere in the financial statements or including the scope verbatim from ISA (UK and Ireland) 700 at paragraph 16(c).

- **Opinion:** The opinion paragraph clearly states the auditor's opinion on the financial statements.

- **Opinion on other matters:** An auditor's opinion on the other reporting responsibilities is set out in a separate section of the auditor's report following the opinion(s) on the financial statements. If the auditor is required to report on matters by exception, such matters will be reported on under the heading *'Matters on which we are required to report by exception'* and incorporate a suitable conclusion in respect of such matters.

- **Date of the audit report:** This is the date on which the auditor signed the report expressing an opinion on the LLP's financial statements. The date of the auditor's report cannot be earlier than the date on which all other information contained in a report of which the audited financial statements form a part have been approved by the members and the auditor has considered all necessary available evidence.

- **Location of auditor's office:** The auditor's report shall contain the location of where the auditor is based.

- **Auditor's signature:** The auditor's report is to be signed in the name of the auditor and dated. Legislation requires that audit reports have to identify the 'senior statutory auditor', who is the person within the audit firm who takes overall responsibility for the audit. Where the auditor is a firm, the senior statutory auditor will sign the audit report on the set of financial statements for the LLP in his or her own name, for and on behalf of the firm. The audit report on other copies of the financial statements, including those for filing with the Registrar of Companies and distribution to members, will have the name of the senior statutory auditor included but will not be signed in their own name.

In addition to reporting on whether the accounts of the LLP give a true and fair view, there are certain other matters which legislation requires auditors to report on by exception. These are as follows:

- Whether adequate accounting records have been maintained.

- Whether the accounts are in agreement with the accounting records and returns.

- Whether the auditors have obtained all of the information and explanations which they consider to be necessary to enable them to perform their audit.

Where the content of any other information accompanying the financial statements including the members' report is inconsistent with the accounts, the auditors may decide that this should be referred to in their audit report.

Auditors are also required to report on the circumstances when financial statements do not comply with applicable accounting standards and the SORP, unless the departure is considered necessary in order for the accounts to give a true and fair view and the accounts contain adequate disclosure of the reasons for the departure.

9   REGULATORY REPORTS REQUIRED FROM AUDITORS

3.9   In some sectors, for example financial services, additional reports covering an LLP's compliance with regulations are required to be given by the auditors to the regulators. The format of these reports is usually specified by the relevant legislation and, to the extent that it is of a recurring nature, will be covered in the letter of engagement.

In certain regulated businesses, legislation places a duty on auditors to report certain rule breaches, sometimes without the prior knowledge of the entity concerned. Such circumstances will usually be referred to in the terms of engagement.

10   REPORTING TO THIRD PARTIES

3.10   From time to time, third parties may request auditors to provide reports on certain aspects of the financial information of an LLP. The request may come from a trade body (for example the Civil Aviation Authority), a government department (for example, in relation to a grant application), and a whole range of other possible parties. Provision of such reports goes beyond the statutory duties of an auditor and will always require additional terms of engagement to be agreed.

Dependent on the precise nature of the report, the audit firm may require the third party to be included in the engagement letter before it will report to them. Alternatively, the audit firm may carry out the assignment directly for the LLP and only allow the third party access to the report after receiving confirmation that the auditors owe no duty of care to that third party.

11   CHANGES IN AUDIT APPOINTMENT

3.11   The procedures surrounding the changes in audit appointment mirror those contained in Part 16, Chapter 4 of the Companies Act 2006 (CA 2006) *Removal, Resignation, etc of Auditors* with respect to company audit appointments.

A resigning auditor is required to deposit a written notice of resignation at the registered office of the LLP. The notice of resignation must also be accompanied by a statement setting out any circumstances surrounding the resignation which the auditor considers should be brought to the attention of the members or creditors of the LLP or, where there are no such circumstances, a statement to that effect. A copy must also be lodged with Companies House no later than 14 days following its issuance.

Where the notice of resignation was accompanied by a statement of circumstances, the auditor may lodge, together with his notice of resignation, a requisition calling on the designated members to convene a meeting of the LLP to consider the explanation of the circumstances surrounding the resignation.

The designated members may remove an auditor and appoint a replacement by giving at least seven days' notice to the incumbent auditor. The auditor is entitled to make representations in writing to the LLP and may ask for those representations to be circulated to members. Notice is required to be given to the Registrar of Companies on the prescribed form, which can be obtained from Companies House, within 14 days.

Additional notification requirements are also placed upon both the auditor and the LLP, irrespective of the reason the auditor ceased to hold office. The requirements, which again mirror those in CA 2006, are for the 'appropriate audit authority' to be informed of the change in appointment. Who the appropriate audit authority is, and whether notification is required, will depend upon whether or not the LLP is a 'major audit client'.

Whilst the term 'major audit client' is used in LLPAAR 2008, there is no definition. Determination of the types of entity that will fall within the definition has been left to the Professional Oversight Team (POT). The parameters are primarily by reference to turnover and external debt, and are subject to regular updating.

Where the LLP is a major audit client, the appropriate audit authority is the POT and, where it is not a major audit client, the appropriate audit authority is the supervisory body of the audit firm (eg ICAEW, ACCA).

Notification is always required when the LLP is a major audit client and, for other LLPs, it is required in circumstances where the auditor ceases to hold office before the end of his term of office.

The notification is required to include a copy of the auditor's statement to the LLP in relation to the circumstances surrounding their resignation or removal. Where there were no circumstances that are needed to be brought to the attention of members or creditors, the notification to the appropriate audit authority should explain the reason for the change. In the case of major audit clients, notification is required at the same time as the auditor deposits their resignation statement with the LLP. For other LLPs, the period of notification is set by the supervisory body.

The requirements placed upon the LLP are similar to those relating to the auditor, with the necessary notifications being required no later than 14 days after the auditors' statement is deposited with the LLP.

APPENDIX 1 – EXAMPLE AUDIT LETTER OF ENGAGEMENT

3.12   The following engagement letter is an illustrative letter only and is not to be taken as definitive. Each engagement is different and will inherently require tailored terms.

The members of An LLP

Dear Members,

We are pleased to accept the instruction to act as auditors for your limited liability partnership (LLP) and are writing to confirm the terms of our appointment.

The purpose of this letter together with the attached terms and conditions is to set out our terms for carrying out the work and to clarify our respective responsibilities.

We are bound by the ethical guidelines of [name of professional body], and accept instructions to act for you on the basis that we will act in accordance with those ethical guidelines. A copy of these guidelines can be viewed at our offices on request or can be seen at [insert website URL].

1   Period of Engagement

1.1   This letter is effective from [insert date].

1.2   It replaces our letter dated [insert date]. The previously agreed commencement date for this engagement still applies.

1.3   We will not be responsible for earlier periods. The partnership's previous accountants, [insert name of accountants], will deal with outstanding returns, assessments and other matters relating to earlier periods and will agree the position with the relevant authorities.

2   Scope of services to be provided

2.1   Our audit will be made with the objective of expressing an opinion on the financial statements.

3   Our responsibility to you

3.1   We have set out the agreed scope and objectives of your instructions within this letter of engagement. Any subsequent changes will be discussed with you and, where appropriate, a new letter of engagement will be agreed. We shall proceed on the basis of the instructions we have received from you and will rely on you to tell us as soon as possible if anything occurs which renders any information previously given to us as incorrect or inaccurate. We shall not be responsible for any failure to advise or comment on any matter which falls outside the specific scope of your instructions. We cannot accept any responsibility for any event, loss or situation unless it is one against which it is the expressed purpose of these instructions to provide protection.

4   Your responsibility to us

4.1   The advice that we give can only be as good as the information upon which it is based. Insofar as that information is provided by you, or by third parties with your permission, your responsibility arises as soon as possible if any circumstances or facts alter as any alteration may have a significant impact on the advice given. If the circumstances change therefore or your needs alter, advise us of the alteration as soon as possible in writing.

5   Statutory responsibilities

5.1   As members, you are required by statute to prepare accounts (financial statements) for each financial year which give a true and fair view of the state of affairs of the LLP and of its profit or loss for that period. In preparing those accounts you must:

(a)   Select suitable accounting policies and then apply them consistently;

(b)   Make judgements and estimates that are reasonable and prudent; and

(c)   Prepare the accounts on the going concern basis unless it is not appropriate to presume that the partnership will continue in business.

5.2   It is your responsibility to keep proper accounting records which disclose with reasonable accuracy at any particular time the financial position of the LLP. It is also your responsibility to safeguard the assets of the LLP and for taking reasonable steps for the prevention of and detection of fraud and other irregularities with an appropriate system of internal controls.

5.3   You are also responsible for making available to us, as and when required, all the LLP's accounting records and all other relevant records and related information, including minutes of all members' meetings.

5.4   The intended users of the report are the members. The report will be addressed to the members.

5.5   As independent auditors we will report to you whether in our opinion the accounts of the LLP which we have audited give a true and fair view of the state of the partnership's affairs, and of the profit or loss for the year, and whether they have been prepared in accordance with the Limited Liability Partnership Act 2000, Limited Liability Partnership Regulations 2008, Statement of Recommended Practice and Companies Act 2006. In arriving at our opinion we are required to consider the following matters, and to report on any in respect of which we are not satisfied:

(a)   Whether proper accounting records have been kept by the LLP and proper returns adequate for our audit have been received from branches not visited by us.

(b)   Whether the LLP's balance sheet and profit and loss account are in agreement with the accounting records and returns;

(c)   Whether we have obtained all the information and explanations which we think necessary for the purpose of our audit; and

(d)   Whether the information in the members' report is consistent with that in the audited accounts.

5.6   We have a professional duty to report if the accounts do not comply in any material respect with applicable accounting standards (UK GAAP) and the Statement of Recommended Practice, unless in our opinion the non-compliance is justified in the circumstances. In determining whether or not the departure is justified we consider whether:

(a)   The departure is required in order for the accounts to give a true and fair view; and

(b)   Whether adequate disclosure has been made concerning the departure.

5.7   Our professional responsibilities also include:

(a)   Stating in our report a description of the members' responsibilities for the accounts, where the accounts or accompanying information do not include such description; and

(b)   Considering whether other information and documents contained in audited accounts is consistent with those accounts; and

(c)   Reporting to you on a timely basis in respect of any issues, such as material weaknesses in your accounting system, which we feel need to be brought to your attention.

5.8   Should you instruct us to carry out any alternative report then it will be necessary for us to issue a separate letter of engagement.

6   Our service to you

6.1   We will conduct our audit in accordance with International Standards on Auditing (UK and Ireland). Those standards require that we plan and perform the audit to obtain reasonable assurance about whether the financial statements are free from material misstatement whether caused by fraud or error. An audit includes examining, on a test basis, evidence supporting the amounts and disclosures in the financial statements. An audit also includes assessing the accounting principles used and significant estimates made by management, as well as evaluating the overall financial statement presentation.

6.2   When undertaking the assignment we will take due consideration of the contents of the partnership agreement or where one does not exist with the Partnership Act 1890.

6.3   Because of the test nature and other inherent limitations of an audit, together with the inherent limitations of any accounting and internal control system, there is an unavoidable risk that even some material misstatements may remain undiscovered.

6.4   In addition to our report on the financial statements, we expect to provide you with a separate letter concerning any material weaknesses in accounting and internal control systems which come to our notice.

6.5   Our auditing procedures will be carried out in accordance with the International Auditing Standards (UK and Ireland) issued by the Financial Reporting Council, and will include such tests of transactions and of the existence, ownership and valuation of assets and liabilities as we consider necessary. We shall obtain an understanding of the accounting and internal control systems in order to assess their adequacy as a basis for the preparation of the accounts and to establish whether proper accounting records have been maintained by the LLP. We will need to obtain sufficient relevant and reliable evidence to enable us to draw reasonable conclusions therefrom.

6.6   The nature and extent of our tests will vary according to our assessment of the LLP's accounting and internal control systems, and may cover any aspects of the LLP's operations that we consider appropriate. Our audit is not designed to identify all significant weaknesses in the LLP's systems, but we shall report to the management any significant weaknesses in, or observations on, the LLP's systems which come to our notice and which we think should be brought to management's attention. Any such report may not be provided to third parties without our prior written consent. Such consent would be granted only on the basis that such reports are not prepared for the interests of anyone other than the LLP in mind and that we accept no duty or responsibility to any other party as concerns the reports.

6.7   The responsibility for safeguarding the assets of the LLP and for the prevention and detection of fraud, error and non-compliance with law or regulations rests with the management. We will plan our audit so that we have a reasonable expectation of detecting material misstatements in the accounts resulting from irregularities, fraud or non-compliance with law or regulations, but our examination should not be relied upon to disclose all such material misstatements or frauds, errors or instances of non-compliance as may exist.

6.8   As part of our normal audit procedures, we may request you to provide formal written representations concerning certain information and explanations we have received from you during the course of our audit.

6.9   In order to assist us with a review of your accounts, which constitutes part of our audit, we will request sight of any documents or statements which will be issued with the accounts. We are also entitled to attend all general meetings of the LLP, and to receive notice of all such meetings.

6.10   Once we have issued our report we have no further direct responsibility in relation to the accounts for that financial year. However, we expect that you will inform us of any material event occurring between the date of our report and that of the annual general meeting that may affect the accounts.

6.11   As members you acknowledge and understand your responsibility:

(a)   For the preparation of the financial statements in accordance with the applicable financial reporting framework, including where relevant their fair presentation;

(b)   For such internal control as the members determine is necessary to enable the preparation of financial statements that are free from material misstatement, whether due to fraud or error; and

(c)   To provide us with:

(i)   Access to all information of which the members are aware that is relevant to the preparation of the financial statements such as records, documentation and other matters;

(ii)   Additional information that we may request from the members for the purposes of the audit; and

(iii) Unrestricted access to persons within the LLP from whom we determine it necessary to obtain audit evidence.

7   Limitation of liability

7.1   You have agreed that our liability as auditors to the partnership will be limited in accordance with sections 532 to 538 of the Companies Act 2006. A separate letter dated insert date sets out the terms of this agreement. Or

7.2   We specifically draw your attention to paragraph XX of our standard terms and conditions which sets out the basis on which we limit our liability to you and to others. You should read this in conjunction with paragraph XX of our standard terms and conditions which excludes liability to third parties. Or

7.3   There are no Third Parties that we have agreed should be entitled to rely on the work done pursuant to this engagement letter.

8   Other Services

8.1   You may request that we provide other services from time to time. If these services exceed £ [insert value], we will issue a separate letter of engagement and scope of work to be performed accordingly.

8.2   Because rules and regulations frequently change you must ask us to confirm any advice already given if a transaction is delayed or a similar transaction is to be undertaken.

9   Agreement of terms

9.1   This letter supersedes any previous engagement letter and applies for accounting periods commencing on or after [insert date]. For periods commencing before this date the previous letter will apply. Once it has been agreed, this letter will remain effective until it is replaced.

9.2   You or we may vary or terminate our authority to act on your behalf at any time without penalty. Notice of variation or termination must be given in writing.

9.3   We shall be grateful if you could confirm your agreement to the terms of this letter by signing the enclosed copy and returning it to us immediately.

9.4   If this letter is not in accordance with your understanding of the scope of our engagement or your circumstances have changed, please let us know.

9.5   This letter should be read in conjunction with the firm's standard terms and conditions.

Yours sincerely

Insert firm name

I/We confirm that I/We have read and understood the contents of this letter and related terms and conditions and agree that it accurately reflects my/our fair understanding of the services that I/We require you to undertake.

Signed .... Date ....

For and on behalf of

Insert LLP name

APPENDIX 2 – EXAMPLE WRITTEN REPRESENTATION

3.13   *The following letter is not intended to be a definitive letter. Representations by members will vary from one LLP to another and from one period to the next. The letter will normally be printed on the LLP's letterhead to include relevant statutory information. This letter should be used as a reference only but keeping in mind that every audit is inherently difference.*

To: [Auditors]

Dear Sirs

The following representations are made on the basis of enquiries of members and staff with relevant knowledge and experience such as we consider necessary in connection with your audit of the LLP's financial statements for the year ended [date]. These enquiries have included inspection of supporting documentation where appropriate. All representations are made to the best of our knowledge and belief.

GENERAL

1.   We have fulfilled our responsibilities as members, as set out in the terms of your engagement letter dated [insert date] under the Companies Act 2006, Limited Liability Partnership Act 2000, Limited Liability Partnership Regulations 2008, Statement of Recommended Practice – Accounting by Limited Liability Partnerships and Companies Act 2006 for preparing financial statements and for being satisfied that they give a true and fair view and for making accurate representations to you.

2.   All the transactions undertaken by the LLP have been properly reflected and recorded in the accounting records.

3.   All the accounting records have been made available to you for the purpose of your audit. We have provided you with unrestricted access to all appropriate persons within the LLP, and with all other records and

related information requested, including minutes of all management and members meetings.

4.   The financial statements are free of material misstatements, including omissions.

5.   The effects of uncorrected misstatements (as set out in the appendix to this letter) are immaterial both individually and in total.

INTERNAL CONTROL AND FRAUD

6.   We acknowledge our responsibility for the design, implementation and maintenance of internal control systems to prevent and detect fraud and error. We have disclosed to you the results of our risk assessment that the financial statements may be misstated as a result of fraud.

7.   We have disclosed to you all instances of known or suspected fraud affecting the LLP involving members, management, employees who have a significant role in internal control or others that could have a material effect on the financial statements.

8.   We have also disclosed to you all information in relation to allegations of fraud or suspected fraud affecting the LLP's financial statements communicated by current or former employees, analysts, regulators or others.

ASSETS AND LIABILITIES

9.   The LLP has satisfactory title to all assets and there are no liens or encumbrances on the LLP's assets, except for those that are disclosed in the notes to the financial statements.

10.   All actual liabilities, contingent liabilities and guarantees given to third parties have been recorded or disclosed as appropriate.

11.   We have no plans or intentions that may materially alter the carrying value and, where relevant, the fair value measurements or classification of assets and liabilities reflected in the LLP's financial statements.

ACCOUNTING ESTIMATES

12.   Significant assumptions used by us in making accounting estimates, including those measured at fair value, are reasonable.

LEGAL CLAIMS

13.   We have disclosed to you all claims in connection with litigation that have been, or are expected to be, received and such matters, as appropriate, have been properly accounted for and disclosed in the financial statements.

LAWS AND REGULATIONS

14.   We have disclosed to you all known instances of non-compliance or suspected non-compliance with laws and regulations whose effects should be considered when preparing the financial statements.

RELATED PARTIES

15. Related party relationships and transactions have been appropriately accounted for and disclosed in the financial statements. We have disclosed to you all relevant information concerning such relationships and transactions and are not aware of any other matters which require disclosure in order to comply with the requirements of company law or accounting standards.

SUBSEQUENT EVENTS

16. All events subsequent to the date of the financial statements which require adjustment or disclosure have been properly accounted for and disclosed.

GOING CONCERN

17. We believe that the LLPs financial statements should be prepared on a going concern basis on the grounds that current and future sources of funding or support will be more than adequate for the LLP's needs. We have considered a period of 12 months from the date of approval of the financial statements. We believe that no further disclosures relating to the LLP's ability to continue as a going concern need to be made in the financial statements.

We acknowledge our legal responsibilities regarding disclosure of information to you as auditors and confirm that so far as we are aware, there is no relevant audit information needed by you in connection with preparing your audit report of which you are unaware.

Each member has taken all the steps that he/she ought to have taken as a member in order to make himself/herself aware of any relevant audit information and to establish that you are aware of that information.

Yours faithfully

....

DESIGNATED MEMBER

[Date]

Chapter 4

The audit and UK and Ireland auditing standards

SIGNPOSTS

- In the broadest terms, an audit involves the collection and evaluation of sufficient and appropriate audit evidence to enable the auditors to express an opinion on the truth and fairness of the LLP's financial statements (see **4.1**).

- Auditors will carry out their work in accordance with International Standards on Auditing (UK and Ireland) issued by the Financial Reporting Council (previously issued by the Auditing Practices Board) (see **4.2**).

- Audit evidence gathered by the auditor must be both 'sufficient' and 'appropriate'. The term 'sufficient' refers to the quantity of the audit evidence. The term 'appropriate' refers to the quality of the audit evidence (see **4.2**).

- There are broadly six stages in an audit involving planning then assessing risk right through to eventual reporting (see **4.3**).

- Audit planning is a critical aspect of the audit and involves the development of an approach which is not only effective in minimising the risk that material errors will go undetected, but also ensuring the audit is carried out efficiently (see **4.4**).

- An audit team discussion will be held at the planning stage to exchange knowledge and gain an understanding of the client and among other things discuss the susceptibility of the financial statements to material misstatement (see **4.4**).

- At the planning phase, the audit strategy is developed which then leads on to the development of the detailed audit plan (see **4.4**).

- Planning is viewed as a 'continuous and iterative process' and it follows that the plan must be continuously updated and amended (where applicable) for any unexpected developments which may arise during the detailed audit (see **4.4**).

- The auditor must obtain an understanding of the LLP and any changes in the LLP's business during the period (see **4.5**).

- It is the members' responsibility to prevent and detect fraud and the auditors will develop procedures which will address their risk assessment that the financial statements contain material misstatement due to fraud, although it is not an auditor's responsibility to detect fraud (see **4.6**).

- Auditors must consider the possibility of management override of internal controls for personal financial gain and, in general, must apply professional scepticism when carrying out an audit (see **4.6**).

- There are other considerations at the planning stage which the auditor must consider including the use of service organisations by the LLP, consideration of laws and regulations and the nature of related parties (see **4.7**).

- An external audit gives a high, but not absolute, level of assurance that the financial statements give a true and fair view and the auditor will apply the concept of materiality to the financial statements (see **4.8**).

- There are two levels of materiality: *financial statement* materiality and *performance* materiality (see **4.8**).

- External auditors may choose to place reliance on an LLP's internal controls and such controls will be documented by the auditor (see **4.9**).

- In developing the audit strategy, the auditor is required to undertake certain procedures to ensure the strategy they develop is appropriate – this is because the audit strategy then leads on to the creation of the detailed audit plan (see **4.10**).

- The audit plan includes the nature, timing and extent of planned risk assessment procedures, further audit procedures at the assertion level and other planned procedures to ensure the audit complies with the UK and Ireland ISAs (see **4.10**).

- There are various sources from which auditors can obtain their audit evidence to ensure the evidence gathered is both sufficient and appropriate (see **4.11**).

- Third-party and auditor-generated audit evidence is considered the most reliable, although such evidence may be more expensive to obtain (see **4.11**).

- An inherent limitation in an external audit is the use of audit sampling (see **4.12**).

- Sampling offers the auditor the opportunity to obtain the minimum amount of audit evidence which is both sufficient and appropriate to form valid conclusions about the population to which the sample represents (see **4.12**).

- Errors found during audit work are recorded on an 'audit error schedule' or 'summary of unadjusted misstatements' and then assessed as to whether, or not, they are material in the context of the financial statements (see **4.13**).

- Misstatements can be factual misstatements, projected misstatements or judgemental misstatements (see **4.13**).

- The audit file must be reviewed to ensure the audit work carried out is sufficient and this review process should be adequately documented (see **4.14**).

- Unadjusted misstatements must be reviewed at the completion phase as well as undertaking analytical procedures to ensure compliance with the UK and Ireland ISAs (see **4.15**).

- Once the review process and completion phase is finished, the audit engagement partner can then form their opinion as to whether the financial statements give a true and fair view and there are a number of opinions which can be expressed depending on whether the auditor considers the financial statements to give a true and fair view or otherwise (see **4.16**).

- Audit working papers must be kept confidential although Regulations allow incoming auditors to review the working papers of the outgoing auditors so the incoming auditors can obtain evidence for their audit (eg on opening balances) (see **4.17**).

1   WHAT IS AN AUDIT?

4.1   The general requirement that the accounts of an LLP are subject to audit has been discussed in Chapter 3. To many, particularly those transferring from partnership to LLP status, whilst they may be aware of the general concepts of audit, the detail of the audit process may be less familiar. This chapter explains in overall terms what an audit is, and the processes and procedures typically performed by the auditors.

At the most general level, an audit involves the collection and evaluation of sufficient and appropriate audit evidence to enable the auditors to express an opinion on whether the accounts are prepared, in all material respects, in accordance with the applicable accounting framework and whether they give a true and fair view of the state of the LLP's affairs.

2   UK AND IRELAND AUDITING STANDARDS

4.2   The auditors of an LLP are required to carry out their work in accordance with International Standards on Auditing (UK and Ireland) ('auditing standards') which are issued by the Financial Reporting Council (previously they were issued by the Auditing Practices Board). Whilst auditing standards do not dictate the exact nature of the work which auditors should carry out, they do set out both principles and essential procedures which must be applied when carrying out audit work. Individual firms are then able to develop their own methodologies to comply with those auditing standards.

Compliance with auditing standards is usually achieved through an 'audit programme'. An audit programme is a collection of procedures which set out various steps to undertake in order to achieve compliance with the UK and Ireland auditing standards. Some firms have been criticised in the past by regulatory bodies for relying too heavily on standard audit programmes and not tailoring such programmes to be client-specific.

Whatever methodology the audit firm uses it must ensure that the audit evidence it gathers to support the amounts and disclosures within the LLP's financial statements is both sufficient and appropriate. 'Sufficient' audit evidence refers to the quantity of the evidence needed and this is affected by the assessment of the risks of material misstatement and the quality of such audit evidence. 'Appropriate' audit evidence refers to the quality of the audit evidence, that is, the relevance and reliability of the evidence in providing support for the conclusions on which the auditor's opinion is based.

At the time of writing the following UK and Ireland auditing standards were in extant:

- ISQC (UK and Ireland) 1 *Quality Control for firms that Perform Audits and Reviews of Financial Statements, and Other Assurance and Related Services Engagements*

- ISA (UK and Ireland) 200 *Overall Objectives of the Independent Auditor and the Conduct of an Audit in Accordance with International Standards on Auditing (UK and Ireland)*

- ISA (UK and Ireland) 210 *Agreeing the Terms of Audit Engagements*

- ISA (UK and Ireland) 220 *Quality Control for an Audit of Financial Statements*

- ISA (UK and Ireland) 230 *Audit Documentation*

- ISA (UK and Ireland) 240 *The Auditor's Responsibilities Relating to Fraud in an Audit of Financial Statements*

- ISA (UK and Ireland) 250A *Consideration of Laws and Regulations in an Audit of Financial Statements*

- ISA (UK and Ireland) 250B *The Auditor's Right and Duty to Report to Regulators in the Financial Sector*

- ISA (UK and Ireland) 260 *Communication with Those Charged with Governance*

- ISA (UK and Ireland) 265 *Communicating Deficiencies in Internal Control to Those Charged with Governance and Management*

- ISA (UK and Ireland) 300 *Planning an Audit of Financial Statements*

- ISA (UK and Ireland) 315 *Identifying and Assessing the Risks of Material Misstatement through Understanding the Entity and its Environment*

- ISA (UK and Ireland) 320 *Materiality in Planning and Performing an Audit*

4.2 *The audit and UK and Ireland auditing standards*

- ISA (UK and Ireland) 330 *The Auditor's Responses to Assessed Risks*

- ISA (UK and Ireland) 402 *Audit Considerations Relating to an Entity Using a Service Organisation*

- ISA (UK and Ireland) 450 *Evaluation of Misstatements Identified During the Audit*

- ISA (UK and Ireland) 500 *Audit Evidence*

- ISA (UK and Ireland) 501 *Audit Evidence – Specific Considerations for Selected Items*

- ISA (UK and Ireland) 505 *External Confirmations*

- ISA (UK and Ireland) 510 *Initial Audit Engagements – Opening Balances*

- ISA (UK and Ireland) 520 *Analytical Procedures*

- ISA (UK and Ireland) 530 *Audit Sampling*

- ISA (UK and Ireland) 540 *Auditing Accounting Estimates, Including Fair Value Accounting Estimates and Related Disclosures*

- ISA (UK and Ireland) 550 *Related Parties*

- ISA (UK and Ireland) 560 *Subsequent Events*

- ISA (UK and Ireland) 570 *Going Concern*

- ISA (UK and Ireland) 580 *Written Representations*

- ISA (UK and Ireland) 600 *Special Considerations – Audits of Group Financial Statements (including the work of component auditors)*

- ISA (UK and Ireland) 610 *Using the Work of Internal Auditors*

- ISA (UK and Ireland) 620 *Using the Work of an Auditor's Expert*

- ISA (UK and Ireland) 700 *The Independent Auditor's Report on Financial Statements*

- ISA (UK and Ireland) 705 *Modifications to Opinions in the Independent Auditor's Report*

- ISA (UK and Ireland) 706 *Emphasis of Matter Paragraphs and Other Matter Paragraphs in the Independent Auditor's Reports*

- ISA (UK and Ireland) 710 *Comparative Information – Corresponding Figures and Comparative Financial Statements*

- ISA (UK and Ireland) 720A *The Auditor's Responsibilities Relating to Other Information in Documents Containing Audited Financial Statements*

- ISA (UK and Ireland) 720B *The Auditor's Statutory Reporting Responsibility in Relation to the Director's Report*

3 THE AUDIT PROCESS

4.3   Whilst the methodologies of individual audit firms vary, all audits can be analysed broadly into the following stages:

- planning;
- risk assessment;
- developing the audit strategy and audit plan;
- obtaining audit evidence;
- review; and
- reporting.

4 PLANNING THE AUDIT

4.4   Auditors invest a considerable amount of time on each assignment in ensuring that the work is planned, to take full account of the circumstances of the individual client. Planning is essential to developing an approach which is not only effective in minimising the risk that material errors will go undetected (detection risk) and in turn result in the auditor forming the incorrect opinion on the financial statements (audit risk), but also makes the most efficient use of audit staff and client time. Auditing standards contain considerable guidance and requirements with respect to the information the auditors should obtain and the assessments they should make when planning the audit.

The first stage in the planning process is for the auditors to establish the terms on which they are going to act by issuing an engagement letter (see Chapter 3), or to assess whether the provisions of a letter issued in a previous year are still appropriate. Revisions to the letter will be issued where this is considered to be necessary.

Planning the audit involves the audit team discussion where members of the audit team will discuss the susceptibility of the financial statements to material misstatement (whether due to fraud or error) and exchange knowledge of the client and the matters pertinent to the audit. Key high risk areas of the financial statements are discussed and sensitive issues such as fraud and fraud in relation to related parties are also discussed. In terms of fraud and the audit team meeting, the team must discuss *how* the financial statements could be materially misstated due to fraud (for example *how* management *could* override internal controls or *how* employees *could* manipulate weaknesses in internal controls). The discussion itself is not just about *if* fraud has occurred in the current or previous audits. This is required because the auditor must apply professional scepticism at all times during the course of the audit and set aside all beliefs about previous experiences relating to members' honesty and integrity.

Planning will also involve the development of the audit strategy. The audit strategy sets out the overall direction of the audit and includes consideration of:

- the overall approach to the conduct and management of the audit;

- the approach in organising the nature and timing of expected communications with the LLP;

- the timing and extent of involvement of experts, client personnel and other third parties; and

- direction, supervision and review.

Once the audit strategy has been developed, this leads onto the development of the audit plan. The audit plan is more detailed than the audit strategy and is essentially the means by which the team will gather sufficient appropriate audit evidence to support the amounts, assertions and disclosures in the financial statements by way of specific audit procedures,

The UK and Ireland auditing standards regard planning as a *'continuous and iterative process'*. This means that audit planning is not simply done at the start of an audit and then finished just before the audit fieldwork commences – the audit plan must be continuously updated and amended (where applicable) for any (unexpected) developments which might arise during the course of carrying out the detailed audit work.

5   UNDERSTANDING THE LLP AND RISK ASSESSMENT

4.5   At an early stage (more often than not at the planning stage of the audit), the auditors will want to obtain a copy of the members' agreement, find out about the LLP's business, any changes therein and its financial performance during the period, together with any significant transactions or other events which may require specific focus during the audit. In the first year of the auditors' appointment, the amount of information required will be substantially more than in subsequent years, as the auditors seek to build up their understanding of the business and the environment in which the LLP operates which is a mandatory requirement under ISA (UK and Ireland) 300 and 315. This understanding will not just encompass the LLP's business but will also take into account:

- The appropriateness of the selection and application of accounting policies, including those relating to revenue recognition (see Chapter 7) and the classification of members' interests (see Chapter 5).

- The objectives and strategies of the LLP.

- How the LLP measures and reviews its financial performance.

- The internal controls operated by the LLP, including:

    — its overall control environment (ie the governance and management functions and attitudes thereto within the LLP);

    — its risk assessment processes, so far as they affect the financial statements;

— the information systems and business processes relevant to financial reporting (including controls over IT systems); and

— controls operated by the LLP and how they are monitored.

- The regulatory framework within which the LLP operates.

- The structure of the LLP.

- The goods/services provided by the LLP and any other pertinent information considered important and relevant to the audit.

The methods adopted to obtain this information will vary, but could include meetings, telephone conversations and/or use of a questionnaire (for example an internal control questionnaire).

The auditors consider the risk of misstatement both at overall financial statement level and at what is termed the assertion level for each component of the financial statements (for example completeness, existence, rights and obligations).

6   FRAUD

4.6   It is the responsibility of the members of the LLP to take reasonable steps to prevent and detect fraud, and this responsibility is specifically referred to in the statement of members' responsibilities accompanying the accounts. Therefore, whilst the detection of fraud is outside the role of the auditors, in order to assess fully the risk of a material misstatement in the accounts, they are required to identify and assess the risk of material misstatement due to fraud, and evaluate the controls the LLP has in place to mitigate the risk. The inherent weaknesses of auditing mean that despite the audit procedures being effective and gathering sufficient and appropriate audit evidence, even material misstatements (due to fraud) may go unnoticed. It is for this reason that ISA (UK and Ireland) 240 *The auditor's responsibilities relating to fraud in an audit of financial statements* outlines the responsibility of the auditor as being that of obtaining reasonable assurance that the financial statements, taken as a whole, are free from material misstatement, whether caused by fraud or error.

Auditing standards specifically require that the auditors perform procedures to obtain information that they can use to identify and assess the risk that fraud could give rise to a material error in the accounts. There are two types of fraud that the auditors need to consider: fraudulent financial reporting, and the misappropriation of assets. ISA (UK and Ireland) 240 also regards management override of internal controls as being a significant risk, regardless of the auditor's past experience of the LLP. In this respect, the procedures outlined in paragraph 32 to ISA (UK and Ireland) 240 must be carried out as a minimum to address this significant risk.

In respect of fraud, auditors should also consider the susceptibility of material misstatement due to fraud because of management override of internal controls (ie how fraud *could* occur due to management override of controls). Employee fraud tends to arise because of a manipulation of weaknesses in internal controls, so auditors should consider the effectiveness of the LLP's internal control environment and consider how an employee *could* perpetrate a fraud, bearing in mind that no internal control system can be 100% effective against fraud or error (robust systems might mitigate the occurrence of fraud or error, but they would not be able to prevent it in its entirety).

The auditors are required to discuss the risk of fraud with management, including the processes that management have put in place for identifying and responding to the risk of fraud. The auditors are also required to obtain information with respect to actual or suspected fraud. To the extent that a risk of misstatement is identified, specific audit tests are designed to mitigate that risk.

Auditing standards contain a presumption that there is always a risk of fraudulent financial reporting with respect to revenue recognition and, therefore, ordinarily this is an area that the auditors will pay particular attention to. In addition, ISA (UK and Ireland) 550 *Related Parties* acknowledges that the nature of related party relationships may, in some circumstances, also give rise to higher risks of material misstatement than with unrelated parties and paragraph 12 to ISA (UK and Ireland) 550 makes a specific requirement for the audit team to consider the susceptibility of the financial statements to material misstatement due to fraud or error that could arise from the LLP's related party relationships and transactions.

7   OTHER PLANNING CONSIDERATIONS

4.7   Auditing standards also require that a number of other specific matters are considered when planning the audit. These include:

- Establishing the extent to which the LLP uses service organisations for processing data, maintaining accounting records, the safe custody of assets such as investments, or initiating transactions on the part of the LLP. Where the activities of the service organisation are considered to be significant, ISA (UK and Ireland) 402 *Audit considerations relating to an entity using a service* organisation requires the auditors to carry out additional procedures in relation to the information held by the service organisation. The auditors must also obtain an understanding of the services provided by a service organisation and the internal controls present at the service organisation.

- Ascertaining whether there are any laws and regulations which provide the legal framework within which the LLP conducts its business and which are central to its ability to conduct that business. Where such laws and regulations are identified, ISA (UK and Ireland) 250A *Consideration of laws and regulations in an audit of financial* statements requires the auditor to obtain sufficient and appropriate evidence of compliance with those laws and regulations. Auditors are not, however, required to consider all laws and regulations which might be applicable to the LLP, only those where non-compliance might result in the LLP being unable to continue in business. The provisions of some laws and regulations have a direct effect on the LLP's financial statements in that they determine the amounts and associated disclosures. Other laws and regulations must be complied with by management so that the LLP can continue in business but which do not have a direct effect on the LLP's financial statements.

- Ascertaining the nature of related parties (see Chapter **9.37–9.42**) and designing procedures to minimise the risk that the accounts will fail to disclose the existence of a material related party transaction. ISA (UK and Ireland) 550 *Related parties* requires the auditor to identify, assess and respond to the risks of material misstatement which arising from the LLP's failure to appropriately account for, or disclose, related party relationships, transactions or balances in accordance with the requirements of the financial reporting framework.

- Consideration of the applicability of the going concern assumption (see Chapter 10). The concept of going concern is considered a material issue in all businesses and ISA (UK and Ireland) 570 *Going concern* requires the auditor to form a conclusion as to whether management's use of the going concern presumption is appropriate in the LLP's circumstances (in other words whether the LLP has the ability to continue in business for the foreseeable future – ie for at least 12 months from the date the financial statements are authorised for issue and the audit report signed).

With regards to the final point concerning the going concern presumption – care must be taken to correct apply the UK and Ireland version of ISA 570 correctly. The mainstream ISA 570 issued by the International Auditing and Assurance Standards Board requires the period of assessment for going concern to be 12 months from the date of the financial statements (ie 12 months from the balance sheet date). ISA (UK and Ireland) 570 is more onerous in its requirements and requires the assessment to be 12 months from the date of approval of the financial statements.

8   MATERIALITY

4.8   In issuing the auditor's report on a set of accounts, the auditors are not stating that they are absolutely 100% correct, but instead they are saying they have obtained *reasonable assurance* that the financial statements are free from material misstatement. The term 'reasonable assurance' is not absolute assurance, but is a high level of assurance. Materiality is an expression of the relative significance or importance of a particular matter. ISA (UK and Ireland) 320 *Materiality in planning and performing an audit* says that a misstatement (or multiple misstatements), including omissions, are considered to be material if they, individually or in the aggregate, could reasonably be expected to influence the economic decisions of users taken on the basis of the financial statements.

Materiality is not only considered in the context of the accounts as a whole, but may also be applied in the context of any individual primary statement (profit and loss account and balance sheet) or of individual items included therein. There is no specific mathematical definition of materiality, due to the fact that it has both qualitative and quantitative aspects and audit firms develop their own methodologies for applying the requirements. Often materiality is calculated as ½–1% of turnover, 5–10% of pre-tax profit and 1–2% of gross assets and then an average struck to arrive at a financial statement materiality level (known as the 'averaging method'), however there is no 'one-size-fits-all' where materiality levels or the calculation of such are concerned. Materiality is very much a judgement call on the part of the auditor.

At the beginning of the audit, an indicative level of materiality will be calculated, which is usually based on a percentage of turnover, profit or gross assets or a combination. This serves as a guideline to the auditors to enable them to assess the areas where there is the potential for the greatest risk of material error. Items in the financial statements falling below the calculated materiality figure may be subject to either fewer audit procedures than other areas or, in some cases, no procedures at all.

When the clarified ISA (UK and Ireland) 320 was introduced it brought with it a new concept of materiality which is known as 'performance materiality'. The idea of performance materiality is that modern day audit techniques are concerned with sampling (ie the auditor will only test a selection of items to obtain reasonable assurance that the financial statements are free from material misstatement). There is always an unavoidable risk that items will go undetected so the idea of performance materiality is to reduce the possibility that the total of all errors which have been found during the audit, together with the undetected errors in the accounts do not exceed overall materiality levels. There is no prescribed calculation in ISA (UK and Ireland) 320 to arrive at a materiality, or a performance materiality, level but the application of performance materiality can be illustrated in the following example:

Example – application of performance materiality

An LLP operates in the pharmaceutical industry developing drugs for medical conditions and as such has a highly significant amount of research and development expenditure.

The audit engagement team has planned the audit of the financial statements for the year-ended 31 December 2014. The firm has determined a materiality level for the financial statements as a whole of £90,000 which has been calculated using the traditional 'averaging' method (1% of turnover, 2% of gross assets, 10% of pre-tax profit). Recently there has been a lot of interest by potential investors and initial talks have been entered into by potential investors to purchase the LLP due to its reputation. The potential investors are particularly interested in the results of the audited financial statements as at 31 December 2014.

The LLP's draft financial statements show that capitalised development expenditure has a net book value of £2.5 million which is clearly material to the financial statements. However, the audit engagement partner has emphasised the point that he is aware the members are keen to capitalise as much development expenditure as possible in order to boost the balance sheet and has therefore advised the audit engagement team to apply performance materiality to the development expenditure.

This is because paragraph 18.8H in FRS 102 *The Financial Reporting Standard applicable in the UK and Republic of Ireland* only allows development expenditure which meets the recognition criteria to be capitalised – any expenditure which does not meet the recognition criteria is written off to the profit and loss account as incurred (because it is classed as research expenditure), hence there is a risk of material misstatement within the area of research and development.

Performance materiality is based on professional judgement. There is no guidance in ISA (UK and Ireland) 320 as to how to calculate it. In the case of the LLP, performance materiality needs to be applied to an area which could influence the economic decisions of the user of the LLP's financial statements (i.e. potential investors). Performance materiality could well be determined as a percentage of financial statement materiality, say, 60%. As a result, a performance materiality of $(60\% \times £90,000) - £90,000 = £36,000$ could be set for the audit of research and development expenditure. The auditor could set higher or lower percentages, or even come up with a more complex formula, depending on their professional judgement.

9 ASSESSMENT OF INFORMATION SYSTEMS AND INTERNAL CONTROLS

4.9 The LLP's own systems of internal control and recording of accounting information will influence the audit approach. In some circumstances, the auditors may determine that the internal controls that the LLP has in place in a particular area are sufficiently robust to reduce significantly the risk of a material error arising. In these circumstances, the auditors may rely on these controls (having first tested them) to reduce the level of their own work. This is generally known as a compliance approach. Care must be exercised by the auditor when placing reliance on an LLP's internal control systems and where the auditor does place greater reliance on the effectiveness of a control, ISA (UK and Ireland) 330 *The auditor's responses to assessed risks* requires the auditor to obtain more persuasive audit evidence.

Irrespective of whether the auditors intend to rely on the LLP's own systems and controls, auditing standards require that they obtain an understanding of the information system, including the related business processes relevant to financial reporting, and of control activities. This usually results in the auditors documenting the key transaction flows of the LLP (eg the sales cycle, the purchases cycle and the payroll cycle etc), together with the internal controls operating over those transaction flows. Some testing will also be carried out to ascertain that the systems operate as described and documented.

Different audit firms will document their understanding of an LLP's systems and controls differently. The most common methods of documenting systems and controls includes:

- *Narrative notes* which consist of a written description of the system showing what occurs in the system at each stage and the controls that operate at each stage.

- *Questionnaires* can consist of internal control questionnaires (ICQs) or internal control evaluation questionnaires (ICEQs). These questionnaires contain a list of questions relevant to the systems and controls; ICQs are used to assess whether controls exist, whereas ICEQs are used to test the effectiveness of the controls.

- *Flowcharts* are graphic illustrations of the internal control system for each cycle of the LLP's business. Lines usually demonstrate the sequence of events and standard symbols are used to signify controls or documents.

10 AUDIT STRATEGY AND PLAN

4.10   Based on the information obtained, the auditors will then develop both an overall strategy as to how the audit work should be scoped, which then allows a detailed plan to be developed, usually in the form of work programmes for each area of the accounts. These programmes will then be used by the staff carrying out the fieldwork to guide them through the performance of that work. The audit strategy and programmes may be updated during the performance of the work, where circumstances are not as envisaged at the time the overall strategy was prepared.

Many audit firms use automated audit software which already includes audit programmes. Whilst such programmes are perfectly acceptable to use, it is important that the auditor ensures they are tailored to be specific to the LLP audit. Many software programmes contain 'generic' audit tests which can sometimes be used as a 'tick box' approach by audit firms. The danger in using a tick-box approach is that it may result in audit evidence being obtained which is not sufficient nor appropriate, which is time-consuming and costly. Careful reviews of audit programmes by the audit engagement partner may be necessary (particularly where the LLP is a complex audit) to ensure that they are appropriate.

In developing an audit strategy, ISA (UK and Ireland) 300 *Planning an audit of financial statements* requires the auditor to:

- identify the characteristics of the LLP's engagement which defines its scope;

- establish the reporting objectives so that the auditor can plan the timing of the audit and the communications which will be required;

- consider significant issues relating to the LLP which will direct the audit team's efforts;

- review the work performed on other preliminary engagement activities and the knowledge gained on other engagements performed by the engagement partner for the LLP and consider its relevance; and

- determine the nature, timing and extent of resources required in order to perform the audit engagement.

Once the audit strategy has been developed, the audit plan can then be produced. The audit plan is more detailed than the audit strategy and includes a description of:

- the nature, timing and extent of planned risk assessment procedures;

- the nature, timing and extent of planned further audit procedures at the assertion level; and

- other planned procedures which are required in order that the audit engagement complies with the UK and Ireland ISAs.

The audit plan is prepared at the start of the engagement so the team is aware of the procedures to be carried out. An important aspect to emphasise where audit planning is concerned is that it does not stop once the audit plan is completed. ISA (UK and Ireland) 300 *Planning an audit of financial statements* recognises that planning is a 'continuous and iterative process' and therefore changes to the audit plan may be needed during the detailed audit fieldwork because of issues arising during the course of the audit. This may also include revisions to financial statement and performance materiality. Where changes to the audit plan are required due to issues arising during the audit, such changes must be adequately documented.

Example – changes to an audit plan

During the course of the planning an LLP's audit, the auditor's initial analytical review confirmed that gross profit margins had remained static on the previous year and therefore she devised audit procedures to determine this was the case. During the on-site audit fieldwork, the auditor discovered several purchase invoices that had not been accrued for at the year-end resulting in a significant reduction in the gross profit margins in the year under audit.

Clearly in a situation like this, the original planned audit procedures would have to be changed (resulting in a change to the audit plan) because more work will have to be undertaken to ascertain why the gross profit margins have disproportionately reduced (other than the unaccrued purchase invoices), but also establishing why the internal controls had also not picked up this omission which would also result in creditors being understated as well as costs.

---

11 OBTAINING AUDIT EVIDENCE

4.11   The evidence which auditors obtain is one of the most crucial aspects of the audit. ISA (UK and Ireland) 500 *Audit evidence* says that the evidence obtained by the auditor must be 'sufficient' and 'appropriate'. The term 'sufficient' refers to the quantity of the evidence needed and the evidence is affected by the assessment of the risks of material misstatement and the quality of such evidence. The term 'appropriate' refers to the quality of the audit evidence, that is, the relevance and reliability of the evidence in providing support for the conclusions on which the auditor's opinion is based.

As part of the planning process, the auditors will have determined the sources from which they will obtain their audit evidence. The evidence can come from one of three sources: (1) the LLP itself (for example, work in progress/accrued income calculations), (2) third parties (for example, confirmation of bank balances provided directly to the auditors), or (3) generated by the auditors (for example, the re-performance of a bank reconciliation). The independent nature of an audit means that third-party and auditor-generated evidence are considered to be more reliable, but such evidence is also more expensive to obtain. In planning their work, the auditors will usually seek to obtain a balance of evidence from all sources, but a level of third-party evidence will always be necessary.

ISA (UK and Ireland) 500 acknowledges that there is more than one way in which the auditors can obtain evidence, and the most appropriate method or methods will be adopted for each item in the accounts. The following are the principal categories:

- *Inspection of records or documents*. This tends to be the most commonly used procedure and involves substantiating amounts in the accounting records by reference to documents. Revenue, for example, will be audited in part by agreement to the related contracts and invoices, together with any proof of delivery of goods or services.

Example – inspection of records or documents

The financial statements of an LLP show the addition of a large number of computers during the year of £80,000 which is very material to the accounts. The audit senior has emailed the purchase ledger clerk and asked for a copy of the invoice to be scanned and sent to the audit firm so that they can verify the rights and obligations assertion relating to this equipment.

The invoice from the supplier could have been altered by the LLP to put the invoice in the name of the LLP. The auditor should have inspected the original invoice whilst carrying out the detailed audit work at the LLP's premises as it is considered that original documents are more reliable than photocopies, scanned copies or copies transmitted by facsimile.

- *Observation and physical inspection.* Whilst, in general, observation tests are of limited application because they are only valid at a point in time, in some circumstances there is no alternative procedure that can be performed. Probably the most common observation test carried out by the auditors is attendance at the stock count of a client where there are material amounts of stock.

Example – observation and inspection

The audit senior has attended the year-end stock count of an LLP and is observing a team of counters checking the quantities and pricing of stock.

While errors or omissions may not be made when the auditor is in attendance at the stock count, the procedures adopted by management may not be followed in their entirety once the auditor has left.

- *Inquiry and confirmation.* This covers a wide range of possible tests, from simply seeking clarification from the LLP's staff of something within the accounting records to requesting third-party confirmation of items such as bank or sales ledger balances.

Example – inquiry and confirmation

As part of the audit process, the audit senior has written to the LLP's bank and ask for a bank audit letter (sometimes called a 'bank confirmation letter') at the balance sheet date to confirm the balances per each bank account operated by the LLP during the financial year.

The bank audit letter is external confirmation from the bank (hence third party) and is more reliable than internally-generated evidence provided by the LLP.

- *Recalculation and re-performance.* Re-performance of calculations to check their mathematical accuracy, for example, depreciation calculations or testing ageing of accounts receivables.

Example – recalculation

The accounting policy for depreciation of assets in an LLP is to depreciate on a pro-rata basis only. The LLP's year-end is 31 March 2015 and on 1 July 2014 an item of machinery was purchased.

In this example, the auditor will be checking that the accounting policy in respect of depreciation has been correctly calculated by recalculating the depreciation charge based on 9/12 of a full year's depreciation charge.

Example – reperformance

The audit senior is auditing an LLP's payroll for the year and is checking that the year-end PAYE and NIC is fairly stated. This can be done by calculating the amount of PAYE and NIC for the entire year, deducting the payments made to HMRC during the year as well as any deductions from PAYE/NIC that the LLP is eligible to claim. This will help to identify any potential over- or under-payments of taxes during the year or at the year-end. It will also offer comfort to the auditor if their reperformance of the PAYE control account agrees to the year-end financial statements.

- *Analytical procedures.* The analysis of the relationships between amounts included within the accounts, either within the same period, or between comparable amounts from different periods or, in some circumstances, industry statistics. In carrying out analytical procedures, the auditors will firstly develop their own estimate of the figures they expect to see, compare this estimate with the actual outcome, obtain an explanation for any differences, and then corroborate that explanation by reference to other information available from the LLP.

Example – analytical procedures

The audit senior has undertaken an analytical review of an LLP's profit and loss account. He has noticed that gross profit margins in 2014 were 40% and in 2013 were 55%.

The fluctuation in gross profit margins would need to be investigated by the audit senior to ensure that they are, in fact, correct as gross margins usually (although not always) are expected to remain fairly consistent from one reporting period to the next.

---

12 SAMPLING

4.12   The auditors are required to obtain reasonable, but not absolute, assurance as to the amounts included within the accounts. As a result of both this requirement and the need for efficiency, audit evidence is usually obtained on the basis of sample testing which is dealt with in ISA (UK and Ireland) 530 *Audit sampling*. Some audit firms have developed elaborate statistical models to enable them to select their samples whereas other firms take a more judge-mental approach. Irrespective of the precise methods adopted for ascertaining the sample to be tested, there are some general principles to which the auditors will always adhere:

- Items are selected in such a way as to give a reasonable expectation that they are representative of the total population. For example, it would be inappropriate to test sales by only looking at transactions in one month. Where an LLP has more than one business stream, samples will need to be selected so that, as a minimum, all material types of business are covered.

- Selection must be made without any conscious bias – all items should have an equal chance of being selected. Items should not be selected for sampling simply because they are easy to locate.

- Where possible, the population to be tested should be stratified. A small number of high-value items covering a relatively large proportion of the population will usually be the most efficient approach.

- Specific key items should be tested – in particular, those which are particularly prone to error or misstatement – for example, all debts over a certain age.

The use of sampling methods means that auditors will not usually test all the information available to them because this would be both impractical and uneconomical. However, auditors may well deem 100% selection to be appropriate when there are a small number of high value items which make up a population, or when there is a significant risk of material misstatement and other audit procedures will not provide sufficient appropriate audit evidence.

Sampling offers the auditor the opportunity to obtain the minimum amount of audit evidence which is both sufficient and appropriate in order to form valid conclusions on the population. In addition, the use of sampling reduces the risk of 'over-auditing' in certain areas resulting in a much more efficient review of the working papers at the review stage of the audit.

13 ERRORS FOUND DURING AUDIT WORK

4.13   Where errors are found by the auditors during the course of their work, these will be recorded within the audit working papers on an 'audit error sched-ule' or an 'uncorrected misstatements schedule' and assessed as to whether or not they are material in the context of the accounts. In making this assessment, both the effect of individual errors and the cumulative effect of items which are essentially immaterial will be considered and they are combined to see if the cumulative effect of all the immaterial misstatements become material in aggregate. ISA (UK and Ireland) 450 *Evaluations of misstatements identified during the audit* requires the auditors to evaluate the effect of identified mis-statements on the audit as well as evaluate the effect of uncorrected misstate-ments (if any) on the financial statements. The auditors will discuss the errors with the members, and request that the accounts be amended to deal with those which are, in their opinion, material. The members may choose to process all amendments but, where they decide that this is not necessary, the written representation given to the auditors (see **3.6**) will need to explain the reasons for non-adjustment – namely that, in the opinion of the members, they are not considered to affect the overall truth and fairness of the accounts.

Where material misstatements are not corrected by the members, this will result in the auditor's qualifying their audit opinion accordingly.

In terms of misstatements, they can be either 'factual', 'projected' or 'judgemental'. *Factual* misstatements are those where there is no doubt and for which documentation is available. *Projected* errors are the auditor's best estimate of misstatements in populations usually derived from sampling. *Judgemental* misstatements are differences arising from the judgements of management concerning accounting estimates.

Example – audit sampling and error projection

The auditors of an LLP are testing sales invoices. The population of sales invoices amounted to £100,000 and the values of the invoices in the sample amounted to £35,000. The following are the results of the sample:

1. The audit senior tested all material items in the sample which amounted to £20,000 and included an error of £1,000. As the audit senior has tested all material items in the sample the error will not be reproduced in the remainder of the population and in this respect the likely error from the sample is limited to £1,000.

2. The audit senior tested a number of other invoices amounting to £15,000 and found an error of £500. In contrast to the testing in 1 above, this error could be reproduced in the sample because both the population and the same are limited to the remaining non-material items. The 'projected' error by extrapolation will be the error discovered (£500) × the remaining population of (£100,000–£20,000) £80,000/the same £15,000 which is £2,667.

The total projected error is £1,000 + £2,667 = £3,667. If the members decide to correct the 'actual' adjustments which are £1,000 found in 1 and £500 in 2 hence £1,500, the projected error will be £2,167. This method is commonly referred to as the 'ratio' method.

If the above samples had not been split into two elements (material and non-material items), the projected error would be found by extrapolating over the total population. This would have increased the errors discovered because the errors would have been calculated as £1,500 × the population of £100,000/the sample of £35,000 = £4,286.

Example – the difference method

The difference method should be used where the error does not have a direct relationship to the monetary value of the item. It is relatively constant for all items, and so will increase in proportion to the number of items in the population. It is calculated as follows:

$$\begin{array}{l} \text{Error found in} \\ \text{the sample} \end{array} \times \frac{\textit{Number of items in the population}}{\textit{Number of items in the sample}} = \textit{Most likely error in population}$$

During the course of the control tests to ensure all goods despatched are invoiced, the auditor has noted the following deviations:

Number of despatch notes not found	1
Number of despatch notes without invoices	3
Authorised cancellations	(1)
Actual deviations	3

Deviation rate = 3/100 = 0.33

The conclusion is that despatches are being invoiced satisfactorily as the error rate in the sample is acceptably low.

14 REVIEW

4.14 ISA (UK and Ireland) 230 *Audit documentation* requires that all working papers be reviewed by a member of the team who is more experienced than the preparer and is a basic quality control requirement of ISA (UK and Ireland) 220 *Quality control for an audit of financial statements*. Reviewing the audit file not only ensures that the work carried out is sufficient to enable an audit opinion to be given, but also ensures that those not involved in the day-to-day work (typically the manager and partner) are aware of all significant issues affecting the LLP and its accounts. The audit engagement partner who will sign the audit opinion is not required to review all working papers but, at a minimum, the review must cover critical areas of judgement, significant risks and such other areas as they consider to be of importance.

The review process should be adequately documented to ensure there is evidence on file that the audit working papers have been reviewed by the audit engagement partner. This can be done either by way of initialling the working papers or having a separate schedule documenting the overall review process. Some 'paperless' audit systems will not allow the audit to be finalised unless there has been a review of the working papers undertaken.

15 COMPLETION OF THE AUDIT

4.15   The completion stage of the audit is crucially important because it is at this stage that the audit engagement partner reviews the evidence obtained with a view to forming their opinion as to whether the LLP financial statements give a true and fair view. The audit engagement partner must review the schedule of unadjusted misstatements to comply with the provisions in ISA (UK and Ireland) 450 and establish the impact on the unadjusted misstatements. This evaluation will be done in conjunction with the materiality levels to determine if the unadjusted misstatements are material both individually and in aggregate.

ISA (UK and Ireland) 520 *Analytical procedures* requires the auditor to perform analytical procedures near the end of the audit to assist the auditor in forming an overall conclusion as to whether the financial statements are consistent with the auditor's understanding of the entity. Such procedures will not be markedly different from those applied at the planning stage (eg ratio analysis and comparisons with prior year financial statements). Undertaking analytical procedures at the end of the audit will provide the auditor with the information needed to explain any unusual trends, fluctuations or relationships within the LLP's financial statements.

In addition to ensuring that all the audit work has been completed satisfactorily, there are a number of other procedures which the auditors are required to carry out prior to issuing their report. These will include the following:

- Discussing with the members the extent to which there have been any events, subsequent to the completion of their fieldwork and through to the date of their report, which provide additional evidence as to any of the amounts included within the accounts or which should be disclosed in the accounts. This is a requirement of ISA (UK and Ireland) 560 *Subsequent events* which requires the auditor to perform procedures to obtain sufficient appropriate audit evidence that all events which have occurred between the balance sheet date and the auditor's report that either require adjustment or additional disclosure within the LLP's financial statements have been identified.

- Ascertaining whether there have been any changes in circumstances which might affect the members' assessment of whether the LLP is a going concern. ISA (UK and Ireland) 570 *Going concern* requires that the auditor remains alert throughout the course of the audit for any events or conditions which may cast doubt on the LLP's ability to continue as a going concern. The concept of going concern is discussed in more detail in Chapter 10.

- Obtaining the written representations from the members. ISA (UK and Ireland) 580 *Written representations* requires the auditor to consider the matters to be included within the members' written representation and ISA (UK and Ireland) 580 requires the representation to be dated as near as possible to, but not after, the date of the auditor's report. Written representations are considered to be audit evidence, but should complement existing audit evidence – in other words they cannot be regarded as sufficient and appropriate audit evidence on their own, primarily because they are internally-generated by the LLP. An illustrative written representation letter is shown in Appendix 2 to Chapter 3.

16 THE AUDIT OPINION

4.16   Chapter 3 sets out the general requirement that an audit report should contain the auditors' opinion as to whether or not the accounts give a true and fair view. A variety of circumstances may lead to the auditor expressing a qualified 'except for', adverse or disclaimer of opinion. Where the auditors have not been able to obtain all of the information they require ('limitation of scope'), or they disagree with the accounting treatment adopted by an LLP or disclosure (or non-disclosure) of an item in the accounts, a qualified audit opinion is expressed. The qualification can take a number of forms:

- *'Except for'*. Where the auditors have been unable to obtain sufficient and appropriate audit evidence with respect to one or more items, but where they are satisfied with the evidence available in all other areas. This form of opinion is also used where the auditors disagree with the accounting treatment or disclosure (or non-disclosure) in relation to an item in the accounts.

- *Disclaimer.* When the possible effect of a limitation in scope is so material and/or pervasive that the auditors have not been able to obtain sufficient appropriate evidence to enable them to form an opinion on the accounts. This can usually occur where the accounting records have been destroyed and the financial statements re-constructed.

- *Adverse opinion.* Where the auditors consider that the matter with which they disagree is so material and pervasive that the accounts are misleading. In these circumstances, the audit opinion will state that the accounts do not give a true and fair view.

In certain circumstances, there may be uncertainties surrounding an issue concerning the accounts, where the effect of the possible range of outcomes could be material. In these circumstances, where the auditors consider that this is a matter to which attention should be drawn, the auditors will make reference to the existence of the issue in their report by way of an 'emphasis of matter' paragraph, but this does not constitute a qualification of the audit opinion. This could arise, for example, where the LLP's ability to continue as a going concern might be called into question due to the occurrence or non-occurrence of future events. An emphasis of matter paragraph is cross-referenced to the relevant disclosure note in the LLPs financial statements.

17 AUDIT WORKING PAPERS

4.17   The auditors will record the results of the work performed on working papers which may be manual, electronic, or a combination of both. The auditors are under a professional obligation to safeguard the confidential nature of the working papers and they will not usually allow access to them by any third party, including the members of the LLP. Audit working papers are the crucial content of an audit file and record the work done and conclusions reached in order to allow the audit engagement partner to form their opinion as to whether the LLP's financial statements give a true and fair view.

However, the regulations require that, where there is a change in auditors, the new auditors may access the predecessor auditor's working papers for the immediately preceding financial period. Where such a request is received, the previous auditors are under a legal obligation to permit access. The outgoing auditors may also charge the LLP for the reasonable costs of allowing the incoming auditors access to the working papers.

ISQC (UK and Ireland) 1 *Quality control for firms that perform audits and reviews of financial statements and other assurance and related services engagements* suggests that the assembly of the audit file and working papers should be done on a timely basis. ISQC (UK and Ireland) 1 suggests a time limit of not more than 60 days after the date of the auditor's report.

Chapter 5

Accounting for members' interests and remuneration – principles

---

SIGNPOSTS

- Section 22 in FRS 102 *The Financial Reporting Standard applicable in the UK and Republic of Ireland* deals with the issue of financial instruments which causes some difficulty where LLPs are concerned (see **5.1**).

- Puttable instruments increase the complexity for LLPs although these are not as common (see **5.1**).

- According to Section 22, financial instruments are either 'debt' or 'equity' depending on the substance of the transaction (see **5.2**).

- Members of an LLP have two sorts of rights: rights which the members have in respect of amounts subscribed or contributed to the LLP and rights to remuneration either by way of salary arrangement or profit share (see **5.2**).

- Accounting for members' capital as either debt or equity depends on whether the LLP has the unconditional right to withhold payment to members (see **5.3**).

- The ways in which members of an LLP are remunerated will vary between LLPs but will reflect the fact that the members are in the position of both owning and working in the LLP (see **5.4**).

- 'Members remuneration charged as an expense' must be shown immediately after 'Profit or loss for the financial year before members' remuneration and profit shares' according to the 2014 SORP (see **5.5**).

- Unpaid profits for the year which the LLP has the unconditional right to withhold at the balance sheet date are treated as available for discretionary division among members (see **5.6**).

- The 2014 SORP requires disclosure of the way in which each type of remuneration has been determined and accounted for (see **5.6**).

- Members' interests can be shown as three types of balance in the balance sheet (see **5.7**).

- A complication for LLPs relates to puttable instruments (see **5.8**).

- The puttable exception can be difficult for LLPs to apply and the 2014 SORP contains some additional guidance (see **5.8**).

- Members' balances are treated as equity only if the LLP has the unconditional right to withhold them from the member (or if they have been paid, the LLP has the unconditional right to reclaim them) (see **5.9**).

- Profit which forms part of 'Profit available for discretionary distribution among members' in the profit and loss account is treated as equity (see **5.10**).

- The 2014 SORP requires the financial statements of an LLP to include a comprehensive statement of components of members' interests and movements during the year (see **5.11**).

- If the LLP is required to produce a cash flow statement under Section 7 of FRS 102, the 2014 SORP requires separate disclosure of transactions with members (and former members) from transactions with non-members (see **5.12**).

- It is fairly common practice for a member of an LLP to borrow in order to fund their initial capital requirements and may not necessarily require disclosure in the LLP financial statements (see **5.13**).

- There are a number of additional disclosures relating to members' remuneration that the Regulations and the 2014 SORP require in the notes to the financial statements (see **5.14**).

- The members' report should include details of the policies adopted by the LLP with regards to capital maintenance including a discussion of the policies adopted in dealing with members' drawings (see **5.15**).

- The LLPs accounting records will need to contain sufficient detail to be able to ascertain the financial relationship between each member and the LLP (see **5.16**).

1   INTRODUCTION

5.1   The area that has probably given rise to the most practical difficulties for LLPs is the application of Section 22 *Liabilities and Equity*. The definition of financial instruments is so widely drawn that the various rights that members have to participate in an LLP, whether by way of capital or sharing of profits, fall within the requirements of this section. However, as Section 22 only applies for accounting periods commencing on or after 1 January 2015 (with early adoption permissible) (and prior to new UK GAAP, FRS 25 only previously applied for periods beginning on or after 1 January 2005), members' agreements prepared before these standards became applicable are in many cases difficult to interpret in the light of the very precise definitions contained in them. The application of the principles of Section 22 to LLPs is considered at some length in the 2014 SORP.

The 2014 SORP also considers another level of complexity, albeit in practice one that is unlikely to apply to many LLPs, which relates to puttable instruments and which is considered further at **5.8**.

This Chapter considers the principles of Section 22 as they apply to LLPs, and some of the practical implications are considered in the following chapter.

2 MEMBERS' INTERESTS AS FINANCIAL INSTRUMENTS

5.2 Section 22 of FRS 102 requires, amongst other things, that financial instruments be classified as either liabilities or equity (the term used for residual interests), by reference to substance rather than legal form. The term 'substance over form' is taken to mean the commercial reality of the transaction. The definition of equity is very tightly drawn and, unless an entity has an unconditional right to withhold payment to an instrument holder, unpaid amounts are classed as a liability and related returns as an expense. Other than in the limited circumstances of what are termed 'puttable instruments', which are considered further below, if an entity (including an LLP) cannot avoid paying an amount to a third party, it has a liability.

The rights that a member has in respect of its relationship with an LLP (referred to in the 2014 SORP as 'participation rights') fall into two types each requiring separate analysis. There are the rights which the members have in respect of amounts they have subscribed or otherwise contributed to the LLP, and their rights to remuneration, whether through salary-type arrangements or profit share.

Whether each right represents either a liability or equity will determine where it is included within the LLP's accounts.

The implications for LLPs are, therefore, wide-ranging, and each LLP needs to examine its members' agreement very carefully to determine the relevant accounting treatments.

3 MEMBERS' CAPITAL

5.3 In the majority of LLPs, members will be required to contribute capital, although in practice there is wide variation as to how this is achieved. The contribution of capital can occur both at the stage someone initially becomes a member and at subsequent dates.

Capital may be contributed either by way of a cash payment by the member or through an arrangement whereby a member agrees to 'capitalise' part of their profit allocation for the year. The latter might typically happen on initial admission, when it might be agreed that the member could reach their capital requirement over a number of years.

Unlike a limited company, an LLP is able to repay to the members any of its capital or convert it to debt without any legal restrictions, and the terms and conditions attaching to members' capital will be determined by the members' agreement. Whilst this appears to create greater flexibility, in practice it is probable that restrictions will exist as a result of external requirements placed on the LLP to maintain a certain level of capital (for example, by banks and the Financial Conduct Authority). LLPs repaying capital will also need to be aware of the risk of this being viewed as a preference over creditors, in the event of the LLP subsequently running into financial difficulties and becoming insolvent.

The accounting classification of members' capital between equity and debt depends on whether the LLP has the unconditional right to withhold repayment to the members. Where the members' agreement entitles a member to the return of capital on retirement from the LLP, the capital is classified as a debt due to members (ie a liability), other than in those cases where the requirements in respect of puttable instruments are met (see below). This is because 'debt' would be considered to be a 'financial liability' and a financial liability is any liability which is:

- A contractual obligation to:

  — deliver cash or another financial asset to another entity; or

  — exchange financial assets/financial liabilities with another entity under conditions which are deemed to be potentially unfavourable to the entity; or

- A contract that will, or might be, settled in the entity's own equity instruments and:

  — under which the entity is, or may be, obliged to deliver a variable number of the entity's own equity instruments; or

  — which will, or may be, settled other than by the exchange of a fixed amount of cash or another financial asset for a fixed number of the entity's own equity instruments. However, in this respect, the entity's own equity instruments do not include instruments which are themselves contracts for the future receipt or delivery of the entity's own equity instruments.

Where there is no requirement to repay capital to members, it will be treated as equity. The terms attaching to capital have wider implications than purely accounting. Where the LLP has the right to refuse capital payments that reduce total capital below a minimum level, this increases the rights of the LLP relative to the individual members. If, for example, the business faced difficult times and an outflow of members, the right of the LLP to hold a minimum level of capital would reduce the extent to which a withdrawal of the firm's working capital would compound the effect of the loss of key members.

In some circumstances, members may be entitled to receive interest on their capital. In determining the accounting treatment of any such interest, the requirements of Section 22 are again relevant. On initial recognition of the capital, it is also necessary to consider any related cash outflows and the extent to which they are at the discretion of the LLP. In circumstances where the LLP has no requirement to repay capital, but there is mandatory interest payable on that capital, it will represent what is termed a compound financial instrument in Section 22. In such cases the debt element (interest) is calculated first, by reference to the net present value of the cash flows and any excess of the capital over that amount will be classed as equity. In a number of cases the debt element will be equal to the amount of the capital, resulting in the capital being classified as a liability in its entirety.

Example – interest paid to members and capital repaid at the discretion of the LLP

The constitution of Westhead LLP requires that its members subscribe capital to the LLP on admission to the partnership. Repayments of this capital amount are made to the outgoing member on retirement and this is subject to the LLP passing a resolution prior to any capital being repaid. If a resolution is not passed, the LLP has the right to retain the capital indefinitely. The terms of the members' agreement also make provision for the member to receive a market rate of interest on all capital which they have subscribed.

In this example, the LLP must pass a positive resolution in order to repay capital amounts to outgoing members and where no positive resolution is passed, the LLP has the ability to retain the capital indefinitely. Notwithstanding this latter possibility, the LLP still has an obligation to pay the subscriber interest on that capital at market rates. As a consequence, Section 22 of FRS 102 would require a liability to be recognised in the LLP's financial statement as a member subscribes to the partnership which reflects the present value of the minimum non-discretionary cash flows (the interest). Because the return is at a market rate at the time the member subscribes the capital, the entire capital will fall to be treated as a liability.

---

4   THE NATURE OF MEMBERS' REMUNERATION

5.4   The way in which members are remunerated will vary between LLPs but will reflect the fact that the members are in the position of both owning the LLP and, usually, working within it. In a company environment the distinction between the rewards a director receives in his or her capacity as a shareholder (ie by virtue of ownership) (dividends) and those received for services provided (directors' remuneration) are more readily distinguished, but within an LLP the distinction between the two is frequently blurred. The accounting treatment and presentation of amounts payable to members is primarily not determined by whether the payments are rewards for working in the LLP or ownership thereof, but by whether or not the LLP has discretion over payment of the amounts.

Members may be rewarded for their involvement with the LLP through one or more of the following:

- *Salaried remuneration.* Changes to the tax legislation from 6 April 2014 effectively mean that some members of an LLP will not be treated as self-employed, but are now taxed as if they are employees (often referred to as 'disguised remuneration') subject to meeting the following criteria:

  Condition A: It is reasonable to expect that at least 80% of the members' pay is fixed, or if variable, then without reference to, or in practice unaffected by, the LLP's profit or loss.

  Condition B: The member has no significant influence over the affairs of the LLP.

  Condition C: The members' contribution to the LLP is less than 25% of the disguised salary.

- *Fixed share.* Members may be 'guaranteed' a certain amount of remuneration each year either within the membership agreement or through individual arrangements between the LLP and the member. This amount will be paid to them irrespective of the level of profits made by the LLP.

- *Share in residual profit.* Members are awarded a share of the profit made by the LLP, after the payment of any salaried remuneration and fixed shares. The basis of allocation will vary but will typically be based on a formula linked to factors such as seniority and the capital introduced by the member. Often, members will be entitled to a fixed amount, as well as a share in residual profit.

- *Drawings.* While salaried remuneration, fixed shares and residual shares refer to the member's entitlement to profit, drawings refer to the cash payments received in respect of that entitlement. Depending on the terms of the members' agreement, drawings may be paid in respect of profit to which the member is already entitled, or may be paid in advance of the division of profit to the member. Whether or not any drawings paid in excess of profit allocation are to be repaid to the LLP will again depend upon the terms of the membership agreement.

5   ACCOUNTING FOR MEMBERS' REMUNERATION

5.5   The 2014 SORP's treatment of members' remuneration and profit share, and the related balance sheet items, reflects the presentation requirements of Section 22 of FRS 102 and whether the participation rights in relation to profits of the LLP are a liability or equity. This assessment should be made independently of the assessment in respect of capital. Those rights that are a liability will be treated as an expense in the current period's profit and loss account; those that are equity will be treated as an addition to the reserves of the LLP.

The provisions in FRS 102 allow entities a choice of whether to present total comprehensive income for the period in one statement (being the 'statement of comprehensive income') or, alternatively, in two statements (being an 'income statement' which is the profit and loss account and a 'statement of comprehensive income'). The LLP Regulations require that the profit and loss account discloses a total for 'Profit or loss for the financial year before members' remuneration and profit shares'. Members' remuneration charged as an expense should be shown immediately after this, with the remainder being profit or loss available for discretionary division among members.

Paragraph 51 of the 2014 SORP requires the following disclosure to be made on the face of the profit and loss account.

Profit or loss for the financial year before members' remuneration and profit shares	X
Members' remuneration charged as an expense	(X)
Profit or loss for the financial year available for discretionary division among members	X

In determining the amount which is charged as an expense, both the amounts payable to the member and any associated employment costs should be included.

6   IDENTIFYING MEMBERS' REMUNERATION CHARGED AS AN EXPENSE

5.6   In determining whether amounts paid to members during an accounting period from that period's profit should be treated as an expense, the 2014 SORP considers whether the LLP has the unconditional right to repayment of these amounts from the members at the balance sheet date. If it does not, the amounts are treated as an expense.

For profit that has not yet been paid to members at the year end, the 2014 SORP considers whether the LLP has the unconditional right to withhold those amounts from members at the balance sheet date. If it does not, the amounts are again treated as an expense. It is in this area that particular care is needed when analysing the members' agreement, in order to determine whether there is an automatic division of profit or whether further action is required by the LLP before the members are entitled to receive those profits.

It is also important that the decision to divide profits, which is the event that creates the obligation to pay those profits to the members, is distinguished from the arrangements for profit sharing. A provision in the members' agreement that sets out the profit shares of members does not of itself constitute an agreement for the sharing of profits.

Unpaid profits for the year that the LLP has the unconditional right to withhold at the balance sheet date are treated as available for discretionary division among members.

In practical terms, remuneration charged as an expense comprises the following:

- *Drawings made against current year profit, of which the LLP does not have the unconditional right to demand repayment at the year end.* This will include salaried remuneration and fixed profit shares. Where the members' agreement stipulates that payments on account of residual profit cannot be reclaimed, except to the extent amounts paid exceed the member's profit division for the year, payments of residual profit made in the year are also treated as an expense.

- *Undrawn profit, which the LLP does not have the unconditional right to withhold from the members at the year end.* This will include, for example, profit-related bonuses to which members are entitled, either through a contract with the LLP or the members' agreement. All undrawn profit will be treated as an expense if, for example, the members' agreement requires automatic division of those profits.

Profit available for discretionary division among members comprises the following:

- *Drawings made from current year profit, of which the LLP has the unconditional right to demand repayment at the year end.* This might occur where payments on account of residual profit are made, and the members' agreement stipulates that no residual profit is divided among the members until some process of post year end approval has taken place.

- *Undrawn profit, which the LLP has the unconditional right to withhold from the members at the year end.* This will relate to undrawn residual profit, the division of which is subject to post year end approval.

The following table, reproduced from paragraph 54 of the 2014 SORP, summarises the treatment of members' remuneration:

Nature of element of member's remuneration	Treat as
Remuneration that is paid under an employment contract	Expense, described as 'Members' remuneration charged as an expense', and deducted after arriving at 'Profit for the financial year before members' remuneration and profit shares'
Other payments, arising from components of members' participation rights in the profits for the year that give rise to liabilities in accordance with section 22 of FRS 102, such as mandatory interest payments	
Automatic division of profits	
Any share of profits arising from a division of profits that is discretionary on the part of the LLP (ie, where the decision to divide the profits is taken after the profits have been made)	Allocation of profit

When profit available for discretionary division among members is subsequently divided, there is no impact on the profit and loss account, and the movement is reflected in the reconciliation of movements in members' interests, of which an example is provided at **5.11**. The balance sheet treatment of amounts paid and payable to members and of undivided profit is explained at **5.15**.

For a large proportion of LLPs the remuneration of members will comprise both an expense element and an allocation of profits, which will need to be separately recorded and accounted for.

In addition to impacting its presentation in the profit and loss account and balance sheet, the extent to which members receive remuneration that falls to be treated as an expense affects the valuation of any work in progress. Remuneration charged as an expense will need to be included within the calculation of work in progress whereas discretionary profit allocation will be excluded. Accounting for work in progress is considered in more detail in **7.7**.

The 2014 SORP requires disclosure of the way in which each type of remuneration has been determined and accounted for and it may be most appropriate to include this within the accounting policy note.

7   THE COMPOSITION OF MEMBERS' INTERESTS

5.7   Within the balance sheet, amounts relating to the interaction of the LLP with its members can give rise to three types of balance:

- *Amounts due from members.* Amounts which are debts owed by the members to the LLP, for example, drawings paid in excess of profit entitlement.

- *Loans and other debts due to members.* Amounts which are liabilities owed by the LLP to the members, for example, undrawn profit allocations and capital that is classed as a liability because the LLP cannot avoid repayment.

- *Members' other interests (equity).* Includes only those amounts that the LLP has the unconditional right to withhold from the members, for example, undistributed profits that the LLP has the right to retain, capital introduced by members whose repayment is subject to approval, and other reserves, for example revaluation reserves.

The 2014 SORP requires 'Loans and other debts due to members' and 'Members' other interests' to be disclosed separately on the face of the balance sheet. 'Loans and other debts due to members' and 'Members capital' should be included in balance sheet item J to the extent that they are classified as a liability. 'Members' capital', 'Revaluation reserve' and 'Other reserves' are classified in equity (balance sheet item K) to the extent that they are classified as equity and the 2014 SORP also requires separate disclosure of these on the face of the balance sheet. Equity cannot include members' capital which is classified as a liability to conform to the requirements in Section 22 of FRS 102. The consequence of this is that some LLPs will classify all capital as a financial liability in cases where individual members have the right to demand repayment of such balances (such as when they retire) and when the LLP does not have the unconditional right to refuse such repayment (except where the conditions for the puttables exception are met).

8   PUTTABLE INSTRUMENTS

5.8   Section 22 of FRS 102 provides additional guidance in respect of a *puttable instrument*. A 'puttable instrument' is a financial instrument which gives the holder of the instrument the right to sell that instrument back to the issuer for cash or for another financial asset. Alternatively, it may be redeemed or repurchased by the issuer on the occurrence of an uncertain future event or on the death or retirement of the holder of the puttable instrument.

For LLPs, there are certain situations when the classification of a financial instrument will meet the definition of a financial liability, but will instead fall to be classified as equity if the conditions are met. Paragraph 22.4 of FRS 102 is drafted in such a way that it applies to individual classes of financial instrument. The overall structure of an LLP may consist of one, or more, classes of financial instrument.

Example – different classes of financial instrument

Whitaker LLP (Whitaker) requires members to subscribe to capital on admission to the partnership. In addition, Whitaker also requires its members to make loans to the LLP as and when required. These loans are separate financial instruments from capital subscriptions.

In this example, Whitaker will have two classes of financial instrument (the capital subscriptions and the loans from the members).

There are certain criteria which have to be met if a puttable instrument is to be classed as equity:

- The instrument entitles the holder to a pro-rata share of the entity's net assets in the event of the entity's liquidation (net assets being the assets which remain after all liabilities have been deducted).

- The instrument is in a class of instruments which is subordinate to all other classes of instruments.

- All the financial instruments in the subordinate class have identical features.

- With the exception of the contractual obligation for the issuer to repurchase or redeem the instrument for cash or another financial asset, there are no other contractual obligations to deliver cash or another financial asset to another entity, or to exchange financial assets or financial liabilities under conditions which are potentially unfavourable to the entity and the contract is not one which will, or may be, settled in the entity's own equity instruments.

- The total amount of expected cash flows which are attributable to the instrument over the life of the instrument are based substantially on the profit or loss, the change in the recognised net assets or the change in the fair value of the recognised and unrecognised net assets of the entity over the life of the instrument.

The second requirement in the criteria above is that the class of instruments is subordinate to all other instruments of the issuer. Therefore, to conform with paragraph 22.4 of FRS 102, where members' interests comprise of more than one class of instrument, equity classification under the puttables exception is only eligible for the class of instrument which is subordinate to all others.

An LLP will typically have at least two individual classes of financial instruments – capital and profit share. Each financial instrument may have more than one component (for example, fixed and variable profit shares). The arrangement in most LLPs mean that the residual interest in the LLP will usually be members' capital. However, this will be applied differently in two sets of circumstances – first, if the residual interest may be 'put' on the LLP (ie redeemed at the option of the member without liquidation of the LLP) and, secondly, where it may be put only on the liquidation of the LLP. In the former, only the whole instrument can be reclassified; in the latter, it is possible to reclassify a component of the instrument. These circumstances are discussed further in Chapter 6.

When a puttable financial instrument obliges the entity to make payments to the holder of the instrument before liquidation, the instrument is classified as a liability (this can be the case where the LLP is required to make mandatory interest or other non-discretionary payments to the holder of the instrument). This treatment is appropriate because of the requirement in paragraph 22.4(iv) of FRS 102 which says that 'apart from the contractual obligation for the issuer to repurchase or redeem the instrument for cash or another financial asset, the instrument does not include any contractual obligation to deliver cash or another financial asset to another entity…'. If the LLP is required to make mandatory interest or other non-discretionary payments to the holder, the instrument will fail to meet the criteria in paragraph 22.4. There is no equivalent restriction for instruments which are only redeemable on liquidation.

Another issue which needs to be carefully considered by LLPs is the distinction between those transactions between the members and the LLP which are undertaken in the members' role as owners and non-owners. Paragraph 42C to the 2014 SORP contains an example of a profit or loss sharing arrangement whereby profit or loss is allocated to the instrument holders on the basis of services rendered or business generated during the current and previous years. The 2014 SORP acknowledges that these arrangements are transactions with instrument holders in their capacity as non-owners and should not be considered when assessing the features listed in paragraph 22.4 of FRS 102. Conversely, the 2014 SORP acknowledges that profit or loss sharing arrangements which allocate profit or loss to instrument holders based on the nominal amount of their instruments relative to others in the class may represent transactions with the instrument holders in their role as owners and hence should be considered having reference to the provisions in paragraph 34 of the 2014 SORP.

The puttable exception can be quite complicated to apply and the 2014 SORP contains some additional guidance in Appendix 2. For LLPs which adopt the FRSSE, at the time of writing there were no proposals to incorporate the principles of the puttable exception into the FRSSE and thus the 2014 SORP confirms that while LLPs should regard the relevant requirements of FRS 102 as a means of establishing current practice, LLPs reporting under the FRSSE may continue to comply with the FRSSE requirements in respect of liabilities and equity.

9   PRESENTATION OF MEMBERS' INTERESTS WITHIN THE ACCOUNTS

5.9   Members' balances are treated as equity only if the LLP has the unconditional right to withhold them from the member (or, in the case of amounts that have been paid to members, if the LLP has the unconditional right to reclaim them). Otherwise they are treated as a liability due to the member. Under the 2014 SORP, all members' balances in the LLP, whether equity or a liability, are shown within 'net assets attributable to members', on the 'bottom half' of the balance sheet. This treatment differs from a company balance sheet, where only equity balances are included in the bottom half of the balance sheet and all liabilities are shown in the top half as a deduction from net assets. As a consequence, any LLP which has zero equity (because, for example, all capital must be returned and all profits are automatically divided) does not present a balance sheet that totals zero but one that shows the net assets attributable to members. The presentation of members' interests is further illustrated in the example accounts in Appendices 1 and 2 in this book.

In an LLP, 'net assets attributable to members' can only include members' balances in the LLP, and, unless the member has the legal right to offset amounts he owes the LLP against amounts it owes him, they must be presented separately, with amounts owed by the member being disclosed within debtors in the top half of the balance sheet.

The 2014 SORP also requires that total members' interests be presented in the accounts by showing the sum of amounts due from members, amounts due to members and members' other interests as a memorandum item on the balance sheet. This is also illustrated in the example accounts.

The presentation of amounts within 'net assets attributable to members' in an LLP also differs from the presentation of partners' balances that is normally adopted in a general partnership. In a general partnership, balances would normally be categorised by their purpose (capital, current, taxation, etc). In an LLP, they are first categorised by whether they are equity or debt, and then subcategorised between capital and other amounts. For example, in an LLP there is no difference in disclosure between current account balances and taxation balances that are payable to or on behalf of, members; both are included within 'loans and other debts due to members – other amounts'.

10 CLASSIFICATION OF PROFIT IN THE BALANCE SHEET

5.10   The balance sheet treatment of profits follows the treatment in the profit and loss account, which is explained at **5.6**.

Profit which forms part of 'profit available for discretionary distribution among members' in the profit and loss account should be treated as equity. To the extent that drawings have been made against profit that is included within equity (which is the case where the LLP has the unconditional right to reclaim drawings), these drawings are shown as 'other debts due from members' within debtors.

Members' remuneration charged as an expense represents profit that the LLP does not have the unconditional right to withhold from the members, and, to the extent it has not been drawn, is presented as a liability due to members in the balance sheet. Where profit that was available for discretionary distribution at the end of the previous year has been divided among the members in the current year, but has not yet been paid, this is also presented as a liability.

The policy for division of profit can significantly impact the shape of an LLP's balance sheet, as demonstrated in the example below.

Example – Division of profit

Members' capital is 100, and members are entitled to have this repaid when they leave.

The LLP has made 350 units of profit for the year, of which 250 have been drawn in the year and 100 remain undrawn.

- In LLP A, all profit is automatically divided (ie the LLP does not have the unconditional right to withhold any profit made from the members), and the undrawn profit of 100 units is presented within loans and other debts due to members.

- In LLP B, drawn profit is divided and cannot be reclaimed by the firm, but the division of undrawn profit is subject to post year end approval. The undrawn profit of 100 units is presented within equity.

- In LLP C, division of all profit is subject to post year end approval. All 350 units of profit are presented within equity and the 250 units that have been drawn are presented as 'amounts due from members'.

Members' capital is presented within 'loans and other debts due to members', as it is a liability rather than 'equity'.

	A	B	C
Cash	200	200	200
Trade debtors	100	100	100
Amounts due from members	–	–	250
Trade creditors	(100)	(100)	(100)
Net assets attributable to members	200	200	450
Loans and other debt due to members			
Members' capital classified as a liability	100	100	100
Other amounts	100	–	–
	200	100	100
Members' other interests			
Members' other interests – other reserves classified as equity	–	100	350
	200	200	450
Total members' interests			
Amounts due from members	–	–	(250)
Loans and other debts due to members	200	100	100
Members' other interests	–	100	350
	200	200	200

11 RECONCILIATION OF MOVEMENT IN MEMBERS' INTERESTS

5.11   FRS 102 at paragraph 4.12 requires certain disclosures to be made which relate to an entity's share capital and reserves. For those entities which do not have share capital (such as an LLP), equivalent information is required to be disclosed which shown the movement in the period for each category of equity, and the rights, preferences and restrictions attaching to each category of equity.

To meet this requirement, the 2014 SORP requires the accounts of the LLP to include a comprehensive statement of the components of members' interests and movements during the year. An example is provided on page 83.

	EQUITY Members' other interests				DEBT Loans and other debts due to members less any amounts due from members in debtors			TOTAL MEMBERS' INTERESTS
	Members' capital (classified as equity)	Revaluation reserve	Other reserves	Total	Members' capital (classified as debt)	Other amounts	Total	Total 2XX1
Amounts due to members						X	X	
Amounts due from members						(X)	(X)	
Balance at [start of the period]	X	X	X	X	X	X	X	X
Members' remuneration charged as an expense, including employment and retirement benefit costs						X	X	X
Profit/(loss) for the financial year available for discretionary division among members			X	X				X
Members' interests after profit/(loss) for the year	X	X	X	X	X	X	X	X
Other divisions of profits/(losses)			(X)	(X)		X	X	–
Surplus arising on revaluation of fixed assets		X		X				X
Introduced by members	X			X	X			X
Repayments of capital	(X)			(X)	(X)		(X)	(X)
Repayment of debt (including members' capital classified as a liability)					(X)		(X)	(X)
Drawings						(X)	(X)	(X)
Other movements	X	X	X	X	X	X	X	X
Amounts due to members					X	X	X	X
Amounts due from members						(X)	(X)	
Balance at [end of period]	X	X	X	X		X	X	X

83

12 MEMBERS' INTERESTS IN THE CASH FLOW STATEMENT

5.12   Where an LLP falls within the scope of Section 7 *Statement of Cash Flows*, it will be required to prepare a cash flow statement. Section 7 is notably different than under previous GAAP in FRS 1 *Cash Flow Statements* and requires a cash flow statement which analyses cash flows during the period between:

● operating activities;

● investing activities; and

● financing activities.

Operating activities are the principal day-to-day revenue-producing activities of the LLP which do not fall to be classed as investing or financing activities. This category is essentially the 'default' category.

Investing activities are the acquisition and disposal of long-term assets and other investments not included in cash equivalents. For example, investing activities would represent cash payments used by the LLP to purchase a fixed asset or show the disposal proceeds from the sale of a fixed asset.

Financing activities are activities which result in changes to the contributed equity and borrowing structure of the LLP. An example could be where the LLP has taken out a loan and the proceeds from the loan would be shown within financing activities.

Paragraph 74A of the 2014 SORP considers the presentation of cash flows with members (and former members) and summarises these as follows:

Nature of transaction	Classification of cash flows
Remuneration that is paid under an employment contract	Operating cash flow
Other remuneration (discretionary or non-discretionary) for services provided	Operating cash flow
Post-retirement payments to former members	Operating cash flow
Capital introduced by members (classified as equity or liability)	Financing cash flow
Repayment of capital or debt to members	Financing cash flow
Payments to members that represent a return on amounts subscribed or otherwise contributed	Financing cash flow

The 2014 SORP requires separate disclosure of transactions with members (and former members) from transactions with non-members. This is to assist with an understanding of the LLPs ability to generate cash flows, and the needs of the LLP to utilise those cash flows.

13 BORROWINGS OF MEMBERS

5.13 It is not uncommon for the members of an LLP to borrow in order to fund at least their initial capital requirements. These arrangements frequently involve the LLP entering into a guarantee, indemnity or similar arrangement with the provider of the funding.

The fact that the members' interests have been funded by way of borrowings is not of itself something which requires disclosure in the accounts. Instead it is necessary to look at the extent of the LLP's obligation to the provider of finance and how this should be treated.

It would be unusual to include a provision in the accounts for the amount of any such loan. Section 21 *Provisions and Contingencies* (see **9.2**) would only require a provision to be recognised when the LLP had a legal or constructive obligation to repay the loan and the requirement for repayment was probable at the year end and the amount of the repayment could be reliably measured. Circumstances where this might arise include the death or early retirement through ill-health of a member. In determining the amount of any provision, the LLP should take into account the extent to which it is legally entitled to offset the liability against the capital interests and other debts due to the member. In addition, in certain circumstances, such as the death of a member, the repayment may be covered by insurance.

Where it is unlikely that the guarantee or indemnity will be called, its existence should, nevertheless, be disclosed as a contingent liability in the notes to the accounts to comply with the provisions in Section 21 of FRS 102, unless the possibility of it being called upon is remote.

14 MEMBERS' REMUNERATION DISCLOSURES

5.14 In addition to the requirement to disclose members' remuneration charged as an expense separately on the face of the profit and loss account, the Regulations and the 2014 SORP require a number of additional disclosures to be made in the notes to the accounts.

For large and medium-sized LLPs, the average number of members during the year should be disclosed in a note to the accounts. An LLP will do this by dividing the total number of members of the LLP for each month (or part thereof) in the financial year by the number of months in the financial year and round the result to the nearest whole number. Whilst not required by either the Regulations or the 2014 SORP, the members may wish to include details of average members' remuneration. Where this option is taken, the 2014 SORP states that it should be calculated by reference to the disclosed average number of members and the amount of 'profit before members' remuneration and profit shares' shown in the profit and loss account.

Where there are factors which distort the amount of profit attributable to members in the year (for example, adjustments to retirement benefits), the members are allowed to disclose an adjusted average members' remuneration, provided that a reconciliation between the basic and adjusted calculations is provided.

For large and medium-sized LLPs, where the profit of the LLP before members' remuneration and profit shares is greater than £200,000, the notes to the accounts are required to disclose the remuneration of the member with the highest entitlement to profit. As well as entitlements from the LLP, this will also include any amounts paid to the member by a subsidiary undertaking or other third party. The 2014 SORP does not specify how the amount should be calculated, although those LLPs that have arrangements whereby some profits will only be allocated in subsequent periods will need to consider which profits are included within the remuneration figure. In these circumstances, it could be either the share of the profit for the period that was agreed after the period end or the amounts allocated in the reporting period relating to profits made in earlier periods. The 2014 SORP requires that the method of calculation should be disclosed, and that a consistent policy should be applied year on year. The 'highest paid' member does not have to be named.

Where it is considered that it will assist an understanding of the financial performance of the LLP, the 2014 SORP recommends that members' remuneration charged as an expense should be further analysed within the notes to the financial statements, for example, between that which is paid under a contract of employment and that which relates to amounts arising from participation rights that give rise to a liability.

15 DISCLOSURE OF MEMBERS' BALANCES

5.15   The extent to which members' balances should be disclosed as equity or as 'loans and other debts due to members' is discussed above.

The Regulations require separate disclosure of the aggregate amount of money advanced by the members by way of loan, the aggregate amount of money owed to members in respect of profits and any other amounts. To the extent that this information is not ascertainable from the reconciliation of movements in members' interests, additional disclosure should be made. The total amount due after more than one year should also separately be disclosed.

In addition, the 2014 SORP requires that the notes to the accounts disclose where amounts due to members would rank on a winding up in relation to other unsecured creditors. In the absence of any agreement to the contrary, amounts due to members will rank equally with other creditors. However, in the absence of any subordination, the LLP may find it difficult to obtain credit from third parties, particularly banks. It is not unusual, therefore, for an LLP to subordinate all or part of the debt due to the members to other creditors in the event of a winding up.

The members' report should include details of the policies adopted by the LLP with respect to capital maintenance. This includes a discussion of the policies adopted in dealing with members' drawings and how these are managed when they come into conflict with the cash requirements of the LLP.

The policy under which members make contributions of equity or debt to the LLP and the terms of their repayment should be disclosed. The members' report must also include details of equity which has been converted to debt (and vice versa) both within the year and for the period from the year end up until the date the accounts are approved.

16 ACCOUNTING RECORDS

5.16   While the published LLP accounts will only show members' interests at an aggregated level, the accounting records maintained with respect to members' interests will need to contain sufficient detail to be able to ascertain the financial relationship between each member and the LLP. They will, therefore, need to include details of the capital introduced by the member, profits allocated, and any salaries paid and drawings made.

Chapter 6

Accounting for members' interests and remuneration – practical considerations

SIGNPOSTS

- Appendix 2 of the 2014 SORP contains a number of examples which seek to assist in determining when members' participation rights are equity and when they are debt (see **6.1**).

- This chapter considers some practical examples to help highlight how the split between debt and equity works (see **6.2–6.8**).

- The 2014 SORP does not address accounting for losses by LLPs as the ways in which losses are addressed vary among LLPs (see **6.9**).

- In some cases the life of an LLP may be deliberately short as it may only have been created for a specific purpose and hence when the project is complete it may be liquidated (see **6.10**).

1   INTRODUCTION

6.1   Chapter 5 considered the principles of accounting for members' interests and remuneration as a consequence of the application of Section 22 *Liabilities and Equity* in FRS 102. This chapter considers some of the implications of applying those principles to the varied ways in which an LLP might choose to operate so far as members' capital and profit shares are concerned.

Appendix 2 of the 2014 SORP contains a number of examples that seek to assist in determining when members' participation rights are equity and when they are debt.

2   ASSUMPTIONS USED IN THE EXAMPLES

6.2   In the following examples, unless otherwise stated, the basic information in respect of 2XX1 is as follows:

- number of members = 10;
- capital subscribed by each member = £10,000;

- profit made in the year = £1,000,000; and

- drawings paid to members = £700,000.

3   CAPITAL AND PROFITS BOTH TREATED AS EQUITY

6.3   *Relevant conditions contained in the members' agreement*

On retirement, capital is not returned to the outgoing member unless agreed by a majority of members.

The decision to divide profit requires agreement of a majority of members. The decision to divide all profits of the year is taken after the year end.

Analysis

The LLP does not have an obligation to return capital or distribute profits to its members.

Accounting treatment

Capital of £100,000 is shown in equity on the balance sheet.

Profits of £1,000,000 are shown as retained profit for the year available for discretionary division among members in the profit and loss account and as part of equity within other members' interests.

Drawings of £700,000 are included within debtors.

Treatment of profit available for discretionary division in subsequent year

Following the year end, the members agreed to divide the £1,000,000. The undrawn £300,000 is paid.

Profit for the year 2XX2 is £1,200,000 and drawings in respect of that year are £800,000.

Total drawings shown in the reconciliation of members' interests will be £1,100,000 (£300,000 + £800,000). £800,000 will also be included within debtors on the balance sheet.

Presentation in reconciliation of members' interests

	EQUITY — Members' Other Interests			DEBT	Total Members' Interests 2XX2	Total Members' Interests 2XX1
	Members' Capital (Classified as equity)	Other Reserves	Total	Loans and other debts due to members less any amounts due from members in debtors		
	£	£	£	£	£	£
Amounts due to members				–		
Amounts due from members				(700,000)		
Balance at start of the period 2XX2	100,000	1,000,000*	1,100,000	(700,000)	400,000	XXXXXX
Profit for the financial year available for discretionary division among members		1,200,000	1,200,000		1,200,000	1,000,000
Members' interests after profit for the year	100,000	2,200,000	2,300,000	(700,000)	1,600,000	XXXXXX
Other divisions of profits/losses		(1,000,000)	(1,000,000)	1,000,000		
Drawings				(1,100,000)	(1,100,000)	(700,000)
Amounts due to members				–		
Amounts due from members				(800,000)		
Balance at end of 2XX2	100,000	1,200,000	1,300,000	(800,000)	500,000	XXXXXX

*assumes no amounts other than the profit and drawings for the previous period.

Part of profits are divided during the year

The members agree to divide £600,000 during the year and the division of the remaining £400,000 is agreed after the year.

Accounting treatment of profits

Profits of £1,000,000 are shown as retained profit for the year, available for discretionary division among members in the profit and loss account and as part of equity within other members' interests.

Drawings of £100,000 (£700,000 – £600,000) are shown in debtors.

Presentation in reconciliation of members' interests

	EQUITY Members' Other Interests			DEBT	Total Members' Interests 2XX1	Total Members' Interests 2XX0
	Members' Capital (Classified as equity)	Other Reserves	Total	Loans and other debts due to members less any amounts due from members in debtors		
	£	£	£	£	£	£
Amounts due to members				XXXXXXX		
Amounts due from members				XXXXXXX		
Balance at start of the 2XX1	100,000	XXXXXX	XXXXXXX	XXXXXX	XXXXXX	XXXXXX
Profit for the financial year available for discretionary division among members		1,000,000	1,000,000		1,000,000	XXXXXX
Members' interests after profit for the year	100,000	1,000,000	1,100,000	XXXXXX	XXXXXX	XXXXXX
Other divisions of profits/losses		(600,000)	(600,000)	600,000	(700,000)	XXXXXX
Drawings				(700,000)	(100,000)	XXXXXX
Amounts due to members				XXXXXX	XXXXXX	XXXXXXX
Amounts due from members				(100,000)	(100,000)	XXXXXXX
Balance at end of 2XX1	100,000	400,000	500,000	XXXXXX	XXXXXXX	XXXXXXX

4   CAPITAL AND PROFITS BOTH TREATED AS LIABILITIES

6.4   *Relevant conditions contained in the members' agreement*

On retirement, capital must be returned to the retiring member.

Profits are automatically divided equally between all members.

Analysis

The LLP has an obligation to return capital and distribute profits to its members.

Accounting treatment

Capital of £100,000 is shown as a liability on the balance sheet (members' capital classified as debt). In the reconciliation of members' interests, it is included within loans and other debts due to members.

Profits of £1,000,000 are shown as members' remuneration charged as an expense in the profit and loss account, and the profit available for discretionary division is nil.

The undrawn element of profit (£300,000) is included within loans and other debts due to members.

5   CAPITAL IS EQUITY AND PROFITS ARE PART EQUITY AND PART LIABILITY

6.5   *Relevant conditions contained in the members' agreement*

On retirement, capital is not returned unless agreed by a majority of members.

25% of profits are divided automatically, the decision to divide the remainder requires the agreement of all members.

Analysis

The LLP has no obligation to return capital.

The LLP has an obligation to pay 25% of profits.

The LLP has no obligation to pay 75% of profits.

Accounting treatment

Capital of £100,000 is shown in equity on the balance sheet.

6.6 *Accounting for members' interests and remuneration*

£250,000 is shown as members' remuneration, charged as an expense in the profit and loss account, and the retained profit available for discretionary division among members is £750,000.

Drawings of £450,000 (£700,000 – £250,000) are included within debtors.

6   REQUIREMENT TO KEEP MINIMUM LEVEL OF CAPITAL

6.6 *Relevant conditions contained in the members' agreement*

On retirement, capital must be returned to the retiring member unless the amount falls below £90,000.

Analysis

The LLP has no obligation to return capital to the extent that total capital is £90,000 or less.

Accounting treatment

Capital of £90,000 is shown in equity on the balance sheet.

Capital of £10,000 is shown as a liability on the balance sheet (members' capital classified as debt).

7   INTEREST ON CAPITAL

6.7 **Capital is a liability**

Relevant conditions contained in the members' agreement

On retirement, capital must be returned to the retiring member.

Members are entitled to interest on capital at 5% per annum.

Decision to divide profit requires agreement of a majority of members.

Analysis

The LLP has an obligation to return capital and pay interest thereon.

The LLP does not have an obligation to distribute profits to members.

Accounting treatment

Capital of £100,000 is shown as a liability on the balance sheet (members' capital classified as debt).

Interest of £5,000 is charged in the profit and loss account within members' remuneration charged as an expense.

To the extent the interest is unpaid, it is included within loans and other debts due to members.

Profits of £999,995 are shown as profit available for discretionary division among members.

Drawings of £700,000 are included within debtors.

Capital is 'equity'

Relevant conditions contained in the members' agreement

On retirement, capital is not returned unless agreed by a majority of members.

Members are entitled to interest at 5% per annum.

Decision to divide profit requires agreement of a majority of members.

Analysis

Whilst the LLP has no obligation to repay capital, it does have an obligation to pay interest. In accordance with the requirements of Section 22 in FRS 102, such an arrangement is regarded as a compound financial instrument requiring a 'split' approach to accounting. This means that the instrument is 'split' between its debt component and its equity component.

The LLP does not have an obligation to distribute profits to members.

Accounting treatment

Section 22 requires that the debt portion of the instrument be valued first, and this is done by calculating the present value of the future committed cash flows. In this example, that would be £5,000 at 5% in perpetuity, resulting in a discounted cash flow of £100,000. Therefore, all of the members' capital will be shown as a liability in the balance sheet. Had the future cash flows been less than £100,000, the lesser amount would have been recorded as a liability and the difference between that amount and £100,000 as equity. Were the cash flows to have exceeded £100,000, then a liability would have been recognised but restricted to the proceeds received by the LLP, namely £100,000.

8   CAPITAL REQUIREMENTS MET THROUGH PROFIT SHARE

6.8   *Relevant conditions contained in the members' agreement*

On retirement, capital is not returned unless agreed by a majority of members.

New members are not required to introduce capital in cash, but can accumulate it from their profit share in equal amounts in the first five years of membership.

Profits are automatically divided equally between all members.

In this example, it is assumed that an 11th member joins in the year.

Analysis

The LLP does not have an obligation to return capital.

The LLP does have an obligation to distribute profits to members.

New members' capital accumulated from profits is accounted for as a transfer within members' interests.

Accounting treatment

Capital of £102,000 is shown in equity on the balance sheet ((£10,000 / 5) + £100,000).

Profits of £1,000,000 are shown as members' remuneration charged as an expense in the profit and loss account, and the retained profit is nil.

The capital accumulated from profits (£2,000) is shown within the reconciliation of members' interests.

Presentation in reconciliation of members' interests

	EQUITY — Members' Other Interests			DEBT	Total 2XX1	Total 2XX0
	Members' Capital (Classified as equity) £	Other Reserves £	Total £	Loans and other debts due to members less any amounts due from members in debtors £	£	£
Amounts due to members				XXXXXXX		
Amounts due from members				XXXXXXX		
Balance at start of 2XX1	100,000	XXXXXX	XXXXXX	XXXXXX	XXXXXX	XXXXXX
Members' remuneration charged as an expense, including employment and retirement benefit costs				1,000,000	1,000,000	XXXXXX
Members' interests after profit for the year	100,000	XXXXXXX	XXXXXXX	XXXXXXX	XXXXXX	XXXXXX
Capital introduced by members	2,000			(2,000)	–	XXXXXX
Drawings				(700,000)	(700,000)	XXXXX
Amounts due to members				XXXXXX		
Amounts due from members				XXXXXX		
Balance at end of 2XX1	102,000	XXXXXX	XXXXXX	XXXXXX	XXXXXX	XXXXXX

97

9   LOSSES

6.9   The 2014 SORP does not address accounting for losses made by LLPs, as the ways in which these are addressed within members' agreements are varied. It is, however, usual for the provisions in respect of losses to be different to those in respect of profits – ie there is often no requirement for members to contribute to losses in the same way they share in profits.

Example 1 – Profits of subsequent periods reduced by past losses (profits are equity)

Relevant conditions contained in the members' agreement

On retirement, capital must be returned to the retiring member.

Decision to divide profit requires agreement of a majority of members.

Members are not required to contribute to losses.

In 2XX0 (the LLP's first year of trading), the LLP makes a loss of £300,000, and drawings were £600,000.

In 2XX1, the LLP makes a profit of £1,000,000, and drawings are £700,000.

In 2XX2, the LLP makes a profit of £1,200,000, and drawings are £800,000.

The remaining undrawn profits from 2XX1 are also paid (£300,000).

Capital remains unchanged throughout at £100,000.

Analysis

The LLP has an obligation to return capital.

The members have no obligation to contribute to losses.

Profits are included within profits available for discretionary division among members in the profit and loss account and equity in the balance sheet.

Accounting treatment

Capital of £100,000 is shown as a liability on the balance sheet (members' capital classified as debt).

In 2XX0:

- A loss of £300,000 is recorded in the profit and loss account (loss available for discretionary division among members). This amount is included within members' other interests on the balance sheet.

- Drawings of £600,000 are included within debtors.

In 2XX1:

- A profit of £1,000,000 is recorded in the profit and loss account (profit available for discretionary division among members). This amount is also included within members' other interests on the balance sheet.

- Drawings of £700,000 are included within debtors.

In 2XX2:

- A profit of £1,200,000 is recorded in the profit and loss account (profit available for discretionary division among members). This amount is also included within members' other interests on the balance sheet.

- The decision to divide the profits of the previous year is reflected within the reconciliation of members' interests, but also takes account of the requirement to make good past losses. A division of £700,000 is therefore reflected.

- Drawings of £800,000 are included within debtors.

Presentation in reconciliation of members' interests

	EQUITY Members' Other Interests		DEBT	Total 2XX0
	Other Reserves	Total	Loans and other debts due to members less any amounts due from members in debtors	
	£	£	£	£
Balance at start of 2XX0	–	–	–	–
Loss for the financial year available for discretionary division among members	(300,000)	(300,000)	–	(300,000)
Members' interests after profit/(loss) for the year	(300,000)	(300,000)	–	(300,000)
Introduced by members			100,000	100,000
Drawings			(600,000)	(600,000)
Amounts due to members	(300,000)	(300,000)	100,000	
Amounts due from members			(600,000)	(600,000)
Balance at end of 2XX0	(300,000)	(300,000)	(500,000)	(800,000)

	EQUITY Members' Other Interests		DEBT	Total 2XX1	Total 2XX0
	Other Reserves	Total	Loans and other debts due to members less any amounts due from members in debtors		
	£	£	£	£	£
Amounts due to members			100,000		
Amounts due from members			(600,000)		
Balance at start of 2XX1	(300,000)	(300,000)	(500,000)	(800,000)	–
Profit/(loss) for the financial year available for discretionary division among members	1,000,000	1,000,000		1,000,000	(300,000)
Members' interests after profit/(loss) for the year	700,000	700,000	(500,000)	200,000	(300,000)
Introduced by members	–	–	–	–	100,000
Drawings			(700,000)	(700,000)	(600,000)
Amounts due to members			100,000		
Amounts due from members			(1,300,000)		
Balance at end of 2XX1	700,000	700,000	(1,200,000)	(500,000)	(500,000)

| | EQUITY Members' Other Interests | | DEBT Loans and other debts due to members less any amounts due from members in debtors | Total 2XX2 | Total 2XX1 |
	Other Reserves	Total			
	£	£	£	£	£
Amounts due to members			100,000		
Amounts due from members			(1,300,000)		
Balance at start of 2XX2	700,000	700,000	(1,200,000)	(500,000)	(800,000)
Profit for the financial year available for discretionary division among members	1,200,000	1,200,000		1,200,000	1,000,000
Members' interests after profit/(loss) for the year	1,900,000	1,900,000	(1,200,000)	700,000	200,000
Other divisions of profits / losses			700,000		
Drawings	(700,000)	(700,000)	(800,000)	(800,000)	(700,000)
Amounts due to members			100,000		
Amounts due from members			(1,400,000)		
Balance at end of 2XX2	1,200,000	1,200,000	(1,300,000)	(100,000)	(500,000)

It should be noted that, in practice, the members' agreement may include clauses with respect to the adjustment of future drawings to take account of past losses. Careful analysis of the members' agreement will, therefore, always be required.

Example 2 – Profits of subsequent periods reduced by past losses (profits are liabilities)

Relevant conditions contained in the members' agreement

On retirement, capital must be returned to the retiring member.

All profits are divided automatically.

Members are not required to contribute to losses.

In Year 1 (the LLP's first year of trading), the LLP makes a loss of £300,000, and drawings are £600,000.

In Year 2, the LLP makes a profit of £1,000,000, and drawings are £700,000.

Capital remains unchanged throughout at £100,000.

Analysis

The LLP has an obligation to return capital.

The members have no obligation to contribute to losses.

Profits are a liability to the extent they exceed past losses.

Accounting treatment

In Year 1:

- Members' remuneration charged as an expense is zero, and the LLP records a loss available for discretionary division of £300,000. This amount is included within members' other interests in the balance sheet.

- Drawings of £600,000 are included within debtors. However, careful consideration is required as to whether such a debtor will be recovered from future profits and whether a provision should be made against it (keeping in mind that assets should not be stated at any more than their recoverable amount).

In Year 2:

- Members' remuneration charged as an expense is £700,000 (£1,000,000 – £300,000). The LLP records a profit of £300,000 available for discretionary division, which is included within members' other interests in the balance sheet.

Presentation in reconciliation of members' interests

	EQUITY — Members' Other Interests		DEBT	Total Year 1
	Other Reserves	Total	Loans and other debts due to members less any amounts due from members in debtors	
	£	£	£	£
Balance at start of Year 1	–	–	–	–
Members' remuneration charged as an expense, including employment and retirement benefit costs				–
Loss for the financial year available for discretionary division among members	(300,000)	(300,000)		(300,000)
Members' interests after profit/(loss) for the year	(300,000)	(300,000)	–	(300,000)
Introduced by members			100,000	100,000
Drawings			(600,000)	(600,000)
Amounts due to members			100,000	
Amounts due from members			(600,000)	
Balance at end of Year 1	(300,000)	(300,000)	(500,000)	(800,000)

104

	EQUITY Members' Other Interests		DEBT	Total Year 2	Total Year 1
	Other Reserves	Total	Loans and other debts due to members less any amounts due from members in debtors		
	£	£	£	£	£
Amounts due to members			100,000		
Amounts due from members			(600,000)		
Balance at start of Year 2	(300,000)	(300,000)	(500,000)	(800,000)	–
Members' remuneration charged as an expense, including employment and retirement benefit costs			700,000	700,000	–
Profit for the financial year available for discretionary division among members	300,000	300,000		300,000	(300,000)
Members' interests after profit/(loss) for the year		–	200,000	200,000	(300,000)
Introduced by members		–	–	–	100,000
Drawings		–	(700,000)	(700,000)	(600,000)
Amounts due to members	–		100,000		
Amounts due from members			(600,000)		
Balance at end of Year 2	–	–	(500,000)	(500,000)	(500,000)

Example 3 – Member has obligation to make good losses

Relevant conditions contained in the members' agreement

All profits are divided automatically.

Members are required to contribute to losses.

Analysis

The members have an obligation to contribute to losses.

Accounting treatment

The profit and loss account reflects the obligation of the members to contribute to the losses of the LLP. This should be included in the line 'Members' remuneration charged as an expense', although 'Members' obligations in respect of losses' might be a more appropriate wording.

An equivalent amount will also be included on the balance sheet within amounts due from members. Consideration will need to be given as to whether such amounts are recoverable and, where they are not, provision should be made so they are carried at recoverable amount.

10 LIMITED LIFE LLP

6.10   LLPs are often used as the vehicle to carry out a specific project – for example, development of a property. Such LLPs may then be liquidated once the project is complete.

Careful analysis of the arrangements is required to determine the appropriate accounting treatment of the interactions with members, particularly in respect of capital. The provisions contained in paragraph 22.4 relating to puttable instruments may well have an effect on the determination of whether that capital is debt or equity. For example, it is not unusual in these circumstances for a members' agreement to include a clause that requires capital to be returned to members, but only upon the liquidation of the LLP. Whilst this might at first sight appear to be a liability, because of an unavoidable obligation to return cash to members, the provisions contained in paragraph 22.4 of FRS 102 may result in a different position, as it sees obligations arising only on liquidation as circumstances that are indicative of a residual interest. Where all of the conditions are met, the capital would be classified as equity.

Chapter 7

Revenue recognition and work in progress

SIGNPOSTS

- The timing of revenue recognition is critical for many LLP's – particularly professional services as the turnover figure is the key driver of profit on which members' will be taxed (see **7.1**).

- Section 23 *Revenue* in FRS 102 *The Financial Reporting Standard applicable in the UK and Republic of Ireland* differentiates between the sale of goods, rendering of services as well as revenue from interest, royalties and dividends (see **7.2**).

- Section 23 uses the 'stage of completion' method as a means of establishing the amount of revenue to be recognised in a service/ construction contract (see **7.2**).

- Service contracts will need to be scrutinised carefully and their terms understood in determining the extent to which revenue should be recognised in an accounting period (see **7.3**).

- Progress payments/advance payments received by the LLP are not revenue because they do not reflect the work performed (see **7.3**).

- The value attributable to the amount of revenue under a service contract is determined with reference to how much can be charged for the work that is being performed (see **7.4**).

- Revenue recognised in respect of work performed but not yet billed is included in turnover and accrued within debtors (or 'amounts recoverable on contracts') (see **7.5**).

- If work has been carried out but the criteria in Section 23 has not been met, work in progress is recognised (see **7.6**).

- Work in progress has to be valued at the lower of cost and estimated selling price, less costs to complete and sell (see **7.7**).

- Various methods of valuing work in progress are used by professional firms, but whichever method is used, the firm will need to determine the amount of overheads to be included in work in progress (see **7.8**).

- A simple method which can be justified and reasonable when valuing work in progress and one which is consistently applied should normally be adequate (see **7.8**).

- Professional judgement needs to be applied to contracts which are undertaken on a contingent fee basis where the work is incomplete at the reporting date (see **7.9**).

- Whilst it is fairly uncommon for LLPs to operate in the construction industry, Section 23 to FRS 102 does contain guidance on the accounting for construction contracts and revenue recognition within a construction contract (see **7.10 and 7.11**).

1   SECTION 23 REVENUE

7.1   FRS 102 *The Financial Reporting Standard applicable in the UK and Republic of Ireland* at Section 23 *Revenue* is the section which deals with the principles involved in revenue recognition. The timing of revenue recognition is critical for many LLPs – particularly professional practices – and this can have a direct tax consequence on the members because the turnover figure (being the headline figure in the accounts) is the key driver of profit on which members will be taxed. The importance of correctly recognising an appropriate amount of turnover at the correct time cannot be over-emphasised. The wording in Section 23 of FRS 102 is not the same as that contained in previous UK GAAP (UITF 40 and Application Note G to FRS 5 *Reporting the Substance of Transactions*) and therefore care must be taken by LLPs in ensuring that the provisions in Section 23 are applied correctly to avoid any contentious issues either with other members of the LLP or with HM Revenue and Customs.

2   THE PRINCIPLES OF REVENUE RECOGNITION

7.2   Section 23 differentiates between revenue which arises from the sale of goods and that which arises from the provision of services. It also deals with revenue which arises in a construction contract as well as revenue which arises from the use by others of assets which generate interest, royalties and dividends to the LLP. Whilst LLPs are often service organisations, this chapter does take a look at the concept of construction contract accounting because such provisions are incorporated within Section 23. In recognition that it is relatively uncommon for LLP's to operate in a construction environment, this particular concept is considered at the end of this chapter.

The underlying principle of Section 23 is that revenue should be recognised when, and to the extent that, an entity has earned the right to payment through a performance-related condition. A *performance-related condition* is defined as '*a condition that requires the performance of a particular level of service or units of output to be delivered, with payment of, or entitlement to, the resources conditional on that performance*'. When dealing with the sale of goods, in most cases a performance-related condition will equate to the delivery of the relevant goods, and hence Section 23 will be relatively easy to apply. However, when dealing with service contracts, the principles can be more difficult to interpret and, under old UK GAAP when Application Note G to FRS 5 and UITF 40 were first issued, many LLPs found that their revenue was being recognised earlier than may previously have been the case. Similar principles are included in Section 23 and thus the remainder of this chapter, therefore, concentrates on accounting for revenue from the rendering of services and revenue in a construction contract.

It can be somewhat problematic for LLPs to decipher the amount of revenue receivable in a service contract at the end of a reporting period. Paragraph 23.14 to FRS 102 says that if the outcome of a transaction which involves the rendering of services can be estimated reliably (ie whether it is a profit- or loss-making contract) then revenue is recognised having reference to the *stage of completion* of the transaction at the end of the reporting period. The stage of completion is often a best estimate and judgement will always be a crucial aspect of arriving at this estimate. In some cases, particularly in construction contracts, professional valuations might need to be obtained to accurately ascertain the stage of completion. For the purposes of Section 23, the outcome of a transaction can be reliably estimated if all of the following conditions can be met:

- the amount of revenue to be recognised can be measured reliably;

- it is probable (ie more likely than not) that cash, or other forms of assets, directly attributable to the transaction will flow to the entity;

- the stage of completion of the transaction can be reliably measured; and

- the costs which have been incurred, and which will need to be incurred to complete the transaction, can also be reliably measured.

When an LLP is undertaking a contract on behalf of a customer/client which involves the rendering of services the LLP must determine the stage of completion which will result in a reliable measure of the work performed. Paragraph 23.22 outlines three possible methods:

- the proportion that costs incurred for work performed as at the reporting date to the estimated total costs (which must exclude any costs which relate to future activity);

- surveys of the work performed; and

- completion of a proportion of the contract or completion of a physical proportion of the contract.

Example – progress payment from a customer

An LLP is undertaking a large project for its customer in developing a bespoke database management system. The work is scheduled to take two years and the

LLP has received an advanced payment from its customer to cover initial costs. The financial accountant has credited the advance to turnover.

Advances received from a customer should not be reflected within turnover because they do not reflect the work performed (this also applies to any progress payments received from a customer). The financial accountant should credit the advance to a 'contract account' within the nominal ledger and only recognise revenue in accordance with paragraphs 23.14–23.16 (paragraphs 23.17–23.20 for construction contracts).

To the extent, therefore, that a service organisation has performed work and the fee is not conditional on a future event outside the entity's control, this will normally represent earned income. As a result, unbilled amounts should be accrued at selling price and be recognised as revenue within the LLP's profit and loss account.

If the outcome of a service contract **cannot** be reliably estimated, the LLP must recognise revenue to the extent of the expenses recognised which are recoverable.

If services are performed by an indeterminate number of acts over a specified period, the LLP must recognise revenue on a straight-line basis over that specified period. There may be occasions when the members regard another alternative measurement method as being more representative of the stage of completion and in such cases the LLP can use an alternative method than the straight-line method.

3   ANALYSING CONTRACTS

7.3   In determining the extent to which revenue needs to be recognised in an accounting period, the contracts in progress at the year end need to be analysed and their terms understood. Many contracts will stipulate when fees on account are to be raised but these may not correlate with the principles of revenue recognition (indeed paragraph 23.22 refers to progress payments and advances which have been received by customers/clients often do not reflect the work performed and so care needs to be taken with such payments/advances to ensure correct accounting treatment). Some contracts, because of their size or complexity, may need to be considered individually. In other cases examination of a single contract may show it to have a number of individually identifiable phases and each of those phases may need to be accounted for separately. More commonly, however, there will be a number of contracts to provide a similar type of service which should be considered together.

In general, achieving the right to payment on a service contract will be related directly to a performance-related condition. As such, revenue should ordinarily be recognised in proportion to the extent of progress on the contract. In most cases, the extent of contract activity can be determined by comparing the amount of time spent or costs incurred in providing the service up to the date of the accounts to the total time or costs that it is expected will be spent or incurred in delivering the service.

Example – completion of a self-assessment income tax return

Consider the position of a tax accountant who is halfway through completing a client's tax return at the accountant's financial year end. Whilst it could be argued that a half-completed tax return is of little practical use, it can also be assumed that the computation will be completed and, by extension, that the accountant will complete all of the tax returns that he is working on at his year end, particularly if the year-end date is 31 January. Section 23 requires that the principles in paragraph 23.14 should be applied in accounting for this contract. The accountant would therefore recognise 50% of the income from the individual contract, and then apply similar calculations to all other contracts.

Not all contracts will be so straightforward and contract terms need to be examined carefully to identify specific circumstances, such as identifiable milestones or contingent fee arrangements, which affect how the associated revenue should be calculated.

Where a contract has identifiable milestones, revenue will be recognised dependent on the milestones that have already been reached and the extent of progress towards the next milestone.

Where there is a contingent fee arrangement and the contingency is outside the control of the LLP, no revenue should be recognised until the contingent event occurs.

Example – law firm operating on a 'no win, no fee' basis

A law firm is acting for a client in a personal injury claim under a 'no win, no fee' arrangement. The case has been ongoing for several months and the year-end financial statements are about to be completed. The bookkeeper is unsure as to whether any revenue should be recognised in this case and the trial is not listed to be heard in court for three months' time.

In this case the outcome of the trial is outside the control of the law firm. As a result, no revenue should be recognised until the case has been won because it is only at that stage that the law firm has a right to consideration.

Even where the contingency is resolved after the financial period end, but before the accounts are approved, no revenue should be recognised in the period. The accounting treatment of work in progress in such circumstances is considered further at **7.9**.

4   DETERMINING THE VALUE OF REVENUE

7.4   The value attributable to the recognised proportion of revenue under a service contract is determined with reference to how much can be charged for the work that is being performed. This will usually be stipulated in the contract, either in the form of a lump sum amount, an hourly rate, or a combination of the two.

Where fees are charged to the client with reference to time spent at an hourly rate, staff members will normally be required to record details of how much time they have spent on different tasks and clients in some form of time recording system. In such situations, firms often calculate accrued income by starting with unbilled time as stated in their time recording systems, valued at standard hourly rates. This will then be adjusted for amounts that are not expected to be fully recoverable, either on a case-by-case basis, or by applying a percentage that reflects past experience of actual recoveries compared to cost.

For certain types of service, contracts may stipulate two different fees dependent upon the outcome of a future event. Revenue should only be recognised based on the value the LLP is certain to get – usually the lowest.

Example – fee outcome depending on a contingent event

A law firm has a contract to advise Company A on the acquisition of Company B. The fees agreed with Company A are that, if the transaction is successful, the law firm will bill £125,000 and, if it is unsuccessful, the fee will be £75,000.

At the year end, it is estimated that 60% of the services have been provided, and so the appropriate level of revenue to be included in the accounts would be £45,000 (60% of £75,000).

---

5   ACCOUNTING ENTRIES

7.5   Where an entity recognises revenue in respect of work that has been performed but not yet billed, this amount is included in turnover and also as accrued income within debtors. The cost of performing the work should not be carried forward within work in progress, but should be recognised as a cost in the profit and loss account. The double-entry is as follows:

DR debtors (amounts recoverable on contracts)	X
CR turnover	X

Where invoices have been raised which exceed the amount of revenue that can be recognised, the excess should not be included in the profit and loss account but as deferred income within creditors. If the amounts have been paid, then they should be disclosed within creditors as 'payments received on account'.

6 WORK IN PROGRESS

7.6 Where an LLP has carried out work but has not yet met the criteria to recognise revenue in paragraph 23.14 of FRS 102, work in progress should be recognised.

Work in progress is an example of the 'matching' concept of accounting. If costs have been incurred to produce goods or services in one period and the related revenue will not arise until a later period, then the costs are deferred and released in the period that the revenue arises so that the two 'match' each other. Costs should only be deferred to the extent that they are expected to be recovered against future revenue, and so work in progress is recognised at the lower of cost and estimated selling price less costs to complete and sell (ie the amount that will be received net of any further costs to be incurred in the process).

7 DETERMINING THE COST OF WORK IN PROGRESS

7.7 As noted at **7.6**, work in progress has to be included in the balance sheet at the lower of cost and estimated selling price less costs to complete and sell. Section 13 *Inventories* deals with the rendering of services insofar as work in progress is concerned. Section 13 says that *cost* does not just include materials (unlikely to be relevant to the majority of LLPs) but also direct labour and overheads.

Direct labour should include the cost of those employees who have been directly involved in the provision of the related service. The employees' cost should include not only their wages or salaries, but also other employment costs, such as national insurance contributions and pensions. Where members' time is included within work in progress, it should be valued to the extent that it is charged as an expense in the profit and loss account (see Chapter 5). Amounts received by members, by way of allocation of profits available for division amongst members, should be excluded from the valuation of work in progress.

Section 23 requires that all 'direct' overheads should be included within the valuation of work in progress. Other overheads should only be included in work in progress to the extent that they are incurred in the provision of the related service. Costs such as administrative overheads and selling expenses must not be included in the cost of work in progress.

Overheads should be allocated to work in progress on the basis of the LLP's normal level of activity. Overhead costs which are the result of inefficiencies, such as the effect of abnormal changes in procedures, should not be included in the valuation.

Irrespective of whether the time input by a member is included within work in progress, the general accounting requirement to match costs and revenues means that any overhead related to the member's time should be included in the valuation.

The above principles will also apply to any stock produced by an LLP involved in manufacturing or production.

8   VALUING WORK IN PROGRESS IN PRACTICE

7.8   In calculating the cost of work in progress, some professional services firms take the value of unbilled fee-earner time at charge-out rates as a starting point, and then reduce this value by the gross profit element included within the charge-out rates. Others build up an hourly cost for each fee-earner from their salary and related costs plus an allocation of overheads.

Whichever method is used, the firm will need to determine the amount of overheads to be included in work in progress (or to be deducted in arriving at gross profit). Particular problems may arise when trying to deal with areas such as central management overheads. Salaries for this area may well include an element of either direct provision of service or the supervision of service delivery, as well as administration. Central costs should be apportioned between direct and indirect costs on a reasonable basis and this should then be consistently applied.

Where an hourly cost is calculated for each fee-earner, further complications can arise in allocating the overheads between fee-earners. The most usual approach is an allocation which is in proportion to direct labour costs.

In practice, a complicated method of calculating the cost of work in progress is often unnecessary, and a simple method, which can be justified as reasonable and is consistently applied, should normally be adequate.

For most firms, a significant part of the standard 'selling price' relates to recovery of indirect costs and profit. As a result, unless the work is subject to an unsettled contingency, which will potentially cause it to be heavily discounted, or no charge to be made for it, it is relatively unusual for further provision against the cost of work in progress to be necessary.

9   WORK IN PROGRESS AND CONTINGENT FEE ARRANGEMENTS

7.9   One area that has given rise to particular debate is contracts undertaken on a contingent fee basis where the work is incomplete at the reporting date.

Where a contract contains a specific deliverable which is much more significant than any other, the LLP must delay the recognition of revenue until that significant deliverable is completed. In such a situation it may be the case that no revenue is recognised, but this should not preclude the LLP from recognising the costs incurred on the contract up to the reporting date as work in progress.

Contingent fee arrangements will normally be accounted for under the provisions laid down in paragraphs 23.14 to 24.16 of FRS 102. Under previous UK GAAP it was acceptable to either expense the cost of the work performed as incurred, or to recognise the costs of work performed as work in progress at the period end (which were subject to the usual considerations relating to recoverability). Where an LLP has always recognised work in progress, the requirements in Section 23 will not result in any difference from what was the case under previous UK GAAP.

10 CONSTRUCTION CONTRACTS

7.10   Whilst it is fairly uncommon for LLPs to operate in the construction sector, it is worth noting that Section 23 incorporates the guidance for construction contracts and recognises that construction contracts themselves may pose a particular accounting issue in that such contracts may well span more than one (if not several, in some cases) accounting periods.

The principles with construction contracts and Section 23 are fairly similar. Revenue and costs in a construction contract are recognised by reference to the stage of completion of the contract activity at the reporting date.

Section 23 is usually applied separately to each construction contract but there may be occasions when the section will have to be applied to those components of a contract which are separately identifiable in a single contract, or to a group of contracts together so as to reflect the substance of a contract or a group of contracts.

Example – one contract treated as separate contracts

Cory Construction LLP has been awarded a construction contract which requires the construction of several retail units on new retail park in a vibrant city centre location in the UK. Whilst the contract is a single contract in itself, the contractor invited separate proposals for each unit which have all been separately negotiated and the costs and revenues associated with each unit can be identified.

For the purposes of Section 23, if a construction contract covers a number of contracts, the construction of each asset (in this case each retail unit) is treated as a separate construction contract. This occurs when:

- separate proposals have been submitted for each asset (in this case each retail unit);

- each asset has been the subject of separate negotiation. Both the contractor and the customer are able to accept, or reject, a specific part of the contract relating to an individual asset; and

- both the costs and the revenues associated with each asset can be identified.

Example – group of contracts treated as a single contract

Cory Construction LLP has tendered for three contracts with a well-known supermarket. The contract is to build a supermarket in a local town centre with a petrol station and car park all on the same location. Separate contracts are available for all three projects but they are only going to be awarded to one contractor and with an overall profit margin and hence are being negotiated effectively as a single package. All three projects have to be completed on the same date so that the supermarket can open as scheduled.

Paragraph 23.20 to FRS 102 requires a group of contracts to be treated as a single construction contract when the following conditions are met:

- the group of contracts are all negotiated as a single package;

- the contracts are so closely interrelated that they are essentially part of a single project and have an overall profit margin; and

- the contracts are undertaken concurrently or in a continuous sequence.

11 ACCOUNTING FOR A CONSTRUCTION CONTRACT

7.11   Construction contract accounting can become very complicated in some areas. Section 23 requires the 'percentage of completion method' to be applied where construction contracts are concerned. Any estimates of revenue and costs are reviewed by the LLP as the contract progresses.

If a contract is profit-making, the LLP must recognise revenue by reference to the stage of completion together with a similar percentage for revenue.

Example – profit-making contract

Cory Construction LLP has been awarded a contract amounting to £100,000 which is expected to make a profit at the end of the contract of £30,000. At the balance sheet date, the valuation agent confirmed the contract was 40% complete.

As the contract is expected to yield a profit of £30,000, Cory Construction LLP will recognise 40% of revenue and 40% of costs to date. Hence the profit and loss account extracts will be as follows:

Turnover	(£100,000 × 40%)	£40,000
Cost of sales	(£70,000 × 40%)	£28,000
Gross profit		£12,000 (ie 40% × £30,000)

There may be occasions when a contract is loss-making. In such cases, paragraph 23.26 says that the expected loss must be recognised immediately with a corresponding provision for an onerous contract.

Example – loss-making contract

Cory Construction LLP has a contract which is expected to make a loss of £1,000. The finance director has calculated that the amount of the contract revenue to be recognised is £800.

The profit and loss account will recognise revenue of £800. The loss is estimated to be £1,000 and must be recognised immediately to comply with the provisions in paragraph 23.26. Hence cost of sales will be £1,800 to generate the required loss (in other words, cost of sales is essentially a balancing figure).

It may not be possible at the reporting date to assess whether a contract will be profit- or loss-making and in these situations the provisions in paragraph 23.25 (a) and (b) will become relevant. Nil profit is recognised in profit or loss when the outcome of a construction contract cannot be reliably estimated and this is achieved by recognising revenue to the extent of costs incurred that it is probable will be recoverable.

Example – uncertainty in a contract

Cory Construction LLP enters into a two-year contract. At the reporting date, the project manager is unable to ascertain whether the contract will yield a profit or a loss. Costs incurred up to the reporting date are £10,000.

As the outcome of the contract cannot be estimated reliably, the amount of turnover to be recognised in the LLP's financial statements is the same as costs incurred, resulting in no profit being taken, hence:

DR debtors	£10,000
CR turnover	£10,000

Chapter 8

Taxation

SIGNPOSTS

- Whilst this chapter deals primarily with taxation, it aims only to give a brief overview and should not be regarded as comprehensive advice (see **8.1**).

- LLPs are partnerships in a 'corporate wrapper' and its member are subject to tax directly on their share of the LLPs profit, including a share of any investment income earned by the LLP and on the proceeds from any capital assets (see **8.2**).

- A 'representative member' must sign the LLP tax return and confirm that the information in the tax return is complete. There are penalties applied by HMRC to each separate member for late returns (see **8.2**).

- The taxation and NI position of salaried members of an LLP is complex (see **8.3**).

- New rules in the Finance Act 2014 were introduced to prevent tax loss in situations where employment is disguised through an LLP (see **8.4**).

- Each member is required to settle his or her tax liability by making two payments on account and a final balancing payment (see **8.5**).

- Setting funds aside in a tax reserve should help to avoid any additional cash flow difficulties, but tax reserve funds will form part of the members' funds available for distribution to creditors in the invent of insolvency (see **8.6**).

- The starting point for assessing taxable profits will be the profit as per the annual accounts which are prepared using Generally Accepted Accounting Practice (see **8.7**).

- Tax legislation does not recognise annuities as being an allowable expense for profits for the purposes of tax (see **8.8**).

- HMRC will generally allow a tax deduction to be claimed for provisions which are made in accordance with Section 21 of FRS 102 *Provisions and Contingencies* (see **8.9**).

- If an LLP borrows money for the purposes of its trade, any interest is likely to be allowable for the purposes of tax as an expense through the profit and loss account (see **8.10**).

> • Proceeds from the disposal of an asset must be reported on the LLP's tax return. The associated capital gain is calculated on the capital gains tax pages of the member's tax return and not collectively on the partnership return (see **8.11**).

1 INTRODUCTION

8.1 Whilst this book deals principally with accounting requirements, the taxation of LLPs and its members cannot be entirely ignored. This chapter aims only to give a brief overview of the taxation of LLPs and will cover some areas where the taxation treatment may differ from the accounts. It should not be regarded as comprehensive advice, and reference should be had to taxation specialists where appropriate.

2 BASIC TAX PRINCIPLES AND COMPLIANCE PROCEDURES

8.2 An LLP is not in itself subject to tax but is, as described by HM Revenue & Customs (HMRC), a 'transparent' entity, which means that, unless certain circumstances apply, such as that the LLP is being wound up, the LLP is 'looked through' and its members are subject to tax. In effect, LLPs are partnerships in a corporate wrapper. Each member will be taxed directly on his share of the LLP's profits, including a share of any investment income earned by the LLP and on the proceeds received from any capital assets. If the LLP is trading, members are also liable to Class 2 and Class 4 national insurance (NI) contributions.

Despite the fact that the LLP is not itself liable to tax, as for a general partnership, it must complete a tax return for each fiscal year. Fiscal years run from 6 April in one year to 5 April in the following year. There are special rules that apply if there is no accounting period ending in the tax year but, in general, the tax return will include the results for the accounting period ended within the fiscal year. For example, if an LLP has a 30 June year end, the 2014/15 return (covering the period 6 April 2014 to 5 April 2015) would include results for the accounting period ended 30 June 2014. Investment income which has been taxed at source, proceeds from the disposal of capital assets, and charges on income are, however, included in the tax return on the basis of the fiscal year in which they arose.

In addition to the general requirement to retain accounting records discussed in Chapter 2, the LLP must also maintain any additional records relating to the tax position for five years and ten months following the end of the tax year in which the accounting period ended.

HMRC may in principle require any member of the LLP to file an LLP tax return but in practice the notice will normally be served on a 'representative member' either selected by HMRC or nominated by the members. The representative member must sign the return to confirm that the information shown thereon is correct and complete. Although it is the representative member who is responsible for filing the return, where the return is filed late and penalties become payable, those penalties are exigible from each member separately. The following penalties may be applied by HMRC *to each member separately* for 2010/11 onwards:

- Return up to three months late – £100 fixed penalty.

- More than three months late – £10 per day (up to 90 days (maximum £900) payable only if HMRC give notice of the penalty and the notice specifies the date from which the penalty is payable).

- More than six months late – the greater of 5% of tax liability and £300.

- More than 12 months late – up to 100% of tax liability. For 2011/12, the penalty may in some special cases be as much as 200% of the tax liability.

- Incorrect LLP return – up to 100% of the tax lost. For 2011/12, the penalty may in some special cases be as much as 200% of the tax liability.

- Failure to keep and maintain records – £3,000.

Whilst certain penalties may sometimes be negotiated with HMRC, the penalties for late submission of a return are mandatory and can in aggregate be substantial depending upon the size of the firm. Although late filing penalties are exigible from members separately it is only the representative member who has any right of appeal against these penalties, in which case the appeal is treated as a composite appeal made on behalf of all relevant members. Thus, although the LLP return notice is issued only to the 'representative member', all members have a very clear interest in ensuring that the representative member fulfils his or her statutory obligations in a timely fashion.

The tax return must be filed with HMRC by 31 January following the end of the fiscal year if this is done electronically, or 31 October if on paper. For example, the 2014/15 return must be filed by 31 January 2016 if it is being filed electronically, and otherwise it should be filed by 31 October 2015.

Following completion of the LLP return, the firm should provide each member with a member's statement, showing their share of income as reported on that return. Each member is then responsible for including this income on his or her personal tax return.

It may sometimes happen that a member disagrees with the amount of taxable profit allocated to him or her on the LLP tax return. The question then arises whether the profit share shown on the LLP return is conclusive as regards the member or whether the member is entitled to enter a different figure on his or her personal return. Obiter dicta in *Self v HMRC* [2009] UKFTT 78(TC) suggest that the proper course is for the member to include on the personal return the amount which is believed to be correct and to explain in the 'white space' any discrepancy with the LLP return.

3   SALARIED MEMBERS

8.3   The taxation and NI position of salaried members of an LLP is complex.

HMRC have historically taken the view that all those who are registered as members at Companies House as members of an LLP fall to be treated for tax purposes as self-employed and not as employees of the LLP. This, despite the fact that Limited Liability Partnerships Act 2000 (LLPA 2000) clearly allows for employee members, which would imply that in some circumstances members are capable of being employees of the LLP, which may appear to be at odds with HMRC's interpretation.

The employment law case of *Tiffin v Aldridge* (2012) 2 All ER 1113 also confirmed that an LLP member could be an 'employee' of the LLP, albeit the claimant in the case was, on the facts, held to be a 'partner (member)'.

Nonetheless, it appears to be the case that the normal case law tests determining whether a person is an employee which would apply, for example, in the case of a salaried member of a general partnership, have no relevance to membership of an LLP: for tax purposes a member of an LLP is treated as self-employed, unless the special rules described below are in point.

Where members of an LLP are treated as partners, not employees, the self-employed (Class 2 and Class 4) rates of NI will apply.

4   DISGUISED EMPLOYMENT

8.4   The Finance Act 2014 introduced rules (effective from 6 April 2014) to prevent tax loss in situations where employment is disguised through limited liability partnerships. Broadly, the changes affect LLP members who work for LLPs on terms that HMRC view as 'tantamount to employment' (ie disguised employment). They will primarily affect LLP members who have a fixed share of profit.

The new rules only apply to individuals that are members of LLPs, and to fall within the rules they have to satisfy three conditions (A–C) as follows: if any of the conditions are not fulfilled the new rules do not apply and the individual will not be treated as an employee.

Condition A is that there are 'relevant arrangements' in place for the individual to perform services as a member of the LLP. 'Relevant arrangements' means arrangements under which amounts are to be, or may be, payable by the LLP in respect of the individual's performance of services for the partnership in his capacity as a member of the partnership. The condition will be met if it is reasonable to expect that at least 80% of the total amount payable by the LLP in respect of the individual's performance during the relevant period of services for the partnership in the individual's capacity as a member of the partnership, will be disguised salary.

An amount will be treated as 'disguised salary' if it:

- is fixed;
- is variable, but is varied without reference to the overall amount of the profits or losses of the LLP; or
- is not, in practice, affected by the overall amount of those profits or losses.

In many cases, this condition will not be fulfilled as partners in an LLP will be remunerated by reference to the overall profits available.

Condition B is that the person concerned does not have significant influence over the affairs of the partnership.

Condition C is that the person's partnership capital is less than 25% of the amount which is reasonably expected to be disguised salary for the tax year. In other words, to avoid being treated as an employee under this test the person concerned has to have at stake capital of at least one quarter of their partnership income. The partnership capital is determined on 6 April 2014 or at the date of appointment of the partner and then at the beginning of each subsequent tax year or whenever the partnership sharing arrangements change.

If a person satisfies all three conditions above, then that person is taxed as if they were an employee of the partnership for all tax purposes, although their wider legal status as a member of the LLP is not changed. In other words, this is purely a tax measure.

Under the new legislation, as outlined above, a salaried member will be deemed to be employed by their LLP for tax and NICs purposes. In these circumstances, the LLP will be liable to deduct and pay tax and NICs on any amount paid to the salaried member as if it were employment income for tax and employed earners' earnings for NICs. The LLP will be the secondary contributor for NICs, and will be responsible for paying NICs on earnings and benefits.

5   TIMING OF TAX PAYMENTS

8.5   Each member is required to settle his or her tax liability by making two payments on account and a final balancing payment. The payments on account fall due for payment on the 31 January during the fiscal year and the 31 July following the end of the fiscal year. Each payment on account is based upon 50% of the previous year's liability to income tax and Class 4 NI contributions. The final balancing payment falls due for payment on 31 January following the end of the fiscal year.

Example – Payment of taxes

For the fiscal year 2014/15, tax will fall due for payment as follows:

1st payment on account	31 January 2015
2nd payment on account	31 July 2015
Balancing payment	31 January 2016*

* The 1st payment on account in respect of the 2015/16 year will also be due for payment on this date.

Class 4 NI contributions are paid at the same time as the tax liability.

6   PROVIDING FOR TAX IN THE ACCOUNTS

8.6   There is no requirement for an LLP to make provision for tax in its accounts. However, many firms choose to set aside a separate tax reserve and a separate tax fund, to ensure that profits are not over-distributed and that members can pay their tax liabilities. There is no requirement to make separate disclosure of the tax reserves, as the LLP is effectively merely holding back profits and in due course acting as agent in making tax payments on behalf of the members.

The basis of reserving for tax will differ depending upon various factors, primarily the general attitude of members to setting aside funds. Perhaps the most common basis is to reserve on the assumption that all of the members will retire on the balance sheet date, setting aside tax on all profits earned to that date and allowing relief for any overlap profit. It may alternatively be considered appropriate to set aside funds which are sufficient to cover tax payments falling due over the course of the following 12 months.

The timing of tax payments means that, if profits fall and members have not themselves been sufficiently disciplined to set aside from drawings funds to pay tax, members can often find that they are required to pay tax on an earlier year's higher profits from reduced current year drawings. Setting aside funds in tax reserves should help avoid these additional cash flow difficulties. It should be borne in mind that, in the event that the firm is insolvent and required to pay its creditors, any tax reserve funds will form part of the members' funds available for distribution to creditors. For this reason, some firms may prefer to keep their tax reserve funds outside the LLP using a 'tax trust account'.

7   PROFITS SUBJECT TO TAX

8.7   The starting point for assessing taxable profits will be the profit as shown in the annual accounts. LLPs are not permitted to use the cash basis for calculating taxable income, and must prepare accounts for *tax purposes* using Generally Accepted Accounting Practice (either UK GAAP or IFRS) principles. The members of an LLP may agree to retain some profit (or losses) in the LLP and allocate to the members an amount which is different from the total profit or loss for the financial year (see Chapter 5). For tax purposes, however, the members will be subject to tax on all profits arising regardless of whether all of those profits have been allocated to them.

The total amount of profit, as adjusted for tax purposes (see below), is divided between the members in accordance with their arrangements for profit sharing and it is this amount that is subject to tax. If the firm holds unallocated profits, a member may be subject to tax on a sum far greater than the amount which has actually been allocated to him. The LLP will need to establish a mechanism (such as equalisation adjustments in tax reserves) to deal with this situation.

Whilst taxable profits will be based upon the profit shown in the accounts, tax legislation provides for certain adjustments to be made before the taxable profit can be established. For example, depreciation is not an allowable deduction for tax purposes, although relief is given for the purchase of some fixed assets by way of capital allowances.

Complications can arise where an LLP incurs a loss. As part of the firm's liability protection for members, many LLPs will have provisions which ensure that the loss is kept within the LLP and is not, for accounting and legal purposes, allocated to the members. However, when submitting the tax return for the LLP, it will be necessary to allocate the tax loss to members.

In the case of trading LLPs, losses may be restricted. The total sideways loss relief that an LLP member can claim, in respect of their share of the LLP's trading losses for any tax year, is restricted to the member's capital contribution as at the end of the tax year less the total sideways loss reliefs previously given at any time in respect of losses from the same trade. From 6 April 2013, a cap applies to certain previously unlimited income tax reliefs that may be deducted from income. The cap is set at £50,000 or 25% of income, whichever is greater.

In the case of a non-active LLP member, losses sustained on or after 2 March 2007 are subject to a £25,000 annual limit. Non-active for this purpose means a partner who does not spend on average at least ten hours per week personally engaged in trading activities. Capital contributions made by a non-active partner on or after 2 March 2007 do not count if the main purpose, or one of the main purposes, for contributing them was for the partner to claim sideways loss relief.

8   RETIREMENT BENEFITS AND ANNUITIES

8.8   As discussed in Chapter 9, the SORP requires an LLP to provide for the present value of the best estimate of the expected liability for future payments to current and former members.

The amounts charged in the accounts can be significant. For this reason, in some cases the remaining partners take on the commitment to pay the annuity to the retiring partner, so that the LLP accounts are not affected.

The tax legislation does not, however, recognise annuities as being an allowable expense from profits for tax purposes. Whether the annuity is paid by the LLP or by the members, relief is given as a charge on income against each member's overall tax liability as and when the annuity is paid. Basic rate tax relief (currently 20%) is given at source on the payment of the annuity to the former member (ie members make the payment net of basic rate tax unless there is a corporate member). If the members are higher rate taxpayers, they may then make a claim on their personal tax return for relief from the remainder of the tax. The amount of the annuity paid in the *fiscal year* is disclosed on the LLP return and on each member's statement. The member must declare the charge on income on the personal section of his tax return and not on the partnership pages relating to the LLP.

Whilst the members eventually receive full tax relief for the annuity, the relief is given over the life of the annuity rather than when a provision is made in the accounts.

9   OTHER PROVISIONS

8.9   Annuities (and pensions) are perhaps the exception to the general rule for allowing provisions for tax purposes. HMRC will generally allow a tax deduction to be claimed for provisions that are made in accordance with Section 21 *Provisions and Contingencies* (see Chapter 9).

10 MEMBERS' BORROWINGS

8.10   An LLP may borrow funds itself or require its members to contribute capital for which they may need to borrow funds from a bank. If the LLP borrows money for the purposes of its trade, any interest is likely to be allowable for tax purposes as an expense through the profit and loss account. Interest on members' personal loans to introduce capital will not be an expense in the profit and loss account but members can, in general, obtain tax relief for the interest paid through their personal tax returns. However, an important exception to this rule is for members of investment LLPs and property investment LLPs, where no relief is available on members' loans to provide capital.

Where capital is withdrawn from the LLP, this will be treated as reducing the amount of capital invested and, therefore, tax relief will not be available on the proportion of the loan interest relating to the withdrawn funds. In order to show a clear trail of capital invested in the LLP, it is recommended that separate records of capital and current accounts are maintained within the LLP, so that profits can be withdrawn without affecting tax relief on borrowings for the firm's capital.

Where members have mortgages or other borrowings which do not attract any interest tax relief, it may be possible to arrange for the borrowing to be taken out in respect of LLP capital and therefore obtain tax relief. This is known as capital recycling, and it is imperative that any recycling is carried out in a strict order and that the transactions are completed and are not mere book entries.

Care must be taken with any capital recycling, particularly in light of the case of *Lancaster v Revenue and Customs Commissioners* [2009] UKFTT (TC), in which interest relief was denied on borrowing to fund a partnership. Advice from a specialist tax adviser should be sought to ensure that any recycling is not caught by this case.

11 CAPITAL GAINS TAX

8.11 The assets of an LLP are treated for tax purposes as owned by the members. Whilst members may own the assets in differing ratios to their income sharing arrangements, in the absence of a separate agreement, any proceeds from the disposal of an asset would be taxed on the members in these same profit sharing ratios.

The proceeds from the disposal of an asset must be reported on the LLP's tax return. However, the gain is calculated on the capital gains tax pages of the member's tax return and not collectively on the partnership return. Where the LLP is carrying on a trading activity, a gain arising on the disposal of a member's share of the firm may be eligible for entrepreneur's relief. The conditions for entrepreneur's relief are tightly drawn but, provided the conditions are met, the net gains will be charged to capital gains tax at a rate of 10%. From 6 April 2011 there is a lifetime limit of £10 million for gains subject to entrepreneur's relief.

Where there has been a revaluation of the firm's assets, followed by a subsequent change in the asset sharing ratios, complications arise because each change in the asset sharing ratios amounts to a disposal by those members reducing their share of the asset, and an acquisition by those increasing their share. This can require complex capital gains tax records to be maintained and the performance of involved computations.

Chapter 9

Other accounting standards

SIGNPOSTS

- There are certain sections within FRS 102 *The Financial Reporting Standard applicable in the UK and Republic of Ireland* which may affect the financial statements of an LLP (see **9.1**).

- The term 'provision' can mean two fundamentally different things in accounting and it is crucial that LLPs make the correct distinction between the two (see **9.2**).

- Care must be taken to ensure that a provision in the context of Section 21 *Provisions and Contingencies* meets the three specific recognition criteria (see **9.3**).

- Provisions should not be made for future repairs and maintenance expenditure, however provisions for dilapidations may be made if the recognition and measurement criteria are met (see **9.5**).

- The time value of money should be taken into consideration for a provision if the time value is material (se **9.6**).

- Provisions for future operating losses should not be made (see **9.7**).

- Provisions should be made for obligations under an onerous contract but should not be made where the contract has merely turned out to be less profitable than originally anticipated (see **9.8**).

- Strict conditions have to be met in order to make a provision for restructuring costs (see **9.9**).

- Amounts in respect of 'reimbursements' should only be provided for in the financial statements if their receipt is 'virtually certain' (see **9.10**).

- Retirement benefits are one of the most complex issues for LLPs (see **9.11**).

- Defined contribution pension plans are fairly straightforward to account for, but defined benefit pension plans are far more complex (see **9.11**).

- Annuities may be payable to members and can either be 'predetermined' or 'profit-dependent' and a combination of these can be possible (see **9.12**).

- The 2014 SORP requires the principles of Section 11 *Basic Financial Instruments*, Section 12 *Other Financial Instruments Issues* and Section 21 *Provisions and Contingencies* be applied in accounting for retirement benefits (see **9.12**).

- There are times when an annuity will meet the definition of an insurance contract and be subject to the accounting requirements in FRS 103 *Insurance Contracts* (see **9.12**).

- The 2014 SORP recognises that in practice any obligations to make post-retirement benefits to members will often to be set out in the members' agreement and reflect significant mortality risk. On transition to new UK GAAP, the obligations will fall under the provisions in FRS 103 although the LLP will still be allowed to continue with its previous accounting policies (see **9.12**).

- A flowchart is reproduced in this chapter which gives guidance on how to determine which guidance applies to a particular obligation (see **9.12**).

- Liabilities in respect of post-retirement benefits are recognised on the expectations of the probable date the member will cease to be a member and the amounts likely to be payable to him/her from that date (see **9.13**).

- Amounts recognised in the profit and loss account relating to current members are included within 'Members' remuneration charged as an expense' (see **9.14**).

- Changes in the liability for former members is recognised within the relevant profit and loss heading (but not in 'Members' remuneration charged as an expense') (see **9.14**).

- Investments made to meet the requirements to fund retirements in the near future should be separately identified in the notes to the LLP financial statements (see **9.15**).

- On conversion to an LLP, the relationship between the LLP and any predecessor entity has to be carefully considered (see **9.16**).

- Tangible fixed assets are recognised when it is probable that future economic benefits will flow to the LLP and the cost of the asset can be reliably measured. Cost can comprise of several parts (see **9.17** and **9.18**).

- Subsequent expenditure on a tangible asset should only be capitalised if it enhances the performance of the asset in excess of its previous capabilities (see **9.19**).

- Tangible fixed assets can be carried under the 'cost model' or be subsequently revalued (see **9.20**)

- Tangible fixed assets must be depreciated over their expected useful lives – although land is typically not depreciated as land has an indefinite useful life (see **9.21**).

- Assets are impaired when their carrying amount falls below a recoverable amount and there are various indicators of impairment (see **9.22** and **9.23**).

- The 'recoverable amount' of an asset is the higher of its fair value less costs to sell and value in use (see **9.24**).

- Impairment losses in respect of a cash-generating unit are allocated in a specific order (see **9.29**).

- There are specific additional requirements in FRS 102 relating to the impairment of goodwill (see **9.30**).

- Assets subject to leasing are classified as either an 'operating' lease or a 'finance' lease and the correct classification is critical as the accounting methods for both are significantly different (see **9.31–9.33**).

- Events which take place after the date of the financial statements but before the financial statements are authorised for issue should be considered as to whether they are 'adjusting' or 'non-adjusting' events' (see **9.34–9.36**).

- Related party transactions are considered in both legislation and in Section 33 *Related Party Disclosures* of FRS 102 (see **9.37–9.38**).

- A transaction is entered into with a related party when the LLP provides goods, services or incurs obligations with a related party regardless of whether a price is charged or not (see **9.40**).

- There are certain disclosure exemptions from disclosing transactions with related parties (see **9.41**).

- For related party transactions which have to be disclosed, there are detailed disclosures which need to be made to ensure the user understands that the financial statements do include the effects of related party transactions (see **9.42**).

1   INTRODUCTION

9.1   An important concept in the world of financial reporting is that financial statements have to be prepared using Generally Accepted Accounting Practice (GAAP). The use of accounting standards enables financial statements to give a 'true and fair view'. The true and fair concept has been enshrined into companies' legislation for many years. In addition to GAAP, Limited Liability Partnerships (LLPs) prepare accounts in accordance with legislation and the Statement of Recommended Practice (SORP) – Accounting by Limited Liability Partnerships. However, in addition to the SORP, there are a number of other sections of FRS 102 *The Financial Reporting Standard applicable in the UK and Republic of Ireland* which may be particularly relevant to LLPs. These are as follows:

- Section 21 Provisions and Contingencies.

- Section 28 Employee Benefits.

- Section 17 Property, Plant and Equipment.

- Section 27 Impairment of Assets.

- Section 20 Leasing.

- Section 32 Events after the End of the Reporting Period.

- Section 33 Related Party Disclosures.

The main provisions of each of the above, as they are likely to affect LLPs, are discussed below. However, this chapter does not cover all aspects of the sections of FRS 102 that might be relevant to the circumstances of any particular LLP, and reference should be made to the detail of the section or abstract as considered appropriate.

Provisions and contingencies

2   USE OF THE TERM 'PROVISIONS'

9.2   The term 'provision' can mean two fundamentally different things in financial reporting and it is important that LLPs correctly distinguish between the two. A provision is defined in the Glossary as a liability of uncertain timing or amount. However, a provision can also be an adjustment to the carrying value of an item within the financial statements.

Example – a provision for a liability

An LLP is currently defending itself in a court case against one of its clients who is claiming damages for loss of earnings. The legal advisers acting for the LLP have advised that it is unlikely the LLP will be successful in its defence and have given an estimate of damages to be £20,000 which will be due for payment in the next accounting period.

In this example, the damages meet the definition of a 'provision for a liability' and must be included as such within the financial statements at the reporting date regardless of the fact that the payment is going to be made in the subsequent accounting period. This is because the conditions giving rise to the legal claim were in existence at the reporting date.

Example – a provision against a carrying amount

An LLP has trade debtors in its balance sheet as at 31 December 2014 amounting to £100,000. The finance director has estimated (based on past practice and experience) that it is likely 5% of these debtors will fail to pay and therefore makes a provision equalling 5% of the trade debtors.

The finance director's write-down of debtors is known as a bad debt 'provision' rather than as a provision for a liability as in the example above.

It can be noted, therefore, that the term 'provision' can be taken to mean different things in the world of accountancy. In the first example the LLP was making a provision for a liability, whereas in the section example, the LLP was making a provision for a bad debt. Other provisions can include a provision for slow-moving or obsolete stock or a provision for depreciation. Such accounting adjustments are not covered by the requirements of Section 21.

3   THE PRINCIPLES OF SECTION 21

9.3   The issue of provisions and contingencies has been a controversial one over the years as they have historically lent themselves to a whole host of accounting manipulations. Prior to the issuance of accounting standards in this area (namely the previous FRS 12 *Provisions, Contingent Liabilities and Contingent Assets* which became Section 21 in FRS 102) there was no guidance for entities which dealt with the definition, recognition, measurement, use and presentation of provisions and hence reporting entities were frequently exploiting this loophole by creating provisions, under the guise of prudence, in one accounting period, only to release them in the next accounting period primarily for the purpose of profit manipulation.

In years when profits were high, management would create a provision to reduce profit to an acceptable level and then in succeeding years would write-down this provision to manipulate profit.

The creation and reversal of artificial provisions became known as 'big bath accounting' or 'big bath provisions' and it was this practice that eventually led to accounting standards being introduced to put a stop to entities manipulating the financial statements.

Before an LLP can recognise a provision within its accounts, it must be able to satisfy each of the three criteria set out in paragraph 21.4 (a) to (c) in Section 21:

● the LLP must have an obligation at its reporting date as a result of a past event;

- it must be **probable** (ie more likely than not) that the LLP will transfer economic benefits (ie pay cash) to settle the obligation; and

- a reliable estimate can be made of the amount involved.

Example – uncertain obligation

Limefields LLP is a city centre firm of surveyors which has been established for several years. One of its clients has instigated legal proceedings on the grounds of negligent advice. The senior partner is refuting the claim on the basis that the client failed to supply accurate and timely information. The LLP has instructed its law firm to defend the legal action and at the year-end the law firm had incurred legal costs of £5,000 and it is likely that further costs are in the region of £10,000 after the hearing. The LLP is considering whether to make a provision in the company's financial statements for £10,000 in the event that they lose the case. The lawyers have confirmed that they are unable to confirm whether the LLP will be successful in the claim and the Barrister who has been engaged on the claim has confirmed that in her experience the claim could go either way.

The criteria in paragraph 21.4(b) says that it must be **probable** (ie more likely than not) that the LLP will be required to transfer economic benefits in settlement. Limefields LLP legal advisers have confirmed that they cannot be certain whether, or not, the LLP will win the case and therefore a provision cannot be made within the financial statements because all three criteria cannot be met. As a result, disclosure as a contingent liability should be made within the financial statements.

---

4 CONSTRUCTIVE OBLIGATION

9.4 A constructive obligation arises where, through custom and practice, the LLP has created a valid expectation on the part of a third party that its claim will be met. Constructive obligations can be very subjective and are not as 'clear cut' as a legal obligation as can be seen in the following example.

Example – constructive obligation

Scanlon Scanning LLP is a very successful document management bureau. They offer a range of products and services to handle customers' document management in the modern age of becoming 'paperless'. They supply scanning equipment to customers and associated software on-site so that their customer can scan paperwork into electronic files and then send the paper files to their storage department where these files are held in secure units. In addition, Scanlon Scanning offers routine upgrades to their customers and on-site maintenance and support for both their software and scanning equipment.

The LLP has been operating successfully for over 30 years and was originally set up by husband and wife, Les and Lisa. As the company grew over the years, Les and Lisa remain as designated members and have a management team in place to deal with the day-to-day routine running of the business. The members introduced a bonus system 11 years ago for management and staff which calculates bonuses using a pre-determined formula on profits.

At a meeting of the members on 27 March 2014 it was confirmed that initial indications suggested that the profit target had been hit and there was going to be a large excess over this target because the LLP had been awarded additional significant contracts in the year. The members agreed that a bonus to management would be provided once the actual figures were confirmed which the accountancy firm have indicated will be around the middle of May 2014.

The final figures were agreed on 15 May 2014 for the year-ended 31 March 2014 and a bonus was accrued in the financial statements.

The question here relates to whether the bonus *should* have been accrued in the 31 March 2014 financial statements or if it should have been provided for in the 31 March 2015 financial statements when it was actually paid.

The designated members, Les and Lisa, introduced the bonus scheme 11 years ago which has not changed and over the years the practice of the LLP has been to pay a bonus based on profit targets. Over the years management have 'expected' this bonus to be paid because the benchmark has been reached and this has then created a constructive obligation on the part of the LLP. Paragraph 21.6 to FRS 102 confirms that such an obligation means that the LLP has no realistic alternative to settling the obligation and therefore such a constructive obligation can be recognised as a provision within the LLP's financial statements as at 31 March 2014.

Where the obligation to pay only becomes apparent after the balance sheet date, but it clearly arises as the result of an event before that date, a provision should be recognised. For example, an unexpected legal claim might be received after the balance sheet date in respect of damage alleged to have occurred before that date. In these circumstances, a provision would be recognised, but it would not be acceptable to create a general provision for possible legal claims arising from work performed. The latter has historically been an approach adopted particularly by professional practices to take account of potential professional indemnity claims. Such provisions are not permitted in the accounts of the LLP, but the members could decide to make an allowance for such possible claims prior to determining the profits available for distribution.

5   REPAIRS AND MAINTENANCE EXPENDITURE

9.5   Future repairs and maintenance do not relate to present obligations of the LLP arising as a result of a past event. Accordingly, no provision should be made for them, even in the circumstances where legislation might require regular maintenance in order for the asset to continue to be used in the business.

The one exception to this general rule is where an asset is held under a lease, and the lease term includes a requirement for the asset to be made good at whatever stage of the lease it is returned to the lessor. In these circumstances, there is both a legal obligation and a past event (the signing of the lease). Such terms are particularly common in the case of property leases, where provision is often required for the future cost of dilapidations.

In the property lease situation, having determined that there is an obligation under the terms of the lease, the LLP must then ascertain whether it is probable that there will be an economic transfer of benefits to settle the obligation. This may arise because the LLP has made the decision to vacate the property and move elsewhere, or perhaps as a consequence of a landlord break clause within the terms of the lease which the members have reason to believe will be activated. Once this criterion has been satisfied, then the potential dilapidations payable must be estimated. In such circumstances, it may be appropriate for the members to instruct a qualified property expert, such as a surveyor. Having quantified the obligation, the charge to the profit and loss account should then be spread, on an appropriate basis, across the periods between when the three criteria in Section 21 were satisfied and when the LLP is likely to vacate the property. Where the LLP has more than one property, it should have a consistent accounting policy across all of its properties.

6   TIME VALUE OF MONEY

9.6   It might be the case that the effect of the time value of money (when discounting provisions to present day values) becomes material. Where the time value of money is material, Section 21 requires the amount of the provision to be the present value of the amount expected to be required to settle the obligation. The LLP must use a pre-tax discount rate (or rates) which reflect(s) current market assessments of the time value of money and risks specific to the liability. The likelihood is that the vast majority of provisions will not require discounting to present day values, but if they do require discounting then the risks which are specific to the liability must be reflected in either the discount rate or in the estimation of the amounts required to settle the obligation – the important part in this respect is that it cannot be both.

7   FUTURE OPERATING LOSSES

9.7   Paragraph 21.11B prohibits provisions being made for future operating losses. This is because there is no past event which puts an obligation on the part of the entity to incur costs or pay out resources and hence they do not meet the definition of a liability. In addition, future operating losses relate to an activity which will continue and are therefore presumed to be avoidable and so no present obligation exists.

Example – future operating losses interacting with impairment

An LLP has a division which has made a loss in the year and the budgets suggest they are going to make future operating losses due to constraints in the marketplace.

Where an entity is expected to incur future losses this is an indication that an impairment review should be carried out on the appropriate division in accordance with Section 27 *Impairment of Assets*. The impairment review would determine whether those assets have suffered an impairment and hence need writing down to recoverable amount. In addition, future operating losses may be indicative that the entity has one, or more, onerous contracts.

8   ONEROUS CONTRACTS

9.8   An onerous contract is defined in the Glossary to FRS 102 as:

'A contract in which the unavoidable costs of meeting the obligations under the contract exceed the economic benefits expected to be received under it.'

Paragraph 21.11A of FRS 102 briefly deals with onerous contracts and cross-refers to Example 2 in the Appendix to Section 21. Provision should be made for the obligations under such a contract. Provision should not, however, be made where the contract has merely turned out to be less profitable than originally envisaged. In these circumstances, the effect on the carrying value of other related assets might, however, need to be considered.

One of the most common types of onerous contract is the lease on a vacated property. In these cases, provision should be made in the accounts, calculated by reference to the likely future rentals to be paid less any rent that can be obtained from subletting the property (sublet income should only be deducted provided that, by the balance sheet date, either the property has been formally sublet or the LLP is actively marketing the property). The provision should also include the other costs associated with the property, such as rates.

Example – an onerous contract

An LLP provides consulting services in respect of pensions and other post-employment benefits and has entered into a lease with an unconnected third party to rent its offices for a five-year period with no break clauses or early cancellation. In year three, due to unprecedented demand for the LLP's services, additional staff have been recruited and the LLP has now outgrown its current offices. The members have sourced larger premises which can house its current and additional staff.

The landlord of the property which is being vacated has refused to allow the property to be sublet and is refusing to allow the company to break out of the lease early. This is representative of an onerous contract – a property lease which has been abandoned by the LLP and which cannot be sublet and the LLP expects to receive no further benefit from the lease but it is still committed to pay the landlord rentals in order to conform to the terms of the original lease.

A provision for future rentals will be recognised and measured in the same way as any other sort of provision.

---

9   RESTRUCTURING COSTS

9.9   In terms of restructuring, this issue is covered in paragraph 21.11C in FRS 102. However, care must be taken when making a provision for restructuring costs because there are strict conditions that have to be met. Essentially, a constructive obligation will only arise in respect of restructuring costs when the entity:

- has drawn up a detailed and formal plan for the restructuring which identifies at least:
    - the business (or part thereof) which is going to be affected;
    - the principal locations which will be affected;
    - compensation for their services which are to be terminated;
    - the costs that will be incurred; and
    - when the restructuring is going to be instigated; and
- has created a valid expectation in the mind-sets of those which will be affected that it will carry out the restructuring either by commencing the restructuring exercise or announcing the plan's main features.

If the above criteria can be met in respect of a restructuring exercise at the balance sheet date, the LLP can recognise a provision to carry out the restructuring.

The decision by the members to go ahead with their plan will not, of itself, be sufficient to constitute a constructive obligation; there must be a valid expectation on the part of those affected that it will take place. This will be indicated either by the LLP having started to implement the plan, or by having announced its main features to those who are affected by it and this is required in order to comply with paragraph 21.11C (b) in FRS 102.

Only amounts which directly relate to the restructuring exercise should be provided for in the LLP's accounts and which are no associated with the ongoing activities of the entity.

10 REIMBURSEMENT OF AMOUNTS INCLUDED WITHIN PROVISIONS

9.10   In certain circumstances, the risk reflected by the provision might be offset by arrangements for reimbursement, for example through an insurance policy. The reimbursement may be recognised in the accounts when it is *virtually certain* that it will be received upon the settlement of the provision (FRS 102 paragraph 21.13). When the reimbursement becomes virtually certain it is not classified as a contingent asset and should then be recognised in the balance sheet as a separate asset and not offset against the related liability. In the profit and loss account, however, the expected income should be netted against the charge arising as a consequence of the provision.

Example – incorrect treatment of a reimbursement

An LLP operates as an accountancy and taxation firm with a year-end of 31 October 2014. The firm has recently been sued by one of its clients for the negligent preparation of a corporation tax return. The firm has received confirmation from its Professional Indemnity Insurers that the insurance company will refund part of the obligation and has provided this confirmation in writing on 30 September 2014. The accountant preparing the firm's financial statements for the year-ended 31 October 2014 has made the following journal entries to incorporate the insurance reimbursement into the LLP's financial statements:

DR provisions for liabilities	£X
CR claims account	£X

The original provision was posted to the claims account in the profit and loss account and hence the claims account is presented net, as is the liability representing the provision in the LLP's balance sheet.

The treatment by the accountant preparing the LLP's financial statements is in contravention of paragraph 21.9 in FRS 102. The reimbursement debtor should be presented in the balance sheet as an asset and must not be offset against the provision. However, in the profit and loss account the expense relating to a provision may be presented net of the amount recognised for a reimbursement.

Employee benefits: retirement benefits

The accounting treatment of retirement benefits within LLPs is probably one of the more complex areas.

11 RETIREMENT BENEFITS OF EMPLOYEES

9.11   Where retirement benefits are provided to employees under an occupational pension plan, this will most probably be through one of two types of plan:

- *Defined contribution plan (often called a money purchase plan).* In this type of plan the employee and/or the employer pays regular contributions fixed as an amount or percentage of pay and do not have an obligation to pay further contributions if the plan has insufficient assets to pay all employee benefits relating to employee service in the current and prior periods. Individual benefits are determined by reference to the contributions paid into the plan in respect of the employee; hence the term 'defined contribution' essentially means the amount of post-employment benefits the employee will receive will be defined by the amount of the contributions the fund has received in respect of that employee.

- *Defined benefit plan (also called a final salary plan).* This is a plan where normally the rules specify the benefits to be paid (usually based on the employee's average or final pay) and the plan is financed accordingly. As actuarial and investment risk are borne, in substance, on the entity the LLP does have an obligation to pay further contributions into the plan if the plan has insufficient assets to pay all employee benefits relating to employee service in the current and prior periods.

Accounting for the provision of benefits under defined contribution plans is reasonably straightforward: the employer's cost recorded in the profit and loss account comprises the contributions payable.

Where an employing LLP makes contributions to the personal pension plans of individuals, these contributions are also accounted for as they are paid.

For a defined benefit plan, the situation is far more complex, because the benefits to be paid are dependent on future events, such as the average or final pay of the employee and the remaining lifetime of both the active and pensioner members of the plan.

LLPs are required to account for any defined benefit pension plans in accordance with Section 28 *Employee Benefits*.

In summary, Section 28 requires the following:

- Plan assets to be valued at fair value at the LLP's balance sheet date.

- The plan liabilities to be valued using the projected unit method discounted using a high quality corporate bond rate.

- The net pension asset or deficit to be shown separately on the balance sheet. Whilst a liability will nearly always be included, a surplus is only included to the extent that the employer will benefit either as a result of reduced contributions or refunds from the plan.

- The profit and loss charge is analysed between:

  — Amounts included within operating costs:

    (i)　current service costs;

    (ii)　past service costs;

    (iii)　any previously unrecognised surplus deducted from past service costs;

    (iv)　gains or losses on settlements and curtailments; and

    (v)　any previously unrecognised surplus deducted from the settlement or curtailment of losses.

  — Amounts included within financing costs and shown adjacent to interest:

    (i)　interest costs (the unwinding of the discount on the plan liabilities); and

    (ii)　expected return on assets.

Actuarial gains and losses are accounted for through the statement of changes in equity.

There is also a significant level of disclosure required in the notes to the accounts, including information about the underlying actuarial assumptions.

Conversion to LLP and, therefore, the adoption of Section 28 causes a number of LLPs a very specific problem not found in similar situations for companies. Where there is a deficit recognised on the 'top' half of the balance sheet, an equivalent amount needs to be recorded within the 'reserves' side of the balance sheet. In the corporate model this is straightforward and is deducted from the profit and loss reserve. However, LLPs do not accumulate a profit and loss reserve in the same way that traditional companies do and all previous profits may well have been distributed. Many LLPs have solved the problem by creating an additional category within members' interests.

The requirements of Section 28 are onerous and forward planning is essential on the part of both those preparing the accounts and those carrying out the audit. Much of the information will probably need to be produced by the actuaries to the pension scheme who will also need reasonable notice of what information is required as it can take some time for the actuaries to complete their work.

There are a number of factors which need to be considered which include:

- The LLP and its pension plan may have different year ends. The consequences of this are that it will not be possible to rely on the plan's accounts to ascertain asset values and the actuarial information may well also need to be prepared to a different date.

- Access may be required by the auditors to the plan's records in order to carry out procedures on movements since the last set of audited accounts.

Where the trustees will not permit this or it is considered more efficient, it may be necessary to involve the auditors of the pension plan.

- The actuarial method required by Section 28 may differ from that used by the actuaries when determining the funding rate of the plan and could result in the need for two different valuations.

- There will be additional costs for both preparing the actuarial information and the audit of the disclosures.

12   RETIREMENT BENEFITS OF MEMBERS

9.12   Where members have an employment contract (see Chapter 5) and have retirement benefits which are awarded based on the remuneration received under those contracts, those benefits should be accounted for in the same way as for employees (see above).

Other retirement benefits payable to members in the future (often referred to as annuities) will usually be of one of the following:

- *Predetermined.* An amount which is fixed at the time of retirement (annuity). This may, for example, be by reference to the profits earned in the last year of membership. Alternatively, it could be a fixed sum, which may be index-linked or linked to some other measure which is independent of the profits of the LLP.

- *Profit-dependent.* An amount which effectively results in the member continuing to receive a share in the profits of the LLP post retirement. There are a wide range of methods used for providing profit-dependent benefits and these may include arrangements whereby the LLP has to achieve a certain level of profits before any payment is made. In addition, a maximum level of benefit payable may be imposed either by reference to a percentage of profits or monetary amount.

A combination of the two types of benefit is also possible. For example, a retiring member may be entitled to a lump sum payment based on a factor such as past profits and an additional amount in future years based on the profits of the LLP. The period of time for which the benefit will be paid may also vary.

Details of the retirement benefits of members will usually be found in the members' agreement. This will require careful review to ensure that all benefits have been identified and correctly accounted for. The members' agreement may not, however, contain all details of retirement benefits and a constructive obligation may have arisen as a result of either custom and practice or discussions held with individual members. These will also need to be considered when determining the accounting treatment of members' retirement benefits.

The 2014 SORP requires that the principles of Section 11 *Basic Financial Instruments*, Section 12 *Other Financial Instruments Issues* and Section 21 *Provisions and Contingencies* be applied to the accounting for retirement benefits of members.

An annuity would meet the definition of a financial liability under Section 11 or Section 12 of FRS 102 if there is a contractual obligation for the LLP to deliver cash or a financial asset to a member. Annuities will more than likely be subject to uncertainties, for example where payments depend on future profits or significant mortality risk exists. The important factor in this respect is establishing whether the liability is, or is not, an unconditional contractual liability. Unconditional contractual liabilities meet the definition of a financial liability and are, therefore, excluded from the scope of Section 21. An annuity will meet the definition of an insurance contract (and hence be subjected to FRS 103 *Insurance Contracts*) if the LLP accepts significant insurance risk (usually mortality risk) and this will apply should the amount payable by the LLP be significantly affected by how long the former member lives. When an annuity is an unconditional contractual obligation for the LLP to deliver cash or a financial asset to a member, and the LLP has not accepted significant insurance risk this will mean the annuity meets the definition of a financial liability and thus fall under the scope of Section 11 or Section 12 of FRS 102 (paragraph 11.9 of FRS 102 outlines the conditions that must be met for such a financial liability to fall within the scope of Section 11). In instances where the conditions are not met, the financial liability is accounted for in accordance with Section 12.

In relation to profit-dependent annuity payments, these will not meet the conditions outlined in paragraph 11.9 and when such annuity payments arise they are to be accounted for either in accordance with FRS 103 (where the payments expose the LLP to significant insurance risk) or in accordance with Section 12 of FRS 102 (where they do not expose the LLP to significant insurance risk).

The 2014 SORP at paragraph 80B recognises that in practice any obligations to make post-retirement benefits to members will often be set out in the members' agreement and reflect significant mortality risk. Where this is the case for an LLP, it is likely that the LLP will historically have accounted for the obligations as provisions under the previous FRS 12. On transition to new UK GAAP, the obligations will fall under the provisions in FRS 103 but the LLP will be allowed to continue its previous accounting policies.

Applying the principles of Section 21 means that an annuity should be recognised once the member has an actual or constructive right to receive it, and the LLP has no discretion to withhold payment.

It is most usually the case that the rights to receive an annuity arise over time (ie whilst the member continues to be a member of the LLP) and it follows, therefore, that the liability should be accrued over that period, building up a liability through to the time of retirement.

In many cases the member may only obtain absolute entitlement to an annuity on reaching a specific milestone, for example achieving a specified number of years service. Even in these circumstances, because the LLP cannot avoid the liability that is accruing in the period through to reaching entitlement, the liability should be built up over the total period of service. Members who choose to leave before reaching the milestone will not be entitled to an annuity.

In certain situations, however, the members may formally agree that, rather than the obligation to the retiring member becoming a liability of the LLP, they instead agree amongst themselves to discharge the obligation out of their profit allocations. As this is a transaction amongst the members, rather than between the LLP and its members, the amounts paid to the retired members are not included within the accounts of the LLP.

Paragraph 76B to the 2014 SORP contains a flowchart which is reproduced below which gives guidance on how to determine which guidance applies to a particular obligation:

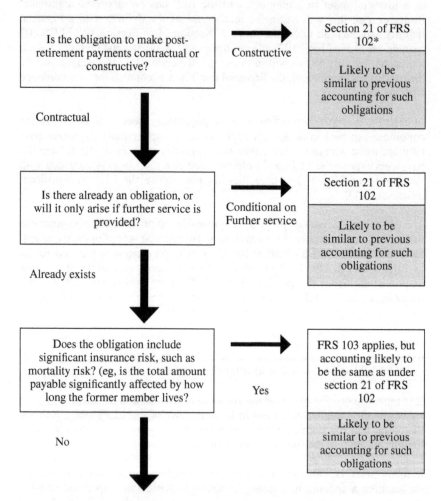

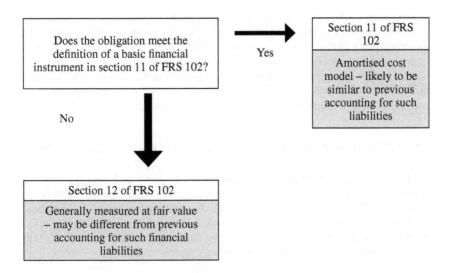

* unless the obligation of certain timing and amount, in which case the general provisions of the Companies Act/GAAP apply.

13 CALCULATION OF THE PROVISION

9.13   To the extent that the liability falls within the scope of Section 21 of FRS 102, the liability that is recognised in the accounts should be based on the expectations, as at the balance sheet date, of:

- the probable date the member will cease to be a member; and

- the amounts likely to be payable to him or her from that date.

LLPs with profit-dependent retirement benefit plans will have to make an assessment of their future profits in order to determine the level of provision. Whilst there will have to be a certain amount of subjectivity attached to these estimates it should be possible for the LLP to determine the range of potential outcomes from which a provision could be calculated.

In determining the value of the liability for members' retirement benefits it will often be appropriate to use the principles of Section 28 *Employee Benefits* and therefore to seek the advice of an actuary who will be able to provide details of factors that should be taken into account, such as life expectancy. Where it is probable that such additional input will be required, in a similar way to obtaining Section 28 information for the LLP's accounts, the actuary will need to be contacted well in advance of preparing the accounts and the auditors will also need to be made aware of the need for their involvement.

The liability may need to be recalculated on an annual basis to take account of changes in membership, eligibility for post-retirement payments, financial estimates and actuarial assumptions.

Where the LLP have offered post-retirement payments consistently to previous members at the point of, but not prior to, retirement this could build an expectation in the mind-sets of all members that they will be offered this benefit at the point of retirement. This constructive obligation would then give rise to earlier recognition of the liability rather than recognising the liability at the point of retirement. In the absence of a formal plan, arrangements to provide post-retirement benefits can arise from the actions of the LLP.

14 PRESENTATION OF MEMBERS' RETIREMENT BENEFITS

9.14   The amounts that are recognised in the profit and loss account (or statement of comprehensive income) with respect to current members should be included within 'Members' remuneration charged as an expense'. The change in liability in respect of former members, however, should not be included within 'Members' remuneration charged as an expense' but within the relevant profit and loss heading, for example 'Administration expenses'.

The liability with respect to current members should be included within 'Loans and other debts due to members' and be described separately where the amount is material. In the year a member retires, the liability should be transferred and included within the balances in respect of former members.

The liability in the balance sheet with respect to former members should be described as 'Post-retirement payments to former members' and be included either within 'Provisions for liabilities' or 'Creditors', dependent upon the circumstances.

Where former members are awarded amounts with respect to past service after their retirement date, this should be recognised in full in the profit and loss account at the time the award is made.

When the LLP discounts liabilities to present day values (to reflect the time value of money) the unwinding of the discount should be presented next to the interest cost line in the profit and loss account (or statement of comprehensive income) to the extent that it relates to former members. Where the unwinding of the discount relates to current members, it should be included in 'Members' remuneration charged as an expense'.

The LLP should disclose the accounting policy adopted with respect to retirement benefits.

15 INVESTMENTS HELD TO FUND FUTURE RETIREMENT BENEFITS

9.15   Whilst the amounts involved mean that LLPs are unlikely to make investments of a size that will cover the liability shown in the accounts, they may, for example, make investments to meet requirements to fund retirements in the near future. Any such investments should be included on the balance sheet as investments, but their purpose should be separately identified in the notes.

16 SPECIFIC ISSUES ON CONVERSION TO AN LLP

9.16   The relationship between the LLP and any predecessor entity will need to be carefully considered. The LLP may assume responsibility for the retirement benefits of a predecessor partnership or other organisation and, in these circumstances, where a legal or constructive obligation exists to pay those amounts, it should be recognised as a provision in the accounts of the LLP.

More commonly, on transition, the predecessor entity may transfer those liabilities to a third party (for example, an insurance company). In these circumstances the former partners or directors may only have recourse to the LLP in the event of the failure of that third party. To the extent that there has been no default and none is probable, the existence of the right of recourse should be disclosed as a contingent liability in the accounts.

Property, plant and equipment

17 TANGIBLE FIXED ASSETS

9.17   Section 17 *Property, Plant and Equipment* deals with accounting for all tangible fixed assets, with the exception of those that are categorised as investment properties, which are subject to the provisions of Section 16 *Investment Property*. A tangible fixed asset can only be recognised on an LLP's balance sheet (statement of financial position) when it is probable (ie more likely than not) that future economic benefits associated with the asset will flow to the entity and the cost of the asset can be measured reliably.

18 THE 'COST' OF A TANGIBLE FIXED ASSET

9.18   Section 17 deals with the issues relating to tangible fixed assets. The section requires that tangible fixed assets should first be recorded at cost although after initial recognition at cost they can be subsequently revalued. Costs which may be capitalised are those that are incremental and would have been avoided only if the asset had not been constructed or acquired. The costs which can be considered for capitalisation are as follows:

- The purchase price including legal and brokerage fees. The cost price should be net of any discounts or rebates.

- Costs which are directly attributable in bringing the asset to the location and condition necessary for it to be used in the manner in which the members intend. This could include the labour costs of employees which are directly attributable to the construction of (say) an architectural practice that chooses to design its own property which may include the time of the staff directly involved in the design project.

- Stamp duty, import duties, non-refundable purchase tax; site preparation and clearance costs; initial delivery and handling costs; and installation costs.

- Where the application of Section 21 (see **9.2–9.10** above) means that a provision is required for the dismantling of an asset and/or restoration of a site at the end of its useful economic life, the estimated cost of dismantling should be included as part of the cost of the asset. For example, if an LLP leases a property and installs partitioning, but the terms of the lease state that this must be removed at the end of the lease, the cost of the partitioning included within fixed assets should also include the estimated cost to dismantle it.

The cost of an asset can include interest on borrowings used to finance the production of that asset, to the extent that those costs arise during the period of production (Section 25 *Borrowing Costs* in FRS 102 deals with these issues). Capitalisation of finance costs is an optional policy, but if the LLP chooses to capitalise finance costs it must do so for all fixed assets where finance costs are a material element of the cost. The interest that may be capitalised should relate only to borrowings that would have been avoided if there had been no expenditure on the asset. This does not mean, however, that there needs to be a separately identifiable loan. The funds could arise from using existing cash which could otherwise have been used to repay existing borrowing or from the extended use of existing facilities. Borrowing costs can only be capitalised in respect of 'qualifying assets'. The Glossary to FRS 102 defines a 'qualifying asset' as one which takes a substantial period of time to get ready for its intended use or sale. It is generally taken to mean that a 'substantial period of time' means more than 12 months.

19 MAINTENANCE EXPENDITURE VERSUS ENHANCEMENT

9.19   Subsequent expenditure, which is necessary to ensure that the fixed asset can continue to operate at the same level, should be charged to the profit and loss account as it is incurred. Subsequent expenditure should only be capitalised where it enhances the performance of the fixed asset in excess of its previous capabilities, for example by increasing its life or capacity. If a fixed asset comprises distinct, different components and these are depreciated at different rates, expenditure to restore 'worn out' parts of the asset can be capitalised.

Example – subsequent expenditure

An LLP owns a light aircraft which it uses in its business and is required, by law, to be overhauled every three years. If the major overhaul does not take place, the aircraft is grounded and cannot be flown.

The LLP must reflect the need to undertake the overhaul or inspection by depreciating an amount of the asset that is equivalent to the expected inspection or overhaul cost over the period until the next inspection or overhaul. Therefore, the cost of the inspection or overhaul is capitalised when incurred because it restores the economic benefits of the aircraft and the carrying amount representing the cost of the benefits consumed is removed from the balance sheet.

20 REVALUATION

9.20   Tangible fixed assets may be revalued, but where an LLP adopts a policy of revaluation all assets within the same class must be revalued (ie the LLP cannot 'cherry pick' which assets it wants to revalue within a certain class) in order to comply with paragraph 17.15. The classes of fixed asset defined by the regulations are very broad, for example land and buildings; plant and machinery; and fixtures, fittings, tools and equipment. An LLP could adopt a narrower class so long as this is reasonable. In practice, it is rare that assets other than property are subject to revaluation.

The decision to revalue a class of assets is one which should only be entered into after careful consideration, as there can be significant costs associated with complying with the requirements contained in paragraph 17.15B. Paragraph 17.15B requires revaluation exercises are carried out with sufficient regularity so as to ensure that the carrying amount of the revalued asset(s) is not materially different from that which would be determined using fair value at the end of the year-/period-end. Paragraph 17.15C acknowledges that the fair value of land and buildings (note land and buildings are separately accounted for in FRS 102) is usually derived from market-based evidence by appraisal and this is usually carried out by professionally-qualified valuers (ie chartered surveyors). In more rare occasions, if the LLP subjects items of plant and equipment to fair value, market values are usually established through appraisal.

If the LLP owns an item of property, plant and equipment which is considered to be of a 'specialised nature' – ie the item is rarely sold (except as part of a continuing business), and this item of property, plant and equipment has been subjected to the revaluation model, then the LLP may need to estimate fair value using an income or a depreciated replacement cost approach to conform with the requirements of FRS 102.

21 DEPRECIATION

9.21   The general principle is that tangible fixed assets should be depreciated to their recoverable amount over their useful expected life. Paragraph 17.16 states that in the event that major components of an item of property, plant and equipment have significantly different patterns of consumption of economic benefits, then component depreciation is appropriate. This is where the LLP will allocate the initial cost of the asset to its major components and then depreciate each component separately over its useful life. A typical example would be land and buildings which have to be separately accounted for under FRS 102 (paragraph 17.8). The land generally has an indefinite life and is therefore not depreciated, but buildings are considered to have a finite life and must be depreciated accordingly.

Example – component depreciation

An LLP has a furnace which requires relining on a five-year cycle.

In accordance with paragraph 17.16, for depreciation purposes the LLP may account separately for the major components (the furnace lining) which have a substantially different useful economic lives from the rest of the asset. In this example, the furnace lining will be depreciated over its useful life of five years so that the depreciation profile of the whole asset more accurately reflects the actual consumption of the asset's economic benefits.

Section 17 to FRS 102 confirms that the depreciable amount of an asset should be allocated to profit and loss using a systematic basis over the useful life of the asset. In this instance, depreciation of an asset will begin when the asset becomes first available for use. An asset becomes first available for use when it is in the location and condition necessary for it to be capable of operating in the manner in which the members intended. Depreciation then ceases when the asset is derecognised from the LLP's balance sheet.

Example – an idle asset

An LLP uses an item of machinery in its production process. The LLP's policy in respect of this machine is to depreciate it under the 'usage method'. This is because the machine is only used at a certain point in the production schedule which occurs only at certain times during the year. The LLP has not depreciated the machine in the months when the machine was idle.

Paragraph 17.20 says that depreciation does not cease when the asset becomes idle or is retired from active use. The only exception to this would be where the asset has been written down to nil (ie fully depreciated). However, in circumstances when the usage method of depreciation is used, the depreciation charge can be zero at times when there is no production.

When considering the depreciation policy, the LLP must take into account a number of factors to ensure that the depreciation method employed is most appropriate in the LLP's circumstances. Such factors can include:

- The LLP's expected use of the asset.

- The expected physical wear and tear.

- Technical or commercial obsolescence.

- Legal or similar limits on the use of the asset.

The depreciation method employed by the entity must be the method that best reflects the pattern in which the LLP will use the asset and therefore consume the economic benefits associated with the asset. The two most common methods of depreciation used in practice are the straight-line method and the reducing balance method (also referred to as the 'diminishing balance' method). In addition, the LLP may consider the units of production method to be applicable in certain circumstances.

Impairment of assets

22 IMPAIRMENT – INTRODUCTION

9.22 An asset (tangible or intangible) is deemed to be impaired when the LLP is unable to recover the carrying value (all, or part thereof) on the balance sheet, either by continued use in its ongoing business or through sale. An impairment may arise either because of something that has happened to the asset or as a consequence of factors affecting the business or economic environment in which the asset is being used. In such circumstances, an adjustment is required to reduce the carrying value of the asset. One of the underlying principles in financial reporting is that assets should not be carried in the balance sheet at any more than their recoverable amount and therefore at each reporting date all assets should be reviewed for any indicators of impairment and consideration given as to whether any write-down to recoverable amount should take place by the LLP.

The principal section in FRS 102 covering impairment is Section 27 *Impairment of Assets*. Section 27 deals with the impairment of all assets (tangible and intangible) including inventories. However, Section 27 does not deal with the impairment of deferred acquisition costs and intangible assets which arise through contracts that fall under the scope of FRS 103 *Insurance Contracts*. In respect of tangible and intangible assets, the objectives of Section 27 are to ensure that:

- fixed assets and goodwill are recorded in the financial statements at no more than their recoverable amount;

- any resulting impairment loss is measured and recognised on a consistent basis; and

- sufficient information is disclosed in the financial statements to enable users to understand the impact of the impairment on the financial position and performance of the reporting LLP.

The term 'fixed assets' will also include investments made by the LLP in other undertakings. In respect of goodwill and fixed assets other than investments, an impairment charge could potentially impact both the LLP's own profit and loss account and the consolidated profit and loss account. In respect of investments, an impairment charge will only affect the LLP's own accounts.

23 INDICATORS OF IMPAIRMENT

9.23   A review for impairment is required if events or changes in circumstances indicate that the carrying value of the fixed asset or goodwill may not be recoverable.

For assets other than inventories, Section 27 sets out examples of events and changes in circumstances that indicate that impairment may have occurred, and these include:

- the decline of an asset's market value during the accounting period in excess of what would otherwise be expected through normal passage of time or use;

- significant changes which have had an adverse effect on the LLP taking place during the accounting period (or which will take place in the near future) relating to the technological, market, economic or legal environment in which the LLP operates, or in the market to which an asset is dedicated;

- increases in interest rates or other market rates of return on investments which are likely to materially affect the discount rate the LLP uses in calculating an asset's value in use and decrease the asset's fair value less costs to sell;

- the net assets of the LLP being more than the estimated fair value of the LLP as a whole.

The above indicators relate to *external* sources of information which the LLP should consider when assessing assets for impairment. There are also some *internal* sources of information which should also be taken into consideration which include:

- evidence of obsolescence or physical damage to the fixed asset;

- a significant event(s) which has an adverse effect on the LLP having taken place (or about to take place in the near future) in the extent to which, or the manner in which, an asset is used or is expected to be used. For example, if the asset will become idle, the LLP plans to discontinue or restructure an operation to which an asset belongs, the LLP plans to dispose of an asset before the previously assessed expected date of disposal or the reassessment of the useful life of an asset to a much lower previously assessed useful life; and

- assessing available evidence from the LLP's internal records which indicate that the economic performance (ie operating results and cash flows) of an asset is, or may be, worse than previously expected.

When the LLP concludes that there is evidence that an asset is impaired, there should be a review undertaken of:

- the remaining useful life;
- the depreciation (or amortisation) method; or
- the residual value for the asset.

Once this review is undertaken, one of the above must be adjusted in accordance with either Section 17 *Property, Plant and Equipment* or Section 18 *Intangible Assets other than Goodwill*. This applies even if no impairment loss is recognised for the respective asset.

24 RECOGNITION AND MEASUREMENT OF IMPAIRMENT LOSSES

9.24 An impairment review comprises a comparison of the carrying amount of the fixed asset or goodwill with its recoverable amount. Recoverable amount is the *higher* of its fair value less costs to sell and its value in use.

Example – calculation of fair value but not value in use

An LLP is undertaking an impairment review of one of its assets. It has established the fair value of the asset less costs to sell but is unable to calculate value in use and is therefore unsure whether, or not, the asset has suffered any impairment. The fair value less costs to sell figure is higher than the asset's carrying amount stated in the LLP's balance sheet.

It is not always considered necessary to determine both fair value less costs to sell and value in use because if *either* of these amounts are higher than the asset's carrying amount, the asset is not impaired and therefore it will not be necessary to calculate the other figure.

To the extent that the carrying amount exceeds the recoverable amount, the fixed asset or goodwill is impaired and should be written down. The impairment loss should be recognised in the profit and loss account unless it arises on a previously revalued fixed asset. Where the impairment is caused by a clear consumption of economic benefits, it should be recognised in the profit and loss account. Other impairments of revalued fixed assets should be treated as a revaluation decrease in accordance with the relevant section of FRS 102 (for example Section 17 *Property, Plant and Equipment*).

Example – impairment of a revalued asset

An LLP has a building in its balance sheet that is accounted for in accordance with Section 17 *Property, Plant and Equipment* under the revaluation model. The amount of the impairment amounts to £70,000 and there is an associated revaluation surplus in the equity section of the LLP's balance sheet directly relating to the building amounting to £80,000.

Paragraph 27.6 says that an impairment loss of a revalued asset is to be treated as a revaluation decrease in accordance with the relevant section of FRS 102 (in this instance it will be Section 17). Section 17 says that a revaluation decrease is recognised in other comprehensive income to the extent of any previously recognised revaluation increase accumulated in equity. Therefore the entries for the impairment loss will be:

| CR land and buildings | £70,000 |
| DR revaluation surplus | £70,000 |

This will result in the revaluation surplus in the LLP's balance sheet going from £80,000 to £10,000.

If, on the other hand the impairment loss amounted to £90,000 then the entries will be:

CR land and buildings	£90,000
DR revaluation surplus	£80,000
DR profit and loss	£10,000

This is because when a revaluation decrease exceeds the accumulated revaluation gains that have been accumulated in equity any excess is recognised in profit or loss.

Fair value less costs to sell

9.25   Fair value less costs to sell is the amount which could be received by the LLP from the sale of an asset in an arm's-length transaction that is entered into between knowledgeable and willing persons. Deducted from this value are the costs directly associated with the sale of the asset. The best evidence of fair value less costs to sell might be found within a binding agreement (which outlines the sale proceeds and any associated costs inherent with the sale). Alternatively, a market value can be sourced from an 'active market'. An 'active market' for the purposes of impairment is a market in which:

• the items traded within the market are homogeneous;

• willing buyers and sellers can normally be found at any time; and

• prices are available to the public.

If a binding sales agreement does not exist, nor an active market for an asset, then fair value less costs to sell should be deciphered using the best information available to the LLP which might reflect the amount that the LLP could obtain at the reporting date from disposal of the asset in an arm's-length transaction (ie on normal commercial terms). The LLP should also consider any other recent transactions for similar assets in the same industry and the outcomes of those transactions.

Value in use

9.26 The value in use of an asset is the present value of the future cash flows obtainable as a result of the asset's continued use, including those that would arise from its ultimate disposal. Whilst value in use should be estimated for individual assets where reasonably possible, in practice, it is the utilisation of groups of assets and liabilities, together with their associated goodwill, that generates cash flows. Hence, value in use will usually have to be estimated for groups of assets and liabilities. These groups are referred to as cash-generating units ('CGU'). Because it is necessary to identify only material impairments, in some cases it may be acceptable to consider a group of CGUs together rather than on an individual basis.

CGUs are identified by dividing the total income of the LLP into as many largely independent income streams as is reasonably practicable in the light of the information available to management. In general terms, the income streams are likely to follow the way in which management monitors and makes decisions about how the different lines of business of the LLP are developed.

Central assets, such as group or regional head offices, and working capital may have to be apportioned across the units using a logical and systematic basis. The resulting CGUs will be complete and non-overlapping, so that the sum of the carrying amounts of the units equals the carrying amount of the net assets of the LLP as a whole.

Cash flows

9.27 Section 27 sets out the rules that need to be applied when determining the expected future cash flows of the CGUs. The calculations should include any allocation of central overheads, but excluding cash flows relating to financing and tax, and they should be based on reasonable and supportable assumptions. The cash flows should be consistent with the most up-to-date budgets and plans that have been formally approved by management. Cash flows for the period beyond that covered by formal budgets and plans should assume a steady or declining growth rate for subsequent years (unless an increasing rate can be justified).

Future cash flows should be estimated for CGUs or individual fixed assets in their current condition. They should not include:

- future cash outflows or related costs savings or benefits that are expected to arise from a future restructuring for which the LLP is not yet committed; or

- future capital expenditure that will improve or enhance the CGU or assets in excess of their originally assessed standard of performance.

In the case of a newly acquired CGU such as a subsidiary, the purchase price will reflect the synergies and other opportunities for making more effective use of the assets as a result of the acquisition. In some of these cases, in order to obtain the benefits from its investment, it may be necessary for the purchaser to undertake related capital expenditure and reorganisations. In these situations, when performing impairment reviews up to the end of the first full year after acquisition (and subsequently, if still appropriate), such capital expenditure and reorganisation costs and benefits should be included in assessing the future cash flows of the investment, to the extent that the investments or reorganisations are still to be incurred. The costs and benefits applied in impairment reviews in subsequent periods should be consistent with those included within the budgets and plans produced and utilised for the initial impairment review.

Discount rate

9.28   The present value of the CGU under review should be calculated by discounting the expected future cash flows. The discount rate used should be an estimate of the rate that reflects current market assessments of the time value of money and the risks specific to the asset for which the future cash flow estimates have not been adjusted. Discount rates used in the present value calculation should be on a pre-tax basis.

Estimates of this market rate may be made by a variety of means, including reference to:

- the rate implicit in market transactions in similar assets;

- the current weighted average cost of capital (WACC) of a listed company whose cash flows have similar risk profiles to those of the CGU; or

- the WACC for the LLP, *but only if* adjusted for the particular risks associated with the CGU.

Using a discount rate equal to the rate of return that the market would expect on an equally risky investment is a method of reflecting the risk associated with the cash flows in the value in use measurement. It is likely that this method will be the easiest method of reflecting risk. However, an acceptable alternative is to adjust the cash flows for risk and to discount them using a risk-free rate (eg a government bond rate). Whichever method of reflecting risk is adopted, care must be taken that the effect of risk is not double-counted by inclusion in both cash flows and the discount rate.

If the LLP chooses to use the third option above, then the WACC for the LLP is based on the combined cost of equity and cost of debt. In terms of calculating the cost of equity, the LLP might consider ascertaining the expected return required by a private equity or venture capital investor for a business in the same industry. For the cost of debt, the post-tax rate of the cost of debt to the business should be used.

25 ALLOCATION OF IMPAIRMENT LOSSES

9.29   To the extent that the carrying amount of the CGU exceeds its recoverable amount, the CGU is impaired. The impairment loss should be accounted for in accordance with paragraph 27.21 of FRS 102 and allocated to reduce the carrying amount of the assets of the CGU in the following order:

- first, to reduce any goodwill in the CGU; and then

- to the other assets in the CGU, on a pro rata basis of the carrying amount of each asset in the CGU.

Care must be taken in allocating impairment losses because an LLP cannot reduce the carrying amount of any asset in the CGU below the highest of:

- its fair value less costs to sell (where this can be established);

- its value in use (where this can be established); and

- zero.

Example – allocation of an impairment loss

An LLP has undertaken an impairment test on one of its groups of assets that is considered to be a CGU. Financial statement extracts for the year-ended 30 September 2014 are as follows:

Goodwill	£130,000
Office equipment	£200,000

The CGU has suffered an impairment loss of £150,000 during the year as the LLP has received widely publicised criticism about the services of its subsidiary which has had a detrimental effect.

The members have undertaken an exercise in calculating fair value less costs to sell and value in use of goodwill. They have determined that the fair value less costs to sell is £60,000 and the value in use is £50,000. The members consider it is not possible to arrive at a figure for fair value less costs to sell or value in use for office equipment.

The impairment loss of £150,000 will first be allocated to goodwill, with the remainder being applied to the office equipment. However, neither the goodwill nor any asset in a CGU can be reduced below the highest of:

- fair value less costs to sell (if determinable);

- value in use (if determinable); or

- zero.

As fair value less costs to sell is higher than value in use, goodwill is to be carried at £60,000, so of the £150,000 impairment £70,000 (£130,000 less £60,000) will be allocated to goodwill, with the remaining £80,000 being charged against office equipment. Following the allocation of the impairment charge, the financial statement extracts will be as follows:

Goodwill	£60,000
Office equipment	£120,000

26   ADDITIONAL REQUIREMENTS FOR GOODWILL IMPAIRMENT

9.30   Paragraph 27.24 of FRS 102 recognises that goodwill, on its own, cannot be sold and it also does not generate cash flow to an LLP which are independent of the cash flows of other assets. This has the consequence that it is not possible to measure the fair value of goodwill directly and hence the fair value should be derived from the measurement of fair value of the CGU of which the goodwill forms part of.

Goodwill acquired in a business combination is impairment tested from the date of acquisition. It is then allocated to each of the acquirer's CGUs which are expected to benefit from the synergies of the combination, regardless of whether, or not, other assets or liabilities have been assigned to those units.

Part of the recoverable amount of the CGU may belong to the non-controlling interests (minority interests) and therefore for the purposes of impairment testing of a non-wholly-owned CGU that has goodwill, the carrying value of that unit is notionally adjusted before being compared with recoverable amount. This is achieved by grossing up the carrying amount of goodwill which has been allocated to the unit to include the goodwill attributable to the non-controlling interest. Once this has been completed, the notionally-adjusted carrying value is then compared with recoverable amount to determine whether the CGU is impaired.

Example – apportionment of an impairment loss

LLP A acquired 80% of the net assets of LLP B on 1 January 2014 (the date of acquisition). The finance manager is undertaking an impairment test on the goodwill acquired in LLP B but is unsure as to the starting point and how the apportionment of such an impairment loss would be split.

Goodwill which has been impaired in a business combination is impairment tested from the date of acquisition. Once this has been established and the impairment calculated, it is then allocated to each of the cash-generating units which are expected to benefit from the synergies of the combination, regardless of whether other associated assets or liabilities of the acquiree are assigned to those units.

20% of the impairment loss will belong to the non-controlling interests (minority interests) as LLP A only acquired 80% of the value of LLP B's net assets. As a result, 20% of the recoverable amount of the cash-generating unit with the goodwill in it will belong to the non-controlling interests. The finance manager should notionally adjust the carrying amount of the cash-generating unit before comparing the unit to its recoverable amount. The finance manager will do this by grossing up the carrying amount of goodwill so it includes the goodwill belonging to the non-controlling interests. It is this 'grossed up' goodwill which is compared to the recoverable amount to determine whether the cash-generating unit is impaired.

Leases

27 LEASES – INTRODUCTION

9.31   The accounting for leases is dealt with in Section 20 *Leases* of FRS 102, which identifies two distinct types of lease arrangement: finance leases and operating leases.

The correct classification of leases cannot be over-emphasised because the accounting treatment between a finance and an operating lease is significantly different. One of the main overarching principles in financial reporting is the concept of *substance over form* and the issue of lease transactions illustrates the need for the substance and not the legal form of a transaction to be considered. When the 'substance' of a transaction is referred to, it means the transaction's 'commercial reality' and it is the commercial reality which will often be markedly different than the transaction's legal form. The concept of 'off-balance sheet finance' has been in existence for several years and leases lend themselves to a host of scenarios which could give rise to leases being off-balance sheet and hence treated as an operating lease when, in reality, the lease should be treated as a finance lease and hence shown on the LLP's balance sheet. Standard-setters are aware of the concept of off-balance sheet finance and hence place emphasis on the substance of the arrangement in an attempt to lessen the scope for off-balance sheet finance to occur. However, the attempts by the standard-setters to close such 'loopholes' in leasing transactions does not stop some LLPs from deliberately engineering leasing arrangements to achieve a desired outcome and hence it is possible that in the future further changes to lease accounting might take place in further attempts to combat off-balance sheet finance.

28 FINANCE LEASES

9.32   A finance lease is a lease that transfers substantially all the risks and rewards of ownership of an asset to the lessee. Whilst there are a number of factors to consider, paragraph 20.5 and 20.6 of FRS 102 outlines various indicators that a lease is a finance lease as follows:

- ownership of the asset is transferred to the lessee at the end of the lease term;

- an option exists in the lease for the lessee to purchase the asset at a lower price than fair value at the date on which the option becomes exercisable and that it is reasonably certain at the inception of the lease that the lessee will exercise this option;

- the term of the lease is for the major part of the useful economic life of the asset being subjected to the lease (regardless of whether title is not transferred);

- at the start of the lease, the present value of the minimum lease payments is equivalent to at least substantially all of the fair value of the leased asset; and

- the asset which is leased is of such a specialised nature that only the lessee can use it without major modifications to the asset being made.

The above indicators can, either individually or in combination, normally lead a lease being classified as a finance lease. There are a further three indicators which could also lead a lease being classified as a finance lease:

- where the lessee can cancel the lease and the lessor's losses associated with the termination of the lease are met by the lessee;

- gains or losses in the residual value of the leased asset accrue to the lessee; and

- the lessee has the ability to continue to lease the asset at the end of the primary lease term at a rent which is substantially lower than market rent (often called a 'peppercorn' rent).

Whilst Section 20 outlines these indicators of a finance lease, the section does acknowledge that these examples are not always conclusive. A key theme in Section 20 is whether the risks and rewards of ownership of the asset passes from the lessor to the lessee. If risks and rewards do not pass from lessor to lessee then the lease is not classed as a finance lease, but is classed as an operating lease.

At the inception of a finance lease, both the leased asset and the related lease creditor should be recorded on the balance sheet at amounts equal to the fair value of the leased asset or, if lower, the present value of the minimum lease payments, determined at the start of the lease. Any incremental costs associated with the lease (eg fees incurred in negotiating the lease) are added to the cost of the asset. Depreciation should be charged in accordance with the provisions in Section 17 *Property, Plant and Equipment*. Depreciation should be charged over the shorter of the lease term and the estimated useful life of the asset when there is no reasonable certainty that the lessee will obtain ownership by the end of the lease term.

Each rental payment is split between the finance charge (the interest) and the capital element. This is done using the *effective interest method*. The effective interest method is a method of calculating the amortised cost of a financial asset or financial liability and then allocating the interest income or interest expense over the relevant period.

Example – lessee accounting calculations for a lease liability

An item of machinery with a useful life of ten years can be purchased outright by an LLP for £42,800. Alternatively, use of the asset may be obtained by means of a finance lease.

Under this arrangement, the LLP (the lessee) would be responsible for insurance and maintenance and would be required to make five annual payments of £11,600 all payable in advance. After the primary period of five years, the lessee would have the option to continue leasing the asset for an indefinite period for a nominal (a 'peppercorn') rental.

It is assumed that the fair value of £42,800 provides an acceptable approximation to the present value of the minimum lease payments determined at the inception of the lease, discounted at the interest rate implicit in the lease.

The total finance charge to be allocated to the periods equals the excess of rentals paid over the amounts capitalised (ie £58,000 *less* £42,800 = £15,200). he finance charge is to be allocated using the effective interest method. The interest rate is calculated at 18% and the following amortisation table shows the movement on the lease liability:

Year	Liability b/f	Lease payment	Finance charge @ 18%	Liability c/f
	£	£	£	£
1	42,800	(11,600)	5,616	36,816
2	36,816	(11,600)	4,538	29,754
3	29,754	(11,600)	3,268	21,422
4	21,422	(11,600)	1,778	11,600
5	11,600	(11,600)	–	
		(58,000)	15,200	

The net book value of assets held under finance leases is required to be disclosed in the accounts, along with the depreciation charged thereon.

29 OPERATING LEASES

9.33   An operating lease is as a lease which does not transfer substantially all of the risks and rewards incidental to ownership. Rentals payable under an operating lease should be charged on a straight-line basis over the lease term, unless:

● another systematic basis represents the time pattern of the LLP's benefit (this can apply even if the payments are not made on this basis); or

● payments to the lessor are structured in such a way so as to increase in line with expected general inflation (which is based on published indexes or statistics) to compensate for the lessor's expected inflationary cost increases. However, it should be kept in mind that if payments to the lessor vary because of factors other than general inflation, this condition will not be met.

Property leases give rise to two particular situations where the cash rental payments may be different from the amount that should be charged to the profit and loss account. These are: (1) where an LLP has been granted a rent-free period; and (2) where it is paying rent on vacant property.

In negotiating a new lease or renewing an existing lease, the lessor may provide incentives for the LLP to enter into the agreement. Examples of such incentives are an upfront cash payment to the lessee or an initial period of the lease term that may be rent-free or at a reduced rent. The nature of the incentives must be examined to establish if they are for the lessee's or the lessor's benefit. This is important because the financial statements must reflect the substance of the transaction.

Lease incentives are dealt with in paragraph 20.15A of FRS 102. Assuming the lease incentive is for the benefit of the lessee, the financial effect (regardless of the form the incentive takes) should be spread over the period of the lease (which is usually on a straight-line basis). This accounting treatment is somewhat different than under previous UK GAAP (UITF 28 *Operating lease incentives*) which required the incentive to be spread over the shorter of the lease term and a period ending on a date from which it is expected the prevailing market rental will be payable.

Example – lease incentive calculation

An LLP is negotiating a ten-year lease. The annual rental will be £20,000 but it is agreed that the lessee will be entitled to an incentive of a rent-free period for the first six months.

The lease incentive is £10,000 (six-months rent-free) and paragraph 20.15A says that this should be spread over the lease term (ten years) hence £1,000 per annum hence £19,000 per annum net of the lease incentive).

The total payment to the lessor over the ten-year period will be £190,000 and the annual lease expense will be £190,000/10 years = £19,000. The LLP's balance sheet at the end of year 1 will show an accrual of £9,000 (the annual expense of £19,000 less the payment made in the first year of £10,000).

Provisions for vacant property are dealt with in **9.8** above.

Events after the end of the reporting period

30 ACCOUNTING FOR EVENTS AFTER THE REPORTING PERIOD

9.34   The Regulations require that all liabilities and losses which have arisen, or are likely to arise, relating to the period prior to the balance sheet date should be taken into account – either by way of recognition within the financial statements or by way of disclosure. This includes those which only become apparent between the balance sheet date and the date on which the accounts are approved by the members. Such items are referred to as 'events after the end of the reporting period' (often referred to as 'post balance sheet events') the accounting for which is dealt with in Section 32 *Events after the End of the Reporting Period.*

Section 32 distinguishes between two types of event:

- adjusting events; and

- non-adjusting events.

31 ADJUSTING EVENTS

9.35   Adjusting events are those occurring after the balance sheet date which provide additional evidence of conditions which were in existence at that date. The accounts should be changed to take account of this additional evidence. Examples of adjusting events include:

- The subsequent determination of the purchase price or of the proceeds of sale of assets purchased or sold before the year end.

- A valuation of a property that provides evidence of an impairment in value.

- The receipt of a copy of the financial statements or other information in respect of an unlisted company in which the LLP has an interest that provides evidence of an impairment in the value of a long-term investment.

- The receipt of proceeds of sales after the balance sheet date or other evidence concerning the net realisable value (or fair/market value) of stocks.

- The receipt of evidence that the previous estimate of accrued profit on a long-term contract was materially inaccurate.

- The renegotiation of amounts owing by debtors or the insolvency of a debtor.

- The discovery of errors or frauds which show that the financial statements were incorrect.

Events after the balance sheet date which indicate a deterioration in operating results and in the financial position of the LLP may highlight issues as to whether the accounts should be prepared on a going concern basis (see Chapter 10).

Example – discovery of fraud

An LLP has a year-end of 30 April each year. The LLP has prepared its financial statements for the year-ended 30 April 2016 and the auditors have completed their detailed on-site fieldwork on 27 June 2016. During the audit work, the audit senior noticed large cash discrepancies throughout the year which had been written off to sundry expenses within the LLP's profit and loss account to agree the bank reconciliation statement. The audit manager and audit senior calculated that the value of the cash discrepancies amounted to £75,000 which is considered material to the financial statements. It was later found that a member of the accounts staff at the LLP had been stealing cash on a regular basis due to a distinct lack of segregation of duties within the accounts department.

The financial statements of the LLP should be adjusted to reflect the discovery of the fraud. This accords with the requirements in Section 32 of FRS 102 at paragraph 32.5(e) which says that the discovery of fraud or errors are adjusting events after the end of the reporting period and therefore should be adjusted within the financial statements.

Example – settlement of a court case

An LLP has a year-end date of 31 March 2016. At that date the company was in dispute with one of its clients who had brought a legal claim against the firm. The client alleged suffering financial loss due to advice received from the LLP. At the year-end date the legal advisers were not able to confirm whether the LLP would be successful in its defence and, as such, the accountant made disclosure of a contingent liability.

On 23 June 2016 (some three days before the financial statements were to be authorised for issue by the members), the court found in favour of the client and ordered the LLP to pay damages of £20,000 plus legal fees of £7,000. The accountant has suggested that the contingent liability disclosure remain within the financial statements and the damages and costs be accounted for within the 2017 financial statements.

Paragraph 32.5(a) is specific on such issues. The settlement of a court case after the end of a reporting period is an adjusting event. While the company was not able to recognise a provision in accordance with Section 21 *Provisions and Contingencies* due to the recognition criteria not being met, the LLP is now required to create a new provision in accordance with Section 32 at paragraph 32.5(a). This particular paragraph is also specific in that the entity must not merely disclose a contingent liability because the settlement provides additional evidence to be considered in determining whether the recognition criteria for a provision has been met in accordance with Section 21 to FRS 102.

32 NON-ADJUSTING EVENTS

9.36   Non-adjusting events relate to conditions which did not exist at the balance sheet date. They do not result in the accounts requiring amendment, but should be disclosed if they are material and hence non-disclosure would affect the ability of users of the accounts to have a proper understanding of the financial position of the LLP. Section 32 includes the following examples of non-adjusting events:

- A major business combination after the balance sheet date or disposal of a major subsidiary.

- Announcing a plan to discontinue an operation.

- Major purchases and disposals of assets, or expropriation of major assets by government.

- The destruction of a major production plant by a fire after the balance sheet date.

- Announcing or commencing the implementation of a major restructuring.

- Issues or repurchases of the LLP's debt instruments.

- Abnormally large changes after the balance sheet date in asset prices or foreign exchange rates.

- Entering into significant commitments or contingent liabilities, for example, by issuing significant guarantees.

- Commencing major litigation arising solely out of events that occurred after the balance sheet date.

Whilst these are listed as non-adjusting events, the circumstances surrounding them should always be considered. In some cases, it may be that they are the best indicator of circumstances at the balance sheet date where no other evidence is available.

Example – contingent asset

LLP A instigated legal proceedings against Company B Ltd on 20 April 2015 because Company B had failed to comply with the terms of a contract to supply goods. As a result of its failure to adhere to the terms of the contract, LLP A has suffered significant losses due to its customers sourcing alternative goods elsewhere. LLP A has a year-end of 31 July 2015.

Company B Ltd has filed a defence with the court and the case was heard on 2 August 2015. Prior to the court case, LLP A's legal advisers were not able to reliably estimate any potential costs which may become refundable if LLP A was successful in its case. However, the court ordered that Company B pay costs of £15,000. The accounts manager at LLP A is proposing to recognise this reimbursement of cost as a debtor in the financial statements to 31 July 2015.

Paragraph 32.7(b) states that an amount that becomes receivable as a result of a favourable judgement or settlement of a court case after the reporting date, but before the financial statements are issued, is a contingent asset at the reporting date. As a result, the LLP would be unable to recognise a receivable, but would instead make disclosure of a contingent asset.

Related parties

33 THE SOURCE OF DISCLOSURE REQUIREMENTS

9.37 The Companies Act 2006 contains specific legislation and disclosure requirements aimed at preventing directors from taking financial advantage from their position. The special relationship that exists between an LLP and its members means that none of this is reproduced in the Regulations. The only disclosure requirements contained within the Regulations are those which deal generally with members' interests (see Chapter 5).

LLPs do, however, have to comply with the full and more onerous requirements of Section 33 *Related Party Disclosures*.

34 THE GENERAL REQUIREMENTS OF SECTION 33

9.38   The objective of Section 33 is to ensure that the LLP's financial statements contain the disclosures necessary to draw attention to the possibility that the reported financial position and results may have been affected by the existence of related parties and by material transactions with them. Section 33 requires disclosure of a material transaction undertaken by the LLP with a related party, irrespective of whether a price is charged. Where the LLP is controlled by another party, disclosure is required of the name of that controlling party, irrespective of whether any transactions have taken place with it.

35 IDENTIFYING RELATED PARTIES

9.39   Under Section 33, a related party is a person (or entity) which is related to the LLP preparing financial statements (a reporting LLP). In addition:

- A person or a close family member of that person is related to the reporting LLP if that person:

  — has control, or joint control, over the reporting LLP;

  — has significant influence over the reporting LLP; or

  — is a member of the key management personnel of the reporting LLP or of a parent of the reporting LLP.

Section 33 then goes on to explain about how businesses may be related to a reporting LLP. This occurs when any of the following conditions apply:

- the entity and the reporting LLP are members of the same group (meaning each parent, subsidiary and fellow subsidiary is related to the others);

- the entity is an associate or joint venture of the LLP;

- both parties are joint ventures of the same party;

- one party is a joint venture of a third party and the other party is an associate of the third party;

- the entity is a post-employment benefit plan for the benefit of employees of either the reporting LLP or an entity related to the reporting LLP. If the reporting LLP is itself such a post-employment benefit plan, the sponsoring employees are also related to the reporting LLP;

- the entity is controlled or jointly controlled by a person or a close family member of that person related to the reporting LLP; and

- the party is an entity that is controlled, jointly controlled or significantly influenced by, or for which significant voting power in such entity resides with directly or indirectly, any individual referred to above or is a member of the key management personnel.

The Glossary to FRS 102 defines control as '*the power to govern the financial and operating policies of an entity so as to obtain benefits from its activities.*'

165

Common control is deemed to exist when both parties are subject to control from boards having a controlling nucleus of directors or members in common.

The difference between control and influence is that control brings with it the ability to cause the controlled party to subordinate its separate interests, whereas the outcome of the exercise of influence is less certain.

Where one party had influence over the financial and operating policies of the other party to an extent that the other party might be inhibited from pursuing, at all times, its own separate interests; or where the parties, in entering into a transaction, were subject to influence from the same source to such an extent that one of the parties to the transaction subordinated its own separate interests, then in both of these situations, control is said to exist and the two parties are deemed related.

The term 'key management personnel' should not be interpreted to mean that all members of an LLP are to be automatically regarded as related parties. Whether the members are related will depend upon the degree of control they have over the day-to-day activities of the LLP. In a small LLP, it may be the case that all the members are directly involved in its management and, as such, should be regarded as related. However, in a large LLP, management may be devolved to a small number of members who should be presumed to be related. The reference to key management in Section 33 means that designated members will usually be related parties. In certain circumstances, key management personnel may also include individuals who are not members of the LLP, for example the Head of Finance or the Head of Human Resources.

The fact that some members of an LLP are also members of another LLP is not of itself sufficient to make the two entities related. The extent to which they have control of both LLPs, and are in a position to influence transactions between the two entities, will have to be considered.

The issue surrounding close family members of a related party has been clarified in Section 33 to FRS 102. Section 33 regards a related party's children, spouse and domestic partner and the dependants of a person or his/her spouse or domestic partner to be related parties.

36 IDENTIFYING RELATED PARTY TRANSACTIONS

9.40   A transaction is entered into with a related party when the LLP provides goods, services or incurs obligations with a related party. A key point to emphasise where this concept is concerned is that a price does *not* have to be charged for the related good, service or obligation. The idea behind related party disclosures is to ensure that the user can understand that the reported financial results may have been affected by the existence of related parties and transactions with those related parties. Regardless of whether a price is charged or not, if the transaction is a material related party transaction ('material' being in the context of both monetary amount and nature) then it should be disclosed in the financial statements.

The following are some examples of transactions that would need disclosure if they are with a related party:

- purchases or sales of goods which covers both finished and unfinished goods;
- the purchase or sale of property or other assets;
- rendering or receipt of services;
- transactions involving lease arrangements;
- the transfer of research or development;
- transfers under licence agreements;
- transfers that arise through financing arrangements (for example a loan);
- guarantees and collateral;
- the settlement of liabilities on behalf of the LLP or by the LLP on behalf of another related party; and
- the participation by a parent or a subsidiary in a defined benefit pension plan that shares risks between the members of the group.

37 EXEMPTIONS FROM DISCLOSURE

9.41   There are some exemptions from disclosure, and these are set out below:

- in a parent LLP's accounts, transactions with wholly-owned subsidiaries;
- in wholly-owned subsidiary entities accounts, transactions with their parent and with other subsidiaries that are wholly-owned within the group;
- remuneration in respect of services as an employee;
- a state (whether it is a national, regional or local government) that has control, joint control or significant influence over the LLP; and
- another entity which is a related party because the same state has control, joint control or significant influence over both the reporting LLP and the other entity.

38 INFORMATION THAT SHOULD BE DISCLOSED

9.42   For each related party transaction, the following should be disclosed:

- Details of parent-subsidiary relationships regardless of whether there have been any transactions between the related parties. The reporting

LLP must disclose the name of its parent and, if different, the ultimate controlling party.

- Compensation paid to key management personnel in total.

- A description of the relationship between the LLP and the other party.

- Information relating to the related party transactions which should also include:

    — the amounts involved;

    — outstanding balances at the reporting date including terms and conditions, whether the outstanding balances are secured and the nature of the consideration to be provided in discharging the obligation as well as any guarantees given or received by the LLP;

    — any provision for doubtful debts due from related parties; and

    — amounts written off in the period in respect of debts due to or from related parties.

Comparative information should also be presented.

The above disclosures are required to be separately presented for each of the following categories:

- entities with control, joint control or significant influence over the entity;

- entities over which the LLP has control, joint control or significant influence;

- key management personnel of the LLP or its parent (in totality); and

- other related parties.

Chapter 10

Going concern

SIGNPOSTS

- LLPs will prepare financial statements on a going concern basis when it is expected the LLP will continue in business for the foreseeable future (see **10.1**).

- If the LLP is going to be liquidated, cease trading or the members have no realistic alternative but to liquidate the LLP or cease trading, an alternative basis is used for preparing the financial statements (see **10.1**).

- Going concern is considered to be a material concept in all entities – regardless of whether they are cash-rich and profit-making or not (see **10.1**).

- Auditors may qualify their audit report if there are uncertainties surrounding the going concern presumption and adequate disclosures have not been made in the financial statements (see **10.1**).

- The members are responsible for assessing the going concern of the LLP when preparing the financial statements (see **10.2**).

- Auditors should consider whether the members have undertaken an assessment of going concern for a period of at least 12 months from the date of approval of the financial statements (not 12 months from the balance sheet date) (see **10.2**).

- There are a number of risk factors which can be regarded as being indicative of a potential going concern problem (see **10.3**).

- If an LLP is part of a group and is relying on its parent or another member of the group for financial support, confirmation should be obtained in writing (see **10.4**).

- There are three possible conclusions relating to an assessment of going concern (see **10.5**).

- Members should ensure disclosure notes are adequate where there is significant doubt about the going concern of an LLP (see **10.6**).

- Auditors will usually consider the going concern presumption up to the point at which the audit report is to be signed (see **10.7**).

- Any concerns the auditor has relating to going concern will be discussed with the LLPs members and management and there are certain issues relating to the going concern assessment which the auditor will pay close attention to (see **10.8**).

- The auditor can express various opinions depending on the effect of going concern assessments (see **10.9**).

1   THE GOING CONCERN CONCEPT

10.1   Going concern is a fundamental principle underlying the preparation of the accounts of all entities. Accordingly, the majority of LLP accounts will be prepared on the basis that the LLP will continue in operational existence for the foreseeable future, known as the 'going concern basis'. The term 'foreseeable future' is taken to mean for a period of at least 12 months from the date of approval of the LLP's financial statements. The Limited Liability Partnership Act (LLPA) states that an LLP is presumed to be carrying on business as a going concern unless the accounts say otherwise. Application of Section 3 to FRS 102 *Financial Statement Presentation* also requires that an LLP should prepare its accounts on the going concern basis, unless the LLP is being liquidated or has ceased trading, or the members have no realistic alternative but to liquidate the LLP or to cease trading. In these circumstances, it may be appropriate to prepare the accounts on an alternative basis (normally the 'break-up' basis). Paragraph 3.9 to FRS 102 does not make specific reference to the 'break-up' basis, but says that where there are material uncertainties which cast doubt on the LLP's ability to continue as a going concern and hence the LLP does not prepare accounts under the going concern basis, the basis on which the financial statements are prepared is disclosed.

Going concern is a central issue to all LLP's regardless of whether they are profitable and cash-rich. Indeed, unforeseen events may take place even in the most profitable of LLP's which may call the ability for the LLP to continue as a going concern into question. In times of economic difficulties (eg recession) going concern needs to be very carefully considered and the auditors need to ensure that sufficient and appropriate audit evidence is obtained where the LLP's going concern status is concerned. In some cases the auditors may deem the going concern basis to be inappropriate in the LLP's circumstances which could have implications for the auditor's overall conclusion on the financial statements.

In preparing the accounts, the members will need to carry out such procedures as they consider necessary to satisfy themselves as to whether the going concern basis is appropriate. There may be factors about the business which cast doubt as to the going concern status of the LLP, for example a downturn in profitability or the renegotiation of necessary bank facilities. In these circumstances, the members will need to consider the actions that can be taken to mitigate those concerns. Disclosure of both the concerns and the mitigating action, together with why the members consider the accounts give a true and fair view of the position of the LLP, is required in the accounts.

Where there are uncertainties associated with the ability of the LLP to continue as a going concern, and the accounts do not include sufficient disclosure, the accounts may not give a true and fair view, and this will be considered by the auditors who, as a consequence, may qualify their audit opinion. The effect on an auditor's report relating to the going concern presumption is considered later in the chapter.

Section 3 to FRS 102 considers the presentation of financial statements under the going concern presumption and also specifies the actions to be taken by the members when they consider the going concern presumption to be inappropriate in the LLP's circumstances.

Example – cessation of trade after the reporting period

An LLP is preparing financial statements to 31 December 2014. Over the last couple of years the LLP has seen a decline in profitability and on 3 March 2015 one of its major customers ceased trading with immediate effect. The liquidators of the customer have confirmed that once the liquidation is complete there will be no funds available to pay unsecured creditors (of which the LLP is one of those creditors). The LLP's bank have also refused to renew borrowing facilities which are due for renewal on 1 April 2015 and the bank have also 'called in' the overdraft. The members have all agreed unanimously that they have no alternative but to also cease to trade with immediate effect. The question arises as to whether the financial statements as at 31 December 2014 should be prepared on a going concern basis in view of the fact that the customer ceased trading and the bank have refused to renew borrowing facilities after the year-end date has passed.

The concept of going concern is also considered in Section 32 *Events after the End of the Reporting Period*. In this context, FRS 102 prohibits an LLP from preparing its financial statements under the going concern concept if, after the end of the reporting period, the members determine it necessary to either liquidate the LLP or to cease trading, or have no realistic alternative but to cease trading. As a result the LLP must not prepare the financial statements under the going concern basis but on an alternative basis (eg the break-up basis).

The above example is an illustration of an issue which might arise after the LLP's year-end has passed. When the members of an LLP conclude that the going concern basis cannot be used to prepare the financial statements, the effect is so pervasive that Section 32 requires a fundamental change in the basis of accounting as opposed to merely adjusting the amounts recognised within the original basis of accounting. In the example above, the requirements in paragraph 3.9 would apply and the LLP should disclose:

● any material uncertainties the LLP may have in making its assessment of the LLP's ability to continue as a going concern; and

- when the LLP does not prepare its financial statements under the going concern basis, it should disclose that fact and the basis on which the LLP has prepared its financial statements (eg a break-up basis).

2   EVIDENCE SUPPORTING GOING CONCERN ASSESSMENTS

10.2   Paragraph 3.8 to FRS 102 requires that, when preparing accounts, the members should assess whether there are significant doubts about the LLP's ability to continue as a going concern. This assessment is required to be made for what is termed the 'foreseeable future'. The term 'foreseeable future' is not defined in accounting standards; however, disclosure is required where the review period considered by members is less than one year from the date of approval of the accounts (not the accounting period end). UK and Ireland auditing standards (specifically ISA (UK and Ireland) 570 *Going concern*) require that, where the period considered is less than one year from the date the accounts are approved and this fact is not disclosed, it should be referred to in the audit report. As a consequence of these requirements, most LLPs will consider a period of at least 12 months from the date of approval of the accounts.

Care needs to be taken with the application of ISA (UK and Ireland) 570 to ensure that the review period is correct (ie 12 months from the date of approval of the financial statements) because this differs from the mainstream ISA 570 issued by the International Auditing and Assurance Standards Board which says the review period should be 12 months from the date of the financial statements. The UK and Ireland version of this standard is more stringent in its approach.

The extent of evidence required to support the members' assessment of going concern will depend on a number of factors. These include:

- The extent to which the LLP's financial resources exceed its requirements.

- The size and complexity of the LLP's operations.

- The extent to which the LLP is operating in a high-risk industry.

For some LLPs, where they are trading profitably and have adequate working capital, the extent of documented evidence could be fairly limited.

In other cases, where the position is less certain, it may be necessary to prepare cash flow projections for subsequent periods comparing these with available, or likely to be available, facilities. Where such projections are considered necessary, they should be completed in sufficient detail to take full account of both future trading and the impact of any major transactions, such as proposed acquisitions or major capital investment programmes.

It is the members' responsibility to consider whether (or not) the going concern basis is appropriate in the LLP's circumstances and the assessment needs to be carefully considered in light of all facts pertinent to the LLP. If the LLP is subjected to external audit, the auditors will not be responsible for considering whether the going concern basis is appropriate, but instead they will be responsible for obtaining sufficient and appropriate audit evidence concerning the members' adoption of the going concern basis and whether the auditors are in agreement that this basis is appropriate. If the auditors disagree and adequate disclosure is not made, there will be implications for the audit opinion.

3   RISK FACTORS INDICATING A SIGNIFICANT LEVEL OF CONCERN

10.3   Whether something is significant or not will depend on the circumstances of the individual LLP. There are, however, a number of risk factors that can be regarded as being indicative of a potential going concern problem. These include:

General business considerations

- Fundamental changes in the market or technology to which the LLP cannot adapt adequately.

- Regulatory changes to which the LLP cannot adapt.

- Political or 'global' factors which may cause a significant effect on the LLP's operations.

- Loss of particular skills or technical expertise which might give it an advantage over competitors.

- The existence of major litigation, where an adverse judgment would imperil the LLP's continued existence or seriously damage its reputation.

General financial considerations

- The LLP's accounts indicate an excess of liabilities over assets.

- The LLP's accounts indicate net current liabilities.

- Significant liquidity or cash flow problems.

- Inability to pay creditors by the due dates.

- Deteriorating relationship with bankers or financiers.

- Denial of trade credit.

- Major losses or cash flow problems since the balance sheet date.

- The LLP has provided significant loans or guarantees, and there is a threat that these might be called in or that the borrower may not be able to make repayments.

- The LLP is dependent on financial support provided by another party (for example, a parent entity or fellow group member), and there is concern that the other party may be unable to provide the level of support needed to enable the LLP to stay in business.

- Cash flow forecasts suggesting net cash outflows.

Difficulties with external financing

- The LLP has experienced difficulties in the past in obtaining external finance facilities and/or complying with the related terms and covenants.

- The LLP has recently undertaken, or is planning to undertake, a major restructuring of debt.

- Borrowing facilities are under negotiation or are due for renewal in the next year.

- There are no planned alternative arrangements should current facilities not be extended.

- Borrowing agreements or executory contracts include clauses relating to debt covenants or subjective clauses (for example, a 'material adverse change' clause) that may trigger a request for repayment.

- The LLP has breached some of the terms or covenants, giving rise to the risk that the facilities may be withdrawn or not renewed.

- Terms or covenants of renewed financing are changed and become more difficult to comply with (for example, increased interest rates or charges).

- The finance facility is secured on assets (for example, properties) that have decreased in value below the amount of the facility.

Dependence on counterparties

- Loss of key members or staff.

- Loss of key customers.

- Evidence that suppliers providing essential goods or services are facing financial difficulties.

- Denial of (or reduction in) normal terms of trade by suppliers.

- The LLP is unable to find alternative suppliers.

The indicators above are not designed to be an 'exhaustive' list and there may be other indicators that the LLP's ability to continue as a going concern is called into question. Essentially, where there is material uncertainty relating to the LLP's ability to continue as a going concern then adequate disclosure should be made in the financial statements.

Example – material uncertainty relating to going concern

An LLP is preparing its financial statements for the year-ended 31 December 2014. 90% of the LLP's income is derived from a government contract which was awarded to the LLP in 2012 for a period of three years.

The contract ends on 31 March 2015 and the LLP is currently putting together a proposal to re-tender for the contract. If the contract is not awarded to the LLP this will cast significant doubt on its ability to continue in existence for the foreseeable future. The government's deadline for the tenders is 30 April 2015 and a decision is expected to be made by 30 June 2015. The LLP is confident that they will be awarded the contract for a further three-years and the financial statements are due to be approved by the members on 30 April 2015.

Clearly there is a material uncertainty regarding the LLP's ability to continue as a going concern because they will not know the outcome of their tender until the end of June 2015, by which time the financial statements will have been approved. The LLP should make disclosure in their financial statements about this material uncertainty and, assuming the disclosures made by the LLP are adequate, the auditors should include an 'emphasis of matter' paragraph within their report which cross-references the user to the relevant note in the LLP's financial statements.

---

4   RELIANCE ON THE SUPPORT OF OTHER ENTITIES WITHIN A GROUP

10.4   Where an LLP which is part of a group relies upon its parent or another member of that group for financial support, confirmation should be obtained in writing. This is usually done by way of a 'letter of support' (or 'comfort letter') issued by the parent to the LLP. The members of the LLP will need to satisfy themselves that the parent is in a strong enough financial position to provide the necessary support. The auditors will require sight of the letter of support, and will also carry out their own procedures in relation to the financial position of the parent and its ability to provide additional support were the LLP to need it. This is because the auditors cannot simply rely on the letter of support from the parent as it is internally-generated – audit evidence must be sufficient and appropriate.

In some cases, a letter of support may be required from the LLP to a subsidiary where that entity's ability to continue as a going concern is dependent upon financial support from the LLP. The LLP should consider the effect such support will have on its own ability to continue in operational existence.

5   CONCLUSIONS IN RELATION TO GOING CONCERN

10.5   Once the members have carried out their assessment, there are three possible conclusions:

- there are no material uncertainties that lead to significant doubt about the LLP's ability to continue as a going concern;

- there are material uncertainties that lead to significant doubt about the LLP's ability to continue as a going concern, but the going concern basis remains appropriate; or

- the use of the going concern basis is not appropriate.

Generally an LLP will not make any disclosures within the financial statements when there are no material uncertainties which lead to significant doubt about the ability of the LLP to continue as a going concern. However, where there are significant doubts about the LLP's ability to continue as a going concern, adequate disclosures should be made in the LLP's financial statements.

6   DISCLOSURE WHERE THERE IS SIGNIFICANT DOUBT

10.6   The adequacy of disclosure made by the members will be assessed by the auditors, but the disclosure will not normally be regarded as adequate, unless it contains the following:

- A statement of the specific nature of the material uncertainties that give rise to significant doubt.

- A statement of the assumptions made by the members, which should be clearly distinguishable from the relevant facts.

- Where appropriate and practicable, a statement regarding the members' plans for resolving the matters giving rise to the uncertainty.

- Details of any relevant actions taken by the members.

- An explanation of why the going concern basis has been adopted.

These statements should be given reasonable prominence within the accounts, and are usually best positioned in the accounting policies note under the 'Basis of preparation' heading although it is not uncommon for some LLP's to make these disclosures under a separate 'Going concern' heading.

Due to the pervasive nature of going concern, if the disclosures are considered to be inadequate by the auditors it will have an impact on the audit opinion. In all cases the auditors will try to resolve any issues as the auditors would ordinarily only issue a qualified opinion as a 'last resort'

All LLPs, whether audited or not, must ensure that any uncertainties relating to going concern are adequately disclosed as the members have a duty to prepare financial statements which give a true and fair view.

7   REASSESSMENT PRIOR TO APPROVING THE ACCOUNTS

10.7   The members' assessment of going concern, and the information supporting that assessment, will usually be prepared at a date in advance of the accounts being approved. In addition, the auditors may perform some of their work on the appropriateness of the going concern basis whilst carrying out other fieldwork. This may be completed some time before the accounts are approved. At the time that the accounts are approved, the members will need to revisit their assessment and consider any further factors that have come to light up until the date the accounts are approved. The auditors will similarly need to update their procedures, both by discussion with the members and by review of any further evidence which has become available.

Care needs to be taken by all parties where the reassessment is concerned. This is because the date of approval of the financial statements and the date of the auditor's report will normally take place on the same day. All events and transactions which may give rise to going concern issues need to be considered and therefore users' of the LLP's financial statements will expect that all such issues have been taken into consideration up to and including the date of approval of the financial statements and the date of the auditor's report. Auditors must therefore ensure that the work they carry out on the LLP's going concern presumption is as near to the date of the auditor's report as possible. Failing to do this may result in a failing to detect a material transaction or event that could call into question the LLP's ability to continue as a going concern and hence increase audit risk (the risk that the auditor forms an incorrect opinion on the financial statements).

8   ASSESSMENTS MADE BY AUDITORS

10.8   In carrying out their work, the auditors will need to assess whether the going concern concept is appropriate and the adequacy of any disclosures about the LLP's ability to continue as a going concern made in the accounts. It is *not* the auditor's responsibility to conclude whether the LLP is a going concern – this is the responsibility of the members. The auditor's responsibility is to obtain sufficient and appropriate audit evidence to corroborate management's assertion about the going concern status of the LLP.

The auditors will discuss factors affecting the ability of the LLP to continue in business with the members and the LLP's management, and also examine the financial information available to support the members' opinion, such as the latest management accounts or budgets and projections. They may also request copies of other supporting details, such as correspondence with bankers and other providers of finance.

The auditors will pay particular attention to the following:

●   the period covered by the projections;

●   how recently those projections have been updated;

●   past history as to the reliability of projections prepared by the LLP;

●   whether the projected income is reasonable in the context of existing clients and customers and known marketing activity for the future;

- whether assumptions as to profit and levels of work in progress, debtors and creditors are consistent with the history of the business;

- whether projected and necessary capital expenditure has been included;

- whether all payments during the period are taken into account, including members' remuneration and drawings, and annuities to former members;

- whether the assumptions made are consistent with each other;

- whether the assumptions used in respect of financing match what is available to the LLP and whether interest rates utilised are realistic;

- whether consideration has been given to the sensitivity of the projections to changes in the underlying assumptions; and

- that periods where cash is most critical have been identified and that an assessment of headroom above available facilities has been made.

Where critical points within the cash flow are identified, the actions which can be taken by the members to mitigate the impact will also be considered. The above list is not an exhaustive list of procedures which the auditor may adopt and further specific procedures may be needed and implemented by the auditor to confirm the appropriateness of the LLP's going concern ability.

9   EFFECT ON THE AUDIT REPORT

10.9   There are a number of effects that going concern can have on the audit report, dependent on the circumstances of the individual LLP. ISA (UK and Ireland) 570 considers all the permutations of circumstances that can arise, the further procedures the auditor may have to undertake, and the effect on the audit report. The effects on the audit report are summarised in Table 10.1:

Table 10.1   Effects of going concern assessments on audit report

Situation	Impact on audit report
No material uncertainty about ability to continue as a going concern	Unqualified
Material uncertainty about ability to continue as a going concern, but the circumstances are explained fully in the notes to the accounts	Unqualified report, but with an 'emphasis of matter' paragraph
Material uncertainty about the LLP's ability to continue as a going concern, but the circumstances are not explained fully in the notes to the accounts	Qualified on grounds of disagreement regarding disclosure ('except for') or adverse opinion (accounts do not give a true and fair view)
The auditors are unable to obtain such information and explanations as they consider necessary from the LLP's management	Qualified on grounds of limitation of scope (insufficient evidence) (disclaimer – auditor is unable to say whether the accounts give a true and fair view)

Situation	Impact on audit report
The period to which the members have paid particular attention in assessing the going concern basis is less than one year from the date of approval of the financial statements, and the auditors believe this to be unreasonably short	Disclaimer as a result of limitation of scope (insufficient evidence), possibly with disagreement regarding disclosure if the members have also failed to disclose the period
The period to which the members have paid particular attention in assessing the going concern basis is less than one year from the date of approval of the accounts, but this has been disclosed	Unqualified (including an 'emphasis of matter' paragraph where appropriate)
The period to which the members have paid particular attention in assessing the going concern basis is less than one year from the date of approval of the accounts, and the members have not disclosed that fact	Qualified on grounds of disagreement regarding disclosure ('except for')
The auditors disagree with the preparation of the accounts on the going concern basis	Adverse opinion ('does not give a true and fair view')
The accounts, in order to give a true and fair view, are prepared on a basis other than the going concern basis	Unqualified. The auditor may include an 'emphasis of matter' paragraph, drawing attention to the basis of preparation

Example audit report extract – use of going concern assumption is appropriate but a material uncertainty exists

Opinion

Express audit opinion.

Emphasis of Matter

Without qualifying our opinion, we draw attention to Note 20 in the financial statements which indicates that the LLP has incurred a net loss of £65,000 during the year ended 31 December 2014 and, as at that date, the LLP's current liabilities exceeded its total assets by £32,000. These conditions, along with other matters as set forth in Note 20, indicate the existence of a material uncertainty that may cast significant doubt about the LLP's ability to continue as a going concern.

Example audit report extract – material uncertainty exists but has not been adequately disclosed and a qualified 'except for' opinion is considered appropriate

Basis for Qualified Opinion

The LLP's overdraft expired and is due to be repaid on 31 March 2015. The LLP has been unsuccessful in negotiating or re-financing this overdraft. This situation indicates the existence of a material uncertainty that may cast significant doubt about the LLP's ability to continue as a going concern and therefore the LLP may be unable to realise its assets and discharge its liabilities in the ordinary course of business. The financial statements (and notes thereto) do not fully disclose this fact.

Qualified Opinion

In our opinion, except for the incomplete disclosure of the information referred to in the Basis for Qualified Opinion paragraph, the financial statements give a true and fair view of the financial position of the LLP as at 31 December 2014 and of its financial performance and its cash flows for the year then ended in accordance with United Kingdom Generally Accepted Accounting Practice and the Statement of Recommended Practice – Accounting by Limited Liability Partnerships and have been prepared in accordance with the requirements of the Companies Act 2006 as applied to Limited Liability Partnerships.

Example audit report extract – material uncertainty exists but has not been adequately disclosed and an adverse opinion is considered appropriate

Basis for Adverse Opinion

The LLP's overdraft expired on 29 December 2014 and the overdraft was repayable on 31 December 2014. The LLP has been unsuccessful in negotiating or re-financing this overdraft and is considering filing for bankruptcy. These events indicate a material uncertainty that may cast significant doubt on the LLP's ability to continue as a going concern and therefore it may be unable to realise its assets and discharge its liabilities in the normal course of business. The financial statements (and notes thereto) do not disclose this fact.

Adverse Opinion

In our opinion, because of the omission of the information mentioned in the Basis for Adverse Opinion paragraph, the financial statements do not give a true and fair view of the financial position of the LLP as at 31 December 2014 and of its financial performance and its cash flows for the year then ended in accordance with United Kingdom Generally Accepted Accounting Practice and the Statement of Recommended Practice – Accounting by Limited Liability Partnerships and have been prepared in accordance with the requirements of the Companies Act 2006 as applied to Limited Liability Partnerships.

Chapter 11

Consolidated accounts

SIGNPOSTS

- An LLP may acquire a controlling investment in another undertaking (see **11.1**).

- When a parent-subsidiary relationship exists, the parent LLP must prepare consolidated financial statements which show the results of the group as a single economic entity (see **11.1**).

- The process of preparing consolidated accounts can be complicated and therefore a logical approach is needed (see **11.2**).

- The parent LLP must have 'control' over the financial and operating policies of the subsidiary in order for a parent-subsidiary relationship to exist and control can be obtained in a variety of ways (see **11.3**).

- Uniform accounting policies and year-ends should be used for all members of the group in preparing consolidated financial statements (see **11.4**).

- If a parent LLP owns less than 100% of the net assets of a subsidiary, the remaining balance will be owned by the non-controlling interests (previously referred to as 'minority interests' in previous UK GAAP) (see **11.5**).

- There are additional considerations which should be taken into account when there has been a change in group structure during the year (see **11.6–11.8**).

- In addition to obtaining a subsidiary (when control is achieved), there are other forms of investment which do not result in control that an LLP can invest in (see **11.10** and **11.11**).

1   INTRODUCTION

11.1   It is not unusual for an LLP to either set up other entities through which to carry out certain parts of its trade or, as discussed in Chapter 12, acquire a controlling investment in another undertaking (ie a subsidiary). Legislation and UK GAAP may, in such circumstances, require the LLP to prepare consolidated accounts, which aggregate the accounts of the LLP and the other undertakings, as well as its own entity accounts.

The main section of FRS 102 which governs the accounting for groups is Section 9 *Consolidated and Separate Financial Statements* although Section 19 *Business Combinations and Goodwill* is also closely related. The objective of a consolidated set of LLP financial statements is to show the results of the group in line with its economic substance – which is that of a single reporting entity. Generally accepted accounting practice (GAAP) recognises that the financial statements of a parent LLP would not, in themselves, present a full picture of the group's economic activities or financial position. The consolidated financial statements will, therefore, reflect the extended business unit which conducts activities under the control of the parent. The cost of the investment in the subsidiary in the parent LLP's individual financial statements is replaced and then on a line-by-line basis the subsidiary's assets, liabilities, income and equity is added in 100% to represent the control obtained by the parent LLP.

All intra-group trading (and the effects thereof) are eliminated during the consolidation process. This is because if intra-group trading (and the effects) were not eliminated on consolidation then the consolidated profit and loss account and consolidated balance sheet would be seriously distorted. For example, intra-group 'sales' are only true sales when the sale occurs with a third party outside of the group structure.

2 PREPARING GROUP ACCOUNTS

11.2 The requirements as to when consolidated accounts must be prepared, and the available exemptions, are considered in Chapter 2. An overview of how group accounts are prepared is shown below:

- Understand the group structure and establish those entities where the LLP has control (keep in mind that control does not necessarily have to be established through a percentage of ownership interest – control can exist even when the LLP owns less than 51% of the net assets of the subsidiary – see the next section).

- Ensure uniform accounting year-ends and accounting policies are used for all members of the group. Where uniform accounting policies are impracticable, adjustments will need to be made to the subsidiary's financial statements for consolidation purposes.

- Eliminate intra-group trading and the results of intra-group trading (intra-group debtors and intra-group creditors).

- Consolidate the results of the parent and all its subsidiaries, paying careful attention to goodwill calculations for any subsidiaries acquired during the reporting period.

For subsidiaries which have been acquired during the accounting period, the fair value of the purchase consideration used in the calculation of goodwill should be carefully assessed. This is because the SORP requires the profit share promised to the new members in the enlarged LLP to be assessed in order to establish if a portion of that remuneration represents consideration for the acquired business rather than future members' remuneration. The substance of the arrangement needs to be carefully scrutinised and legal advice should be obtained where considered necessary.

The SORP contains an example whereby the members of an acquired entity were awarded an increased profit share for a certain amount of time after the acquisition which then falls back to normal levels. It could be suggested that the short-term excess amounts formed part of the purchase consideration and hence the substance of the arrangement should be carefully assessed to ensure appropriate treatment.

Where non-controlling interests (minority interests) are concerned, these are usually shown within the consolidated balance sheet as a deduction from net assets (see section 5).

3   UNDERSTANDING CONTROL

11.3   In accounting terms, an LLP will be the parent LLP of another undertaking if it exercises control over that undertaking. Both legislation and Section 9 refer to undertakings, which means that the LLP needs to consider not just companies and LLPs in which it has an interest, but also other vehicles, such as partnerships and unincorporated businesses.

The Glossary to FRS 102 defines control as 'the power to govern the financial and operating policies of an entity so as to obtain benefits from its activities'. Control is deemed to exist, and hence the LLP is the parent LLP of another undertaking, if any of the following apply:

- The LLP owns (directly or indirectly through subsidiaries) a majority of the voting rights in the undertaking (only in exceptional circumstances could such ownership not constitute the achievement of control).

- The LLP is a member of the undertaking and has the right to appoint or remove directors holding a majority of the voting rights at meetings of the board on all, or substantially all, matters.

- The LLP has the power to govern the financial and operating policies of the undertaking under either a statute or by way of an agreement.

- The LLP has the power to cast the majority of votes at meetings of the undertaking and control of the undertaking is by that board or body.

- The LLP has options or convertible financial instruments that are currently exercisable, or by having an agent with the ability to direct the activities for the benefit of the controlling undertaking.

- The LLP has the power to exercise, or actually exercises, dominant influence or control over the undertaking and the LLP and the undertaking are managed on a unified basis (two or more undertakings are managed on a unified basis if the whole of the operations of the undertakings are integrated and they are managed as a single unit. Unified management does not arise solely because one undertaking manages another).

The term 'dominant influence' refers to the situation where an LLP can use its position to achieve the operating and financial policies which it desires, notwithstanding the rights or influence of any other party. Such influence may, or may not, be explicit in nature. Determining whether there is dominant influence requires consideration of how this is effected in practice, by reference to the way in which the LLP interacts with the potential subsidiary. The fact that the LLP has the ability to exercise dominant influence, but chooses not to, will not of itself be sufficient to establish a parent-subsidiary relationship.

4   THE PREPARATION OF CONSOLIDATED ACCOUNTS

11.4   Consolidation is the process of adjusting and combining financial information from the individual accounts of a parent LLP and its subsidiaries, to prepare consolidated accounts that present financial information for the group in line with that of its economic substance ie as a single economic entity. Paragraph 9.17 of FRS 102 says that uniform group accounting policies should be used in preparing the consolidated accounts for like transactions and other events and conditions in similar circumstances. It may, therefore, be necessary to make adjustments to amounts shown in a subsidiary's accounts at the time of consolidation where the subsidiary uses accounting policies which are different from those adopted in the consolidated financial statements. Particular attention is likely to be required to any overseas subsidiaries, as local accounting practice may differ from that in the UK.

Paragraph 9.16 of FRS 102 requires that the accounts of the subsidiaries to be used in preparing the consolidated accounts should, where practicable, be for the same financial year end, and for the same accounting period, as those of the parent LLP. However, this may not be practicable, particularly in the case of overseas subsidiaries, where legislation in a particular country may dictate the year end. Where possible, interim accounts for that subsidiary should be used; however, if this is impracticable, earlier accounts of the subsidiary may be used, provided they are prepared for a financial year that ended not more than three months earlier. Outside this period, legislation requires that interim accounts be prepared.

All intra-group trading and the effects of intra-group trading should be eliminated on consolidation. The objective of this elimination process is so that the consolidated financial statements show the trading results of the group as if it were a single reporting entity (ie the consolidated accounts show the results of the group's trading with the outside world which does not include any intra-group trading).

Example – intra-group trading

LLP A has a wholly-owned subsidiary (Sub B) and the group's year-end is 31 December 2013. During the year LLP A has provided services to Sub B amounting to £15,000 which have been reflected as cost of sales in Sub B's individual financial statements. At the year-end Sub B owed LLP A an amount of £3,000.

All intra-group trading (and the effects thereof) have to be eliminated on consolidation to show the results of the group as if it were a single reporting entity. Therefore in the consolidated financial statements of the group the eliminations will be:

DR sales	£15,000 (this reduces LLP A's sales)
CR cost of sales	£15,000 (this reduces Sub B's cost of sales)
Being elimination of intra-group sales during the year	
DR creditors	£3,000 (this reduces Sub B's creditors)
CR debtors	£3,000 (this reduces LLP A's debtors)
Being elimination of intra-group debt at the year-end	

This will have the effect of the consolidated financial statements showing the trading with entities which are outside of the group (ie with the outside world) as well as reducing debtors and creditors for the effects of intra-group trading at the year-end.

Intra-group transactions may result in profits or losses being reflected in the book value of assets to be included in the consolidation. Such profits or losses should be eliminated in full, because, for the group as a whole, no profits or losses have arisen.

Example – unrealised profit in in stock at year-end

LLP A has a wholly-owned subsidiary (Sub B) and the group's year-end is 31 December 2015. On 29 December 2015, Sub B sold goods to LLP A for £6,000 which resulted in a profit on sale for Sub B of £3,000. All of these goods were in LLP A's stock at the year-end.

The unrealised profit in stock remains in LLP A's stock figure at the year-end (because this would have been valued at cost of £6,000). However, the £3,000 profit is merely an intra-group profit in stock and in order to reduce stock back down to cost to the group (to accord with the principles in Section 13 *Inventories* which says that stock should be valued at the lower of cost and estimated selling price less costs to complete and sell), LLP A will have to eliminate the profit by:

DR closing stock (consolidated profit and loss account)	£3,000
CR closing stock (consolidated balance sheet)	£3,000

This will then bring the stock value down to cost to the group.

5   NON-CONTROLLING INTERESTS

11.5   Where the LLP controls less than 100% of a subsidiary, the interest it does not control is referred to as a non-controlling interest. The term 'minority interest' may be more familiar with preparers of LLP financial statements but FRS 102 refers to them as 'non-controlling interest'.

Within the consolidated balance sheet, non-controlling interests are most usually shown as a deduction from net assets. The consolidated profit and loss account should show separately the aggregate of profit or loss on ordinary activities for the period attributable to the non-controlling interests. Profits or losses arising in a subsidiary should be apportioned between the controlling and non-controlling interests, in proportion to their respective interests held over the period in which the profit or loss arose. Where the losses in a subsidiary attributable to the non-controlling interest result in its interest being one of net liabilities rather than net assets, the group should make provision to the extent that it has any commercial or legal obligation to provide finance that may not be recoverable in respect of the accumulated losses attributable to the non-controlling interest.

Example – consolidated profit and loss account showing non-controlling interests

	2014	2013
	£'000	£'000
Turnover	10,000	9,000
Cost of sales	(6,000)	(4,000)
Gross profit	4,000	5,000
Other operating costs	(2,000)	(1,000)
Other operating income	700	500
Operating profit	**2,700**	**4,500**
Interest payable and similar charges	(800)	(900)
Profit on ordinary activities before tax	**1,900**	**3,600**
Tax on profit on ordinary activities of subsidiaries	–	–
Profit on ordinary activities after tax	**1,900**	**3,600**
Equity non-controlling interests	102	–

	2014	2013
Profit for the financial year before members' remuneration and profit shares	**2,002**	**3,600**
Profit for the financial year before members' remuneration and profit shares	**2,002**	**3,600**
Members' remuneration charged as an expense	(1,200)	(1,200)
Profit for the financial year available for discretionary division among members	**802**	**2,400**

6   CHANGES TO THE GROUP STRUCTURE DURING A FINANCIAL PERIOD

11.6   Chapter 12 considers in more detail the accounting implications of business combinations during a financial period. However, when preparing consolidated accounts where there has been a change in the group structure during the period, the following specific considerations should be taken into account.

Acquisitions

11.7   In a business combination, Section 19 *Business Combinations and Goodwill* requires that the identifiable assets and liabilities of the acquired subsidiary are brought into the consolidation at their fair values at the date that the undertaking becomes a subsidiary.

There may be occasions when a parent owns, say, 70% of a subsidiary and then increases this ownership interest by acquiring further ownership interest from the non-controlling interests to, say, 90%. When the parent increases its controlling interest in a subsidiary Section 9 does not require the parent to revalue the identifiable assets and liabilities and any provisions for contingent liabilities to fair value; nor does it permit any additional goodwill being recognised. Instead, any increases in the parent's ownership interest is accounted for as a transaction between the equity holders.

Example – increases in ownership interest

LLP A has owned 60% of the net assets of Undertaking B for several years and has a year-end of 31 December. During the year to 31 December 2014, LLP A acquired a further 30% of the net assets of Undertaking B thus taking its ownership interest to 90% at a cost of £4,000.

Paragraph 22.19 to FRS 102 says that changes in a parent's controlling interest in a subsidiary which do not result in a loss of control are to be accounted for as transactions with equity holders in their capacity as equity holders. Any difference (if any) between the amount by which the non-controlling interest is changed and the fair value of the consideration paid or received is recognised directly in equity and attributed to equity holders of the parent. The parent will not recognise any change in the carrying value of assets (which includes goodwill) or liabilities as a result of the transaction. Therefore, LLP A will record the transaction as:

DR non-controlling interests	£4,000
CR cash at bank	£4,000

The above example highlights an example of where the parent increases its ownership interest in stages. It might be the case that the LLP achieves control in stages and in such situations the transaction is accounted for in accordance with paragraphs 19.11A and 19.14 of FRS 102. Paragraph 19.11A says that when control is achieved following a series of transactions, the cost of the business combination is the total of the fair values of the assets given, liabilities assumed and equity instruments issued by the acquirer at the date of each transaction in the series. The cost is then allocated by recognising the acquiree's identifiable assets and liabilities and a provision for contingent liabilities at fair value and any difference will be goodwill and therefore accounted for in accordance with paragraphs 19.22–19.24 of FRS 102.

Example – control achieved in stages

LLP A acquired a controlling interest in Undertaking B in two transactions as follows:

30 June 2015: 15% holding at a cost of £33,000 when the fair value of the net assets of Undertaking B amounted to £180,000.

31 March 2016: 45% holding at a cost of £162,000 when the fair value of the net assets of Undertaking B amounted to £290,000.

The cost of the business combination is £195,000. The group share of the fair value of the assets at the date that control is achieved is £174,000 (60% × £290,000). Goodwill is therefore £21,000.

Disposals

11.8   When an undertaking ceases to be a subsidiary during a period, the consolidated accounts for that period should include its results up to the date that it ceases to be a subsidiary, together with any gain or loss arising on that cessation. If control is lost (hence the subsidiary falls to be classed as either an associate or a simple investment), the gain or loss on the disposal is calculated as the difference between:

- the proceeds from the disposal; and

- the proportion of the carrying value of the amount of the subsidiary's net assets, including any related goodwill, disposed of (or lost) as at the date of disposal (or as at the date that control is lost).

If a disposal occurs but the parent still retains control (ie the disposed element does not result in the LLP owning less than 51% of the net assets of the undertaking) then no gain or loss is recognised on the disposal. Instead the disposal is accounted for as a transaction between equity holders and the non-controlling interests is changed to reflect the parent's partial disposal.

Example – outright disposal of a subsidiary

LLP A has undertaken a strategic review of its business and has decided to dispose of its entire ownership interest in Undertaking B. The group has a year-end of 31 October and the sale completed on 31 August 2015 for a sum of £100,000. The net assets of the subsidiary were valued at £98,700.

The resulting profit on disposal amounts to £1,300 (£100,000 proceeds less disposal of the subsidiary at fair value of £98,700) and this gain will be recognised in the LLP's profit and loss account (income statement).

Accounting for interests in undertakings that do not give rise to control

11.9   Whilst an outright controlling interest via a subsidiary is probably the most common form of interest that an LLP will have in another entity, other lesser interests, where the LLP does not control the activities of the other entity, are also possible.

Associate

11.10   In this situation, the LLP holds a participating interest, and exercises *significant influence* over the other entity. The term 'significant influence' means that the LLP has the ability to participate in the financial and operating polices of the associate but it does not control (or have joint control over) the associate. In practical terms, the LLP has a long-term interest and is actively involved, and influential, in the direction of its investee, through its participation in policy decisions covering the aspects of policy relevant to the LLP, including decisions on strategic issues such as:

- the expansion or contraction of the business, participation in other entities or changes in products, markets and activities of its investee; and

- determining the balance between dividend and reinvestment.

Section 14 *Investments in Associates* in FRS 102 contains an assumption that a holding of 20% or more of the shares of an entity is presumed to be a participating interest, unless the contrary can be clearly demonstrated. The presumption is rebutted if the interest is either not for the long term or is not beneficial.

Section 14 requires that the equity method of accounting be used when including the associate in its own consolidated accounts. It should be noted that equity accounting is only relevant if the LLP is already required to prepare consolidated accounts; it cannot be applied in the financial statements of an individual LLP.

The equity method of accounting is a method whereby the equity investment is initially recognised at the transaction price (which should also include all transaction costs) and it is then subsequently adjusted to reflect the investor's share of the profit or loss, other comprehensive income and equity of the associate.

Example – equity accounting for an associate

On 31 December 2014, Indigo LLP invested a sum of £10,000 in Purple in return for a 25% holding in the net assets of Purple. On 31 December 2015 the resulting profit in Purple was £7,000.

On 31 December 2014, Indigo will account for its investment in its associate as follows:

| DR investment in associate | £10,000 |
| CR cash at bank | £10,000 |

This represents the initial investment in Purple.

Indigo then needs to reflect its share of Purple's profit in its consolidated profit and loss account so under equity accounting the entries will be:

| DR investment in associate (25% × £7,000) | £1,750 |
| CR profit and loss account | £1,750 |

In the consolidated profit and loss account, the LLP's share of its associate's operating result should be included immediately before the group operating result. From the level of profit before tax, the LLP's share of the relevant amounts for associates should be included within the amounts for the group. In the balance sheet, the LLP's share of the net assets of the associate should be included and separately disclosed as part of investments. Goodwill arising on the LLP's acquisition of its associate, less any amortisation or impairment, should be included in the carrying amount for the associate but should be disclosed separately. In the profit and loss account, the amortisation or other write down of such goodwill should be separately disclosed as part of the LLP's share of the associate's results.

Joint venture

11.11 The accounting for joint ventures is dealt with in Section 15 *Investments in Joint Ventures*, and this section applies to:

- accounting for joint ventures in the LLP's consolidated financial statements;

- investments in joint ventures in the individual financial statements of a venturer which is not a parent; and

- investments in jointly controlled operations and jointly controlled assets in the separate financial statements of a venturer which is a parent.

A joint venture will exist where the LLP holds a long-term interest in another venture, and shares control under a contractual arrangement. The joint venture agreement can override the rights normally conferred by ownership interests, with the effect that:

- acting together, the venturers can control the venture and there are procedures for such joint action; and

- each venturer has (implicitly or explicitly) a veto over strategic policy decisions.

There is usually a procedure for settling disputes between investors and, possibly, for terminating the joint venture.

Joint ventures can take the form of jointly controlled operations, jointly controlled assets or jointly controlled entities. The key aspect of the joint venture is that there must be a contractual arrangement in place in which two (or more) parties undertake an economic activity which is subjected to joint control.

When including the joint venture in its consolidated accounts, the LLP should use the equity method showing, in addition to the amounts included under the equity method (as outlined for associates above), on the face of the balance sheet, the LLP's share of the gross assets and liabilities of the joint venture, and, in the profit and loss account, the LLP's share of its turnover (which should be distinguished from that of the group).

7 APPENDIX – ILLUSTRATIVE CONSOLIDATED BALANCE SHEET

11.12 The following illustrative consolidated balance sheet is an example only and some LLP consolidated balance sheets may contain additional information from that shown in the following illustration.

	Note	2014	2013
		£'000	£'000
Fixed assets			
Intangible assets	8	X	X
Tangible assets	9	X	X
Investments	10	X	X
		X	X
Current assets			
Debtors	11	X	X
Cash at bank and in hand	12	X	X
Creditors: amounts falling due within one year		(X)	(X)
Net current assets		X	X
Total assets less current liabilities		**X**	**X**
Creditors: amounts falling due after more than one year	14	**(X)**	**(X)**
Provisions for liabilities	15	**(X)**	**(X)**
Pension scheme liability	26	**(X)**	**(X)**
Equity non-controlling interests		X	X
Net assets attributable to members	1	**Y**	**Y**
Represented by:			
Loans and other debts due to members within one year			
Members' capital classified as a liability	16	X	X
Other amounts	16	X	X
		X	X
Loans and other debts due to members after more than one year			
Other amounts	16	X	X
		X	X

11.12 *Consolidated accounts*

	Note	2014	2013
Equity			
Members' other interests – other reserves classified as equity	16	(X)	(X)
Revaluation reserve	16	(X)	(X)
		Y	Y
Total members' interests			
Loans and other debts due to members	16	X	X
Members' other interests	16	(X)	(X)
Amounts due from members	16	(X)	(X)
Total including pension scheme liability		(X)	(X)
Pension scheme liability		X	X
Total excluding pension scheme liability		X	X

Chapter 12

Business combinations

SIGNPOSTS

- An LLP can acquire another business either by taking a direct investment or by acquiring the assets (see **12.1**).

- Under UK GAAP there are two methods of accounting for a business combination: the 'purchase method' or 'merger accounting' (see **12.2**).

- Strict rules govern the use of merger accounting but are particularly relevant to partnerships which are transferring to LLP status (see **12.2**).

- There are three steps involved in applying the purchase method (see **12.3**).

- The date of acquisition may not necessarily be the date on which control is obtained (see **12.7**).

- The consideration paid by a parent LLP for an ownership interest in another undertaking may take several different forms and not necessarily just be simply in cash (see **12.8**).

- Care needs to be taken to ensure the accounting for 'contingent consideration' is applied correctly (see **12.8**).

- In dealing with a business combination, an LLP should also have regard to not only those parts of the agreement which deal with the consideration, but also to those parts of the agreement which deal with the arrangements entered into for profit-sharing with any new members joining the LLP from the acquired entity (see **12.8**).

- At the date of acquisition, assets and liabilities of the acquired entity are to be valued at fair value and various factors should be taken into account when arriving at fair values (see **12.9**).

- When an LLP acquires the business assets and liabilities of an entity rather than making an investment, the primary difference is that goodwill arising on acquisition will be recorded on the LLP's own balance sheet (see **12.10**).

- Goodwill under FRS 102 does not have an indefinite useful life and must be amortised on a systematic basis over its expenses useful economic life (see **12.11**).

- Internally-generated goodwill cannot be recognised on the LLP's balance sheet (see **12.11**).

- A reassessment exercise should be carried out if the goodwill arising on a business combination is negative (ie a 'bargain purchase' has taken place) to ensure the completeness of assets and liabilities and the accuracy of the cost of the combination (see **12.11**).

- There are additional requirements in respect of goodwill impairment under FRS 102 (see **12.12**).

- There are three criteria which must be met before merger accounting can be applied (see **12.13**).

- The SORP recommends merger accounting be used (where permitted) so as to reflect the initial 'conversion' to LLP (see **12.13** and **12.14**).

- There are accounting consequences in respect of a merger which differ from the investment by a parent in a subsidiary (see **12.15**).

1   INTRODUCTION

12.1   This chapter considers the accounting consequences of an LLP acquiring another business, either by taking a direct investment (equity, partnership share, etc) or by acquiring the assets, liabilities and trade without making a direct investment in the disposing entity.

In each of these circumstances, there are accounting implications both for the LLP's accounts and for consolidated accounts where the LLP is required to prepare them (see Chapter 2 for the exemptions from the requirement to prepare consolidated accounts, and Chapter 11 for more detailed considerations regarding the preparation and presentation of consolidated accounts).

2   GENERAL ACCOUNTING PRINCIPLES FOR BUSINESS COMBINATIONS

12.2   There are currently two possible methods of accounting for a business combination within consolidated accounts: the purchase method or merger accounting. The purchase method was previously referred to as the 'acquisition' method of accounting in previous UK GAAP. With regards to merger accounting, the conditions which must be met before merger accounting can be applied are discussed below. The rules contained within accounting standards are extremely strict and, as a result, mergers in the corporate environment are relatively rare. The strict criteria for merger accounting are particularly relevant to partnerships transferring to LLP status as, historically, most partnerships have regarded any business combination with another partnership as a merger. However, a large number of these combinations would not meet the accounting requirements for merger accounting and, therefore, fall to be treated as acquisitions and hence the purchase method would be applied.

In addition to the requirements set out in legislation, accounting for business combinations is governed by the provisions in Section 19 *Business Combinations and Goodwill*.

Section 19 provides guidance on the identification of the acquirer, measuring the cost of the business combination and the allocation of this cost to the assets acquired and the liabilities and provisions (including contingent liabilities) assumed in the business combination. The accounting treatment for goodwill is also addressed in Section 19.

The scope of Section 19 does not, however, apply to:

● the formation of a joint venture; or

● the acquisition of a group of assets which would not constitute a business.

In financial reporting terms, a business combination is the bringing together of separate businesses into one reporting business. In almost all cases, a business combination will result in one party obtaining control of one or more other businesses within the combination from the date of acquisition (the date of acquisition being the date on which control is obtained by the parent).

Some business combinations can be very complex in terms of how they are structured depending on the reasons for the combination and occur by the issue of equity instruments (shares), the transfer of cash (or cash equivalents) or other assets. In some combinations there may well be a mixture of equity instruments, cash/cash equivalents or other assets, and in some combinations, there may well be a new entity set up that will control the combined entities or net assets transferred or it could involve the restructuring of existing combined entities.

3   PRINCIPLES OF THE PURCHASE METHOD

12.3   The general principle of consolidated accounts is that they should present the financial position and results of the parent and its subsidiary undertakings in line with the group's economic substance, which is that of a single LLP. All business combinations which fall under the scope of Section 19 are accounted for by applying the purchase method with the exceptions of group reconstructions which may be accounted for by applying the merger accounting method and public benefit entity combinations which are in substance a gift or a merger and hence would be accounted for under Section 34 *Specialised Activities*.

There are three steps in applying the purchase method:

● identify the acquirer;

● measure the cost of the business combination; and

- at the date of acquisition, allocate the cost of the business combination to the assets acquired and liabilities (including provisions and contingent liabilities) assumed.

Identify the acquirer

12.4   The acquirer is the parent LLP which obtains control of the other combining business(es). Control has to be obtained and for the purposes of Section 19 'control' is the power to govern the financial and operating policies of an entity or business in order that the parent LLP can benefit from its activities.

Measure the cost of the business combination

12.5   The cost of a business combination is the total of:

- the fair values at the date of acquisition of assets given, liabilities incurred (or assumed) and equity instruments which are issued by the acquirer in exchange for control of the acquiree; and

- costs which are directly attributable to the business combination.

Allocate the cost of the business combination

12.6   The cost of the business combination is allocated at the date of acquisition. This occurs by the parent LLP recognising the acquiree's identifiable assets and liabilities and a provision for contingent liabilities (which satisfy the recognition criteria) at their fair values.

When the group acquires a new subsidiary, the parent LLP is treated as having acquired the assets and liabilities at their 'fair value' at the date of acquisition, and the income and expenditure of the subsidiary is only included in the consolidated profit and loss account from the date of acquisition. For the purposes of business combinations, the date of acquisition is the date on which control is passed to the parent LLP and may not necessarily be the same date on which completion of the transaction occurs and purchase consideration is transferred.

In preparing the consolidation, the cost of the investment in the subsidiary shown on the balance sheet of the parent LLP will nearly always differ from the fair value of the assets and liabilities of the subsidiary at the date of acquisition. The difference between the aggregate fair values of the assets and liabilities and the purchase consideration (cost of investment) represents either positive or negative goodwill, the accounting treatment of which is discussed at **12.11**.

4   DETERMINING THE DATE OF ACQUISITION

12.7   When a parent LLP acquires a subsidiary, the date of acquisition is the date on which control passes to the parent LLP. The date that control passes is a matter of fact and it cannot be artificially altered, for example by including within the purchase and sale agreement some other 'effective' date. It can usually be assumed that control passes on the date on which an offer to purchase becomes unconditional.

Care must be taken in determining the date of acquisition because control may not necessarily pass on the date that the purchase consideration is transferred. Indeed, as is often the case in such matters, consideration may well be paid in instalments or certain portions of the consideration may be contingent on future occurrences (or non-occurrences).

Where there is an earn-out arrangement, or consideration is payable in instalments, the date of acquisition is not usually deferred, and all the circumstances should be considered in order to determine when control passes. Once control passes to the parent LLP, there becomes a parent-subsidiary relationship.

5   PURCHASE CONSIDERATION

12.8   The cost of a business combination is generally the aggregate of:

● the amount of cash paid;

● the fair value of any other purchase consideration given by the acquirer; and

● the directly attributable expenses of the acquisition (ie those costs which would have been avoided had the combination not taken place).

The cost of the combination will determine the initial carrying value of the investment on the parent LLP's own balance sheet.

The fair value of purchase consideration is determined by reference to the following:

● *Cash and other monetary items* (for example, monetary assets given or liabilities assumed) – the amount paid or payable.

● *Interest in the LLP.* Where there has been a valuation of the LLP at, or shortly prior to, the acquisition of the newly acquired entity, it may be possible to value the consideration by reference to such a valuation (for example, where the members or shareholders of the acquired entity become members of the LLP). However the SORP acknowledges that, for any type of entity in which there is no ready market for its securities or other interests, the best estimate of value may be obtained by valuing the acquired entity.

● *Non-monetary consideration.* Estimated by reference to market prices, estimated realisable values, independent valuations or other available evidence.

It is not unusual for an acquisition agreement to provide for part of the purchase consideration to be deferred to a future date (deferred consideration) or to be contingent upon the occurrence of some future event (contingent consideration).

Paragraph 19.12 of FRS 102 says that when a business combination agreement makes provision for an adjustment to the cost of the combination which is contingent on future events, the parent LLP should include the estimated amount of that adjustment in the cost of the combination at the date of acquisition when the adjustment is probable and can be measured reliably.

If, at the date of acquisition, such an adjustment was not recognised because it was not probable or could not be reliably measured (or both), but then subsequently becomes probable and can be reliably estimated, the additional consideration is to be treated as an adjustment to the cost of the business combination. Although it is not explicitly stated in the standard itself, any adjustment made to the cost of the business combination should be made to goodwill until the consideration is finally established and payable in accordance with the sale/purchase agreement. Conversely, the adjustments to provisional fair values of assets and liabilities acquired to reflect new information obtained are finalised within 12 months from the date of acquisition and hence such adjustments are applied retrospectively as if they had occurred at the date of acquisition.

The rules for finalising provisional fair values is a concession which allows the parent LLP to finalise fair values that it was not initially possible to finalise due to time constraints. This is notably different than the situation with contingent consideration whereby an initial estimate is made and is then later adjusted, based on future events.

Example – contingent consideration adjustments

LLP A acquires a wholly-owned subsidiary, Undertaking B, for £15 million. The terms of the sale agreement requires the parent LLP to seek protection from false representation made by Undertaking B's sellers. At the completion date, LLP A will pay the sellers of Undertaking B £14 million in cash and the remaining £1 million will be placed in an escrow account and will be payable to the sellers of Undertaking B one year after the date of completion if no false representations claims have been made.

At the date of acquisition, it would be impossible for LLP A to establish whether any false representation claims will be made and hence no adjustment should be made to the combination's cost by the parent LLP at the date of acquisition.

However, if at the first anniversary of the sale, new facts emerge which indicate that there would be an adjustment to the amount held in the escrow account, the provisions in paragraphs 19.12 and 19.13 would be triggered. If it is assumed that the amount to be released to the previous owners of Undertaking B is to be £300,000, the refund of £700,000 to LLP A would be recognised as an adjustment to the purchase consideration and a consequential reduction in goodwill by that amount.

When considering accounting for a business combination by an LLP, reference should be made not only to those parts of the agreement that deal with the consideration, but also those parts dealing with the arrangements entered into for profit-sharing with any new members joining the LLP from the acquired entity. These arrangements may also include an element of contingent consideration. For example, the members from the acquired entity might be awarded an increased profit share for a limited period after the acquisition, which subsequently reduces back to a 'normal' level. In these circumstances, it will be necessary for the LLP to make an estimate of the future profits which will be earned by the LLP over this period and to include an estimate of the enhanced profit share element payable to such members as part of the cost of the business combination.

Deferred or contingent consideration should generally be included in the balance sheet as a liability at the time of acquisition. FRS 102 does not specify where the liability should be disclosed on the balance sheet; therefore, it could be within creditors or within provisions for liabilities. Where there is any estimation involved, the most appropriate position would usually be within 'Provisions for liabilities'.

Where the deferred or contingent consideration is to be satisfied by an enhanced profit share, rather than include the amount within provisions it should be shown as part of members' other interests, preferably under a separate heading such as 'Members' interests in respect of deferred consideration'. As the conditions for triggering the entitlement to deferred or contingent consideration are reached, transfers should then be made to members' capital accounts or debt due to members, dependent on the terms agreed with the new members.

The cost of the combination should also include any expenses which are directly attributable to the combination. These costs should not include any allocation of costs that would have been incurred irrespective of whether or not the acquisition had been entered into, such as management remuneration.

6   DETERMINING THE FAIR VALUE OF ASSETS AND LIABILITIES

12.9   The assets and liabilities to be included in the assessment of fair value are all those which existed at the date of acquisition. In determining fair value, the following should be taken into account:

- the conditions in existence at the date of acquisition;
- fair value should not reflect any changes resulting from the LLP's intentions or actions taken subsequent to the date of acquisition;

- fair value should not reflect any impairment, or other changes, resulting from events subsequent to the acquisition;

- provisions or accruals for future operating losses or other costs expected to be incurred as a result of the business combination should not be included; and

- only those liabilities for terminating or reducing the activities of the acquiree should be recognised to the extent that the parent LLP has, at the date of acquisition, an existing liability for restructuring which meets the recognition criteria in Section 21 *Provisions and Contingencies*.

Fair value should be assessed by reference to the LLP's accounting policies. Therefore, where accounting policies differ between the LLP and the entity acquired the values of the assets and liabilities should be adjusted to bring them into line with the LLP's accounting policies.

The general requirement within Section 19 is that the fair value exercise should be completed, if possible, by the date on which the first accounts including the acquired business are approved by the members. This may not always be possible, particularly where the date of acquisition is close to the year end. In these circumstances provisional valuations should be made, which should be amended, if necessary, in the next accounts. Although not specifically stated in Section 19, the corresponding adjustment to the combination's cost will be to goodwill. The accounts for the first year post acquisition should make it clear that the fair values are provisional. Any adjustments to the initial accounting for a business combination beyond 12 months from the date of acquisition should only be recognised to correct a material error in accordance with Section 10 *Accounting Policies, Estimates and Errors*.

It is not unusual for purchase and sale agreements to include values for the assets and liabilities of the acquired business. These may however differ from the fair values of such assets and liabilities. Fair value guidance is provided in FRS 102 at paragraphs 11.27 to 11.32 and paragraph 11.28 outlines various valuation techniques which can be employed to arrive at a fair value assessment. Such techniques can include:

- using recent arm's-length market values for identical assets;

- current fair values of other similar assets;

- discounted cash flow analysis; and

- option pricing models.

The general principles for determining the fair values of different classes of assets and liabilities are set out below:

- *Tangible fixed assets.* The lower of the recoverable amount and depreciated replacement cost. Where similar assets are bought and sold on the open market (for example, property), the value should be determined by reference to market value.

- *Intangible fixed assets.* These must be capable of being valued separately to the underlying business before they can be recognised. The fair value should be determined by reference to replacement cost, which will usually be market value.

- *Stocks and work in progress.* The lower of replacement cost or estimated selling price less costs to complete and sell. Replacement cost is the cost at which the stocks would have been replaced by the acquired entity, reflecting its normal buying process and the sources of supply and prices available to it. Current cost would include members' time as discussed in Chapter 5.

- *Quoted investments.* Market price (adjusted if necessary for unusual price fluctuations or for the size of holding).

- *Monetary assets and liabilities.* The fair value should take into account the amounts expected to be received or paid.

- *Contingent assets and liabilities.* Contingent assets and liabilities should only be included if the contingency existed at the date of acquisition. The value should be based on a reasonable estimate of expected outcome.

- *Businesses sold or acquired exclusively with a view to subsequent resale.* Where a purchaser has been identified or is being sought and the disposal is reasonably expected to occur within approximately one year of the date of the acquisition, the operation should be valued at an estimate of the sales proceeds. Such items should be included as a single asset within current assets.

- *Pensions and other post-retirement benefits.* For a funded scheme, the amount of the surplus or deficiency should be recognised as an asset or liability respectively. An asset should, however, only be recognised to the extent that it can be recovered through reduced contributions or through refunds from the scheme. For unfunded schemes the valuation of accrued obligations should be recognised as a liability.

7 ACQUISITION OF BUSINESS ASSETS AND LIABILITIES

12.10 Similar accounting provisions will apply where an LLP acquires the assets and liabilities of a business rather than making an investment therein.

The principal difference is that any goodwill arising will be recorded on the LLP's own balance sheet instead of only on the consolidated balance sheet. In these circumstances, amortisation of goodwill will be charged against, and directly affect, the profits of the LLP available for distribution to the members.

8 GOODWILL

12.11 A successful business will be worth more than the sum of its net assets, and therefore has 'goodwill'. Section 18 *Intangible Assets other than*

Goodwill prohibits the recognition of internally-generated goodwill at paragraph 18.8C(f). FRS 102 deals with goodwill and other intangible assets in a separate section (Section 19 *Business Combinations and Goodwill*) and is defined as *'future economic benefits arising from assets that are not capable of being individually identified and separately recognised.'* Goodwill under the provisions in FRS 102 will only generally appear in the LLP's balance sheet as a result of a business combination. A number of partnerships include goodwill on their balance sheet. In some circumstances, this arises not as a result of the acquisition of another business, but instead as part of a revaluation exercise to calculate the cost of capital for new partners. Such goodwill does not represent goodwill arising as a result of a business combination which brings together separate entities into one reporting entity and, as a result, cannot be recognised on transition to an LLP.

Unlike previous UK GAAP, goodwill is considered to have a limited useful economic life, and paragraph 19.23(a) requires goodwill that satisfies the recognition and measurement criteria in paragraph 19.22 to be amortised on a systematic basis over that useful economic life. If the LLP is unable to make a reliable estimate of the useful economic life of goodwill, then paragraph 19.23(a) says that the life shall not exceed five years. This is a considerable reduction from previous UK GAAP which contained a rebuttable presumption that the useful economic life of goodwill is 20 years or less. An important point to emphasise is that the five-year rule only applies to goodwill (or other intangible assets) where the members are unable to assign a useful economic life and in many cases an amortisation period in excess of five years may well be appropriate and the LLP may have justifiable reasons for choosing such a period. The use of professional judgement in this area is a critical aspect and paragraph 19.25(g) requires the LLP to disclose supporting reasons for the useful life of goodwill where the useful life exceeds five years.

A further point to consider is an LLP which considered its goodwill to have an indefinite useful economic life. Under Section 19 all goodwill and intangible assets will have a finite useful life and therefore on transition to FRS 102, LLP's that have not been previously amortising goodwill on the grounds that they consider it to have an indefinite useful life will need to change the accounting policy and arrive at a reliable estimate of the useful economic life of the goodwill and amortise it systematically over that useful life. If the members cannot ascertain a reliable useful economic life then the LLP should amortise it over a five-year period from the date of transition to FRS 102.

The key to developing an amortisation policy is for the members to assess the LLP's accounting policy in respect of amortisation and to consider whether this policy genuinely reflects the position of the acquired business. Different LLP's operating in different industries will have varied accounting policies in respect of amortisation of goodwill and consideration needs to be given of the nature and stability of the acquired business and its product lifecycles.

In rare circumstances, the cost of a business combination may be less than the fair value of the assets and liabilities acquired. In such cases, 'negative goodwill' arises and the provisions in paragraph 19.24 will be triggered. There are three steps that an LLP should take where negative goodwill is concerned:

- Go back to the identification and measurement of the acquiree's assets, liabilities and provisions for contingent liabilities and assess them for completeness as well as the accuracy of the cost of the combination. The objective of this reassessment is to ensure that assets are not overstated and liabilities have not been omitted.

- Should negative goodwill still exist following this reassessment, then the negative goodwill is recognised separately on the face of the balance sheet immediately below goodwill, followed by a subtotal of the net amount of goodwill and the excess.

- In subsequent accounting periods, recognise the excess up to the fair value of non-monetary assets acquired in profit or loss in the periods in which the non-monetary assets are recovered. Any excess which exceeds the fair value of non-monetary assets acquired are recognised in the LLP's profit and loss account in the periods which are expected to benefit.

9 IMPAIRMENT OF GOODWILL

12.12   The overarching principle in financial reporting is that assets should not be carried in the balance sheet at any more than their recoverable amount. For this reason, the LLP should undertake a review of their assets at each reporting date and consider whether such assets are capable of being recovered at their carrying value. If, as a result of the assessment, the LLP considers that assets will not be recovered at their carrying value then a write-down to recoverable amount will be needed (this is known as an 'impairment').

Section 27 *Impairment of Assets* gives guidance to LLPs on conducting a review for impairment. Paragraph 19.23(b) also specifically requires an LLP to follow Section 27 for the recognition and measurement of goodwill impairment and there are additional specific requirements in respect of goodwill impairment contained in paragraphs 27.24–27.27.

Goodwill acquired in a business combination is allocated to each cash-generating unit which is expected to benefit from the synergies of the business combination regardless of whether other assets or liabilities of the acquiree have been assigned to those units.

For subsidiaries which are not wholly-owned by the parent LLP, part of the recoverable amount of a cash-generating unit (CGU) is attributable to the non-controlling interests in goodwill. In recognition of this, paragraph 27.26 requires the carrying value of that unit to be notionally adjusted before being compared with its recoverable amount. This is done by grossing up the carrying value to include the goodwill attributable to the non-controlling interest. This grossed up value is then compared to recoverable amount to ascertain whether the CGU is impaired.

12.13 *Business combinations*

In situations where the parent LLP cannot allocate goodwill to individual CGUs (or groups thereof) on a non-arbitrary basis, then it should test goodwill for impairment by determining the recoverable amount of either:

- the acquired undertaking in its entirety if the goodwill relates to an acquired entity which has not been integrated into the reporting entity; or

- the entire group but excluding those entities which have not been integrated where the goodwill relates to an undertaking which has been integrated.

In order to carry out this correctly, the LLP must separate goodwill into that portion which relates to entities that have been integrated and the portion which relates to goodwill which have not been integrated.

It might be the case that where goodwill has been written down to recoverable amount following an impairment test, the reasons for the original impairment cease to apply to the LLP. FRS 102 permits impairment losses relating to goodwill to be reversed provided the reasons for the impairment cease to apply.

10 APPLICATION OF MERGER ACCOUNTING

12.13   The 2014 SORP only allows merger accounting for group reconstructions so as to be consistent with the requirements in FRS 102. Merger accounting is not the acquisition of a subsidiary by a parent LLP – it is the combining of entities to create a new reporting entity. There is no controlling party in merger accounting and strict criteria exists to ensure that this is the case. All of the following criteria must be met for an entity combination to meet the definition of a merger:

- no party to the combination is purported to be an acquirer or an acquiree;

- there will be no significant change to the classes of beneficiaries of the combining entities or the purpose of the benefits provided as a result of the combination; and

- all parties in the combination (as represented by the members of the board) participate in establishing the management structure of the combined entity and also participate in the selection of management personnel with such decisions being made on the basis of a consensus between the parties to the combination rather than purely by exercise of voting rights.

Merger accounting is also dealt with in Section 19 of FRS 102. In respect of initial conversions, where the requirements in paragraph 19.27 are met in respect of group reconstructions, the 2014 SORP recommends that the merger accounting method be used (where permitted) so as to reflect the initial 'conversion' to LLP. The initial 'opening' balance sheet should follow the accounting policies of the LLP. Ordinarily, such transactions will be undertaken using book values rather than fair values and therefore the merger accounting method reflects the substance of the transactions.

When there is a 'true' merger, Section 19 of FRS 102 requires merger accounting to be used. Merger accounting may also be used when there is a business combination which meets the definition of a group reconstruction. Whilst Section 19 does not make merger accounting mandatory in the latter case, it is generally considered that merger accounting as opposed to the purchase method should be applied to group reconstructions in order for the accounts to give a true and fair view as merger accounting will reflect the substance of the transaction.

Considerations relating to transition from a partnership to an LLP are dealt with in more detail in Chapter 13. However, in general, these should be accounted for as group reconstructions using merger accounting.

11 CONDITIONS PERMITTING MERGER ACCOUNTING

12.14   FRS 102 allows a group reconstruction to be accounted for using merger accounting provided that three conditions are met:

- the use of the merger accounting method is not prohibited by law;

- the ultimate equity holders remain the same, and the rights of each equity holder, relative to the others, are unchanged; and

- no non-controlling interest in the group's net assets is altered by the transfer.

The 2014 SORP acknowledges that new start-ups and existing businesses (which include both partnerships and limited companies) might choose to become an LLP. When this happens, the 2014 SORP requires merger accounting to be used provided that the transfer complies with the three criteria above.

12 THE ACCOUNTING CONSEQUENCES OF A MERGER

12.15   Where all of the criteria for merger accounting are met, the accounting in the consolidated accounts is as follows:

- the net assets of the two entities are combined using their existing book values – no fair value adjustments are required because existing book values reflects the substance of the transaction;

- adjustments will, however, need to be made as necessary to ensure that the same accounting policies are applied;

- no goodwill or negative goodwill will be recognised;

- the results of all the combining entities are brought into the financial statements of the combined entity from the start of the financial year in which the combination took place and are adjusted in order to achieve uniformity of accounting policies; and

- the comparative amounts should be restated to the aggregate of the amounts recorded by the two entities in the previous period, adjusted as necessary to achieve uniformity of accounting policies.

When comparatives are restated so as to achieve uniformity of accounting policies, there will often be a difference between the amounts reported as attributable to owners by the predecessor undertaking and the members' interests in the opening balance sheet of the LLP. In such cases the 2014 SORP requires that such differences are not dealt with in the financial statements of the LLP.

The 2014 SORP also identifies additional factors which LLPs should consider when adjusting comparative information:

- whether the predecessor undertaking's accounting policies require amendment as they are not compliant with the requirements of FRS 102;

- whether the predecessor undertaking's accounting policies are to be amended voluntarily; and

- whether any of the members' rights change on transition together with the effects of those changes.

Chapter 13

The transition from partnership to LLP

SIGNPOSTS

- Whilst the conversion to LLP may seem attractive, it is not without its costs in terms of internal time and professional fees (see **13.1**).

- In the event of the LLP becoming insolvent, the capital may not be returned to the members (see **13.2**).

- Whilst all, or the vast majority of, assets and liabilities would be transferred from the partnership into the LLP, the former partners may decide that some assets and liabilities remain in the former partnership (see **13.3**).

- Retirement benefits to former partners need careful consideration (see **13.3**).

- When the transfer of assets and liabilities into the LLP is to take place, they should be brought in at amounts which have been calculated in accordance with the LLPs accounting policies which should be compliant with FRS 102 (see **13.4**).

- For new LLPs which are groups, there are a number of steps they must take to establish the basis on which any consolidated financial statements are to be constructed (see **13.5** and **13.6**).

- In order for an LLP to qualify as a group reconstruction and adopt merger accounting, the interests of the members in the LLP should be in the same proportions as their 'share' in the partnership immediately prior to the transfer to the LLP (see **13.7**).

- Pro-forma comparative information should be presented in the financial statements of the first period after incorporation for a single-entity LLP formed from the transfer or incorporation of an existing entity (see **13.8**).

- The 2014 SORP contains some additional guidance where there is a delay in forming the LLP and the transfer of the existing partnership into the LLP (see **13.8**).

- There are specific issues which auditors need to consider in the first year of transition (see **13.9**).

1 INTRODUCTION

13.1 The combination of the advantages of limited liability and the concept of partnership makes conversion of existing partnerships to LLP status attractive and is the main reason why LLPs have increased in popularity over recent years. It is not, however, without its costs, not only in respect of the internal time and professional fees involved in effecting the transfer, but also with regard to the accounting and auditing requirements, a number of which will be unfamiliar to some partnerships that choose to 'convert' (see below). In addition, the financial affairs of the LLP will be in the public domain through the filing of annual accounts with the Registrar of Companies (Companies House).

In this chapter, we look specifically at some of the accounting issues surrounding the transition of a partnership to an LLP.

2 HOW MUCH CAPITAL?

13.2 Whereas the liability of individual members is significantly reduced from that within a partnership (hence 'limited liability'), in the event of the insolvency of the LLP the capital may not be returned to the members. It is important, therefore, to take this into consideration when determining the level of existing partnership capital which should be introduced to the new LLP. Although there are obvious attractions to keeping the level of capital as low as possible, it should be noted that third parties such as banks and regulators may require the subordination of amounts due to members and/or require minimum amounts to be retained within the LLP.

3 THE ASSETS AND LIABILITIES TO BE TRANSFERRED

13.3 In most circumstances, it would be anticipated that all, or the vast majority of, assets and liabilities would be transferred from the partnership to the new LLP. The former partners may, however, decide that some assets and liabilities should remain in the former partnership.

One particular area for consideration is the treatment of liabilities to former partners. Some partnerships have sought to leave the retirement benefits due to former partners as a liability of the partnership rather than transfer that liability to the LLP. Such a course of action will normally require the consent of those former partners, and they may also require the liabilities to be underwritten by the LLP. The accounting treatment of post-retirement liabilities is dealt with in **9.11** to **9.16**. Similar accounting treatment will also apply to any other liabilities of the former partnership—namely whether or not the LLP will be required to recognise the liability will depend upon the probability that it may be required to make any payment. Even if no provision is required to be recognised in the accounts, the possibility of a future liability should be disclosed as a contingent liability of the LLP and the requirements in Section 21 *Provisions and Contingencies* should be considered.

210

4   ALIGNMENT OF ACCOUNTING POLICIES

13.4   On transferring assets and liabilities to the LLP, the amounts at which they are initially recorded in the accounts should be calculated by reference to the accounting policies to be adopted by the LLP. The accounting policies selected must be compliant with the requirements of FRS 102 and (where appropriate) the FRSSE. Dependent on the policies adopted by the partnership, these could vary significantly from those shown in the accounts of the predecessor partnership. This will be particularly relevant where the partnership had prepared accounts for its own purposes other than on the 'true and fair' basis, making adjustments to that basis only for the purposes of its tax return. Areas where differences may arise include:

- Provisions for retirement benefits to former partners to the extent that the liability to meet the cost is transferred to the LLP (see **9.11–9.16**).

- De-recognition of provisions which do not meet the definition within Section 21 (for example, provisions for possible future PI claims) (see **9.2–9.10**).

The particular issues facing partnerships with subsidiary undertakings are discussed below.

5   GROUPS

13.5   The majority of partnerships with subsidiary undertakings, irrespective of whether those subsidiaries are companies or other partnerships, will not historically have prepared consolidated accounts in the form required by UK GAAP. The partnership may well have prepared some form of 'group' accounts, probably an aggregation of the results and balance sheets, but these are unlikely to be sufficient going forward as they will more than likely not accord to the principles in UK GAAP.

There are a number of steps that the LLP must take in order to establish the basis on which any group accounts should be constructed. It will need to:

- Ascertain those investments of the partnership which fall to be treated as subsidiaries. In simple terms, this will be those other entities in which the LLP has a controlling interest (see Chapter 11).

- Determine whether or not group accounts are required by reference to the combined size of the LLP and its subsidiaries. (The circumstances where group accounts are not required are considered in Chapter 2).

- Determine the cost of investment in those subsidiaries. For companies, this will be the amount paid to acquire the shares, which should already be recorded as an investment in the accounts of the partnership. For an investment in a partnership, the cost of investment will be the amount of capital held in that partnership.

- Where a subsidiary has been previously acquired, ascertain whether or not it is practical to determine the fair values of assets and liabilities at the date of acquisition (the date of acquisition being the date on which control is passed to the parent LLP). Where a subsidiary is a company or partnership formed by the previous partnership to undertake certain parts of the partnership's business no further analysis should be necessary.

- If intra-group trading has taken place, identify the amounts as these will need to be eliminated from consolidated accounts (both the intra-group trading and the effects of such trading eg intra-group debtors/creditors) so that the consolidated financial statements present the results of the group as if it were a single reporting entity.

- Where assets are sold between group members at a profit (for example, fixed assets or stock); identify the profit element in order that it can be eliminated from the consolidated accounts.

Example – intra-group profit in stock at the year-end

LLP A sold goods for resale to Subsidiary B (B) for £2,000 which represents cost plus 25%. At the year-end goods of £1,200 were still in stock and included in B's stock count. The selling price is therefore made up as follows:

Cost	£1,600
Profit	£400 (ie 25% of cost)
Sales price	£2,000

The unrealised profit in stock is £240 (£1,200/£2,000 × £400) and is removed by crediting closing stock in the consolidated balance sheet and debiting closing stock in the consolidated profit and loss account. The objective of this is to reduce the closing stock valuation to cost to the group.

In reality, the step which is most likely to cause difficulties is the identification of assets and liabilities associated with past acquisitions. Whether or not it is possible to determine the fair value of assets and liabilities at the date of acquisition will depend on the extent of the records maintained by the partnership and the period of time that has elapsed since the acquisition. The method suggested below may give an adequate approximation, particularly for subsidiaries acquired some time previously.

13.6   As a matter of accounting principle, the consolidated accounts should not include any profits earned by a subsidiary prior to acquisition. An adjustment should therefore be made in the consolidated accounts to remove any such profits from the cumulative reserves of the group. The 'other side' to this adjustment should be made against the cost of investment, along with the elimination of the share capital of the subsidiary. Any difference between the cost of investment and pre-acquisition reserves and share capital, together with any adjustments to reflect fair value, should be treated as goodwill and be amortised in the consolidated profit and loss account on a systematic basis over the estimated useful economic life of the goodwill (note under FRS 102, all goodwill will have a finite useful life).

The following example illustrates the position where it has not been possible to determine the fair values of the assets and liabilities in a previously acquired subsidiary.

Example – Previously acquired subsidiary

X & Co (a partnership) acquired Y Ltd a number of years ago for £200. At that date, share capital was £30 and profit and loss reserves were £70. Net assets, therefore, were £100. At the current year end, the balance sheet of Y Ltd is as follows:

	£
Assets	400
Share capital	30
Profit and loss account	370
	400

In preparing the consolidated accounts, the newly formed LLP first needs to aggregate its balance sheet and profit and loss account with that of Y Ltd. It will then raise a journal which will debit share capital by £30, debit profit and loss by £70, debit goodwill by £100 (£200 – £100), and credit cost of investment by £200. The goodwill will then require amortisation in accordance with the accounting policy determined by the LLP.

---

6   PRESENTING THE TRANSITION IN THE ACCOUNTS

13.7   As discussed in Chapter 12, the transition from partnership to LLP should be accounted for using the merger accounting method, provided that it meets the criteria to be treated as a group reconstruction set out in paragraph 19.27 of FRS 102. Paragraph 19.27 is worded in the context of corporate entities, and states that, in order to qualify as a group reconstruction, *'the ultimate equity holders remain the same, and the rights of each equity holder, relative to the others, are unchanged'* immediately before and after the transaction.

Putting this definition into the context of a partnership, in order for the transfer to an LLP to qualify as a group reconstruction and hence being eligible to apply merger accounting, the interests of members in the LLP should be in the same proportions as their 'share' in the partnership immediately prior to transfer.

Both the amount of capital introduced and profit-sharing arrangements will need to be taken into account when determining if the criteria have been met.

The application of this requirement means that it may be preferable not to combine the retirement or appointment of partners or members with transition to an LLP, nor should the relative benefits of partners/members be altered at this stage. Where the requirements of paragraph 19.27 are not met, the transfer should be accounted for as an acquisition (and hence the use of the purchase method) and the assets and liabilities transferred would need to be restated to their fair values and the 'consideration' for the acquisition determined by reference to the value of the business of the partnership transferred. Goodwill will arise as a consequence of the difference between the two values, and this will have to be recognised on the balance sheet and amortised through the profit and loss account of the LLP. For a partnership in the services sector, the value of the business taken as a whole, compared to the value of its underlying assets and liabilities, could well be significantly different. The amount of goodwill, and the impact on the profit and loss account, could be substantial.

13.8   The 2014 SORP requires that single entity LLPs formed from the transfer or incorporation of an existing entity should present comparative pro-forma information in the financial statements of the first period after incorporation. The corresponding amounts should be stated using the same accounting policies as those adopted by the LLP. For the reasons discussed above, the amounts shown by the comparative figures may differ from those in the equivalent partnership accounts, resulting in a consequential difference between partners' interests and members' interests. This difference should not be reflected in the accounts of the LLP, which should be prepared on the basis that the LLP has always existed and always prepared accounts in accordance with its selected accounting policies.

It is frequently the case that there is a delay between forming the LLP and the transfer of the existing partnership undertaking. In these cases, there is a conflict between the requirements to present a profit and loss account that complies with statutory requirements (ie covering only the period from the transfer of the previous undertaking) and information that provides a meaningful comparative of what is effectively the same business. The 2014 SORP considers this issue in some detail in Appendix 4. Appendix 4 considers two potential alternative ways of presenting the LLP's results based on a scenario where Entity A establishes an LLP on 1 April, transfers its trade and assets to the LLP on 1 July and has a year-end of 31 December and prepares entity-only accounts. The two potential alternative options are as follows:

- bring in the net asset book values at the date of transfer of trade and assets. Profits are recognised which arise in the LLP from the incorporation date (1 April) but will only include transactions from the date of transfer which is from 1 July to 31 December (as the LLP did not undertake any trading transactions before the date of transfer); or

- bring in the net book values at 1 January and include the results for the 12-month accounting period from 1 January to 31 December so as to be consistent and comparable with Entity A's reporting period.

The 2014 SORP recommends the following presentation:

- A statutory profit and loss account for the period from transfer of business to the reporting date.

- Disclosure of the 12-month period to the reporting date.

- Pro-forma comparatives for the previous reporting period.

This can be contrasted with the position where a group transfers to LLP status. In these circumstances, the group reconstruction provisions of Section 19 require that comparative figures be presented for the previous year. These will not be pro-forma and will, therefore, fall within the scope of the audit report. Whilst an LLP presenting consolidated accounts does not have to present the individual LLP's profit and loss account within the financial statements, Companies Act 2006 requires that it still be prepared for the information of members. Similar principles to those discussed above will therefore apply.

It is recommended that those partnerships considering transfer to LLP status carry out some initial calculations of the impact that changes in accounting policies could have and how this affects existing partners' interests. Such changes can then be explained and discussed with the partners.

7 AUDIT ISSUES ARISING IN THE FIRST YEAR OF TRANSITION

13.9 There are a number of potential issues which will affect the audit of an LLP formed from a partnership in its first year.

The majority of partnerships do not have their accounts audited and, therefore, it will be for the auditors to determine whether they are able to obtain sufficient and appropriate audit evidence as to the accuracy of the opening balance sheet of the LLP to enable them to state that the accounts for the current reporting period give a true and fair view. Whilst it should usually be possible to form an opinion on the closing balance sheet, the opening figures will impact the amounts included in the profit and loss account, and qualification with respect to limitation in audit scope may be required.

It may be possible to restrict the qualification to a specific account area, for example work in progress, if the auditors are able to perform audit procedures that allow them to meet the requirements of ISA (UK and Ireland) 510 *Initial audit engagements – opening balances*.

Further complications may arise in considering the status of any comparative figures and their impact on the audit report.

For a single entity LLP formed from an existing partnership, the comparative information is only included as a pro-forma and can therefore be excluded from the scope of the audit report. Where this is the case, the presentation of the comparatives in the accounts should make it clear that they are unaudited pro-forma information, and this fact should also be made clear in the scope paragraph of the audit report.

The position for a group headed by a new LLP which is required to present comparative information in accordance with paragraph 19.30 of FRS 102 may be more complex. In particular, where the comparative information has not been subject to audit, reference to this fact will be required in the audit report in a similar way to that referred to above.

LLP pro forma financial statements – group

XYZ LLP

REPORT AND FINANCIAL STATEMENTS

FOR THE YEAR ENDED

31 MARCH 201X

NOTE – in this example all profits require the approval of members before they are divided and division occurs after the year end. Capital is returned to members on their retirement.

The terminology used for the primary financial statements is that in FRS 102, although paragraph 3.22 to FRS 102 allows the use of alternative titles provided they are not misleading (hence the terms 'balance sheet' and 'profit and loss account' etc would still fall to be permissible).

LLP pro forma financial statements – group

Contents

Designated members and advisers

Designated members
A Designate
B Smith
C Jones

Registered office
1 The Long Street
Longtown
Longshire
LL1 1XY

Bankers
Big Bank plc
85 The Long Street
Longtown
Longshire
LL1 1YZ

Auditors
Stuart & Wilson LLP
5 The Short Street
Longtown
Longshire
LL2 1AB

Solicitors
Wright & Prentice LLP
25 The Short Street
Longtown
Longshire
LL2 1BC

Members' report

The members present their report and the financial statements for the year ended 31 March 201X.

Activities

The principal activity of the Group continues to be [   ].

Review of business

[The 2014 SORP requires disclosure of the principal activities of the LLP and its subsidiary undertakings, indicating any significant changes during the year. Whilst there are no statutory requirements with respect to additional information that might be included here, the members may wish to include further information about the performance of the LLP in support of the financial disclosures.]

Designated members

The following were designated members during the year:

A Designate

B Smith

C Jones

Members' drawings and the subscription and repayment of members' capital

During the year members receive monthly drawings representing payments on account of profits which may be allocated to them. The amount of such drawings is set at the beginning of each financial year, taking into account the anticipated cash needs of the LLP and may be reclaimed from members until such time as profits have been allocated to them.

Profits are determined, allocated and divided between members after the finalisation of the accounts. Prior to the allocation of profits and their division between members, drawings are included as 'amounts due from members' within debtors. Unallocated profits are included within equity as 'members' other interests'.

Capital requirements are determined by the designated members and are reviewed at least annually. All members are required to subscribe a proportion of that capital, with the amounts being determined by reference to experience.

On retirement, capital is repaid to members.

Auditors

[A resolution to reappoint Stuart & Wilson LLP as auditors will be proposed at the next members' meeting.] Or [Stuart & Wilson LLP have indicated their willingness to be reappointed and the members have made appropriate arrangements for them to be deemed reappointed as auditors].

Approved by the members

and signed on their behalf

A Designate

Designated member

Statement of members' responsibilities in respect of the financial statements[1]

The members are responsible for preparing the financial statements in accordance with applicable law and regulations.

The Limited Liability Partnerships (Accounts and Audit) (Application of Companies Act 2006) Regulations 2008 (the 2008 Regulations) requires the members to prepare financial statements for each financial year. Under the law the members have elected to prepare financial statements in accordance with United Kingdom Accounting Standards (United Kingdom Generally Accepted Accounting Practice). The financial statements are required by law to give a true and fair view of the state of affairs of the group and of the profit or loss of the group for that period. In preparing these financial statements, the members are required to:

- select suitable accounting policies and then apply them consistently;

- make judgements and accounting estimates that are reasonable and prudent;

- state whether applicable UK Accounting Standards have been followed, subject to any material departure disclosed and explained in the financial statements;

- prepare the financial statements on the going concern basis unless it is inappropriate to presume that the group will continue in business.

The members are responsible for keeping proper accounting records which disclose with reasonable accuracy at any time the financial position of the LLP and to enable them to ensure that the financial statements comply with the 2008 Regulations. They are also responsible for safeguarding the assets of the group and thence for taking reasonable steps for the prevention and detection of fraud and other irregularities.

These responsibilities are exercised by the designated members on behalf of the members.

Disclosure of information to the auditor

Each of the persons who is a member at the date of approval of this report confirms that:

- So far as the member is aware, there is no relevant audit information of which the group's auditor is unaware; and

- The member has taken all the steps that he/she ought to have taken as a member in order to make himself/herself aware of any relevant audit information and to establish that the group's auditor is aware of that information.

The following is an illustrative unqualified auditor's report

---

1 This statement can alternatively be included within the members' report and is only required where the LLP is subject to audit.

Independent auditors' report to the members of XYZ LLP

We have audited the financial statements of XYZ LLP for the year-ended 31 March 201X which comprise the principal accounting policies, the consolidated income statement, the consolidated statement of comprehensive income, the consolidated statement of financial position, the partnership statement of financial position, the consolidated statement of cash flows and related notes. The financial reporting framework that has been applied in their preparation is applicable law and United Kingdom Accounting Standards (United Kingdom Generally Accepted Accounting Practice).

Respective responsibilities of members and auditor

As explained more fully in the Members' Responsibilities Statement set out on page X, the members are responsible for the preparation of the financial statements and for being satisfied that they give a true and fair view.

Our responsibility is to audit and express an opinion on the financial statements in accordance with applicable law and International Standards on Auditing (UK and Ireland). Those standards require us to comply with the Financial Reporting Council's Ethical Standards for Auditors.[2] This report is made solely to the members of the partnership, as a body, in accordance with Chapter 3 of Part 16 of the Companies Act 2006, as applied by regulations 39 and 40 of the Limited Liability Partnerships (Accounts and Audit) (Application of Companies Act 2006) Regulations 2008. Our audit work has been undertaken so that we might state to the partnership's members those matters we are required to state to them in an auditor's report and for no other purpose. To the fullest extent permitted by law, we do not accept or assume responsibility to anyone other than the partnership and the partnership's members as a body for our audit work, for this report, or for the opinions we have formed.

Scope of the audit of the financial statements

A description of the scope of an audit of financial statements is provided on the Financial Reporting Council's website at www.frc.org.uk/auditscopeukprivate.

Opinion on the financial statements

In our opinion the financial statements:

- give a true and fair view of the state of the group's and the partnership's affairs as at 31 March 201X and of the group's profit for the year then ended;

- have been properly prepared in accordance with United Kingdom Generally Accepted Accounting Practice; and

---

2   This is still sometimes referred to as the 'Auditing Practices Board's Ethical Standards for Auditors' although the Auditing Practices Board now no longer exists.

- have been prepared in accordance with the requirements of the Companies Act 2006 as applied to limited liability partnerships by the Limited Liability Partnerships (Accounts and Audit) (Application of Companies Act 2006) Regulations 2008.

Matters on which we are required to report by exception

We have nothing to report in respect of the following maters where the Companies Act 2006 as applied to limited liability partnerships requires us to report to you if, in our opinion:

- adequate accounting records have not been kept by the partnership, or returns adequate for our audit have not been received from branches not visited by us; or

- the partnership financial statements are not in agreement with the accounting records and returns; or

- we have not received all the information and explanations we require for our audit.

A B Smith (Senior Statutory Auditor)
For and on behalf of Stuart & Wilson LLP
5 The Short Street
Longtown
Longshire
LL2 1AB

[insert date]

Consolidated income statement for the year ended 31 March 201X

	Notes	201X £'000	201X £'000	201Y £'000
Turnover	3			
– Acquisitions		_____		
Operating costs				
Staff costs	5			
Depreciation and other amounts written off tangible fixed assets				
Other operating charges				
Other operating income			_____	_____
Operating profit				
– Acquisitions		_____		
Share of operating profits of associated undertakings				
Profit/(loss) on sale of fixed asset investments				
Interest receivable and similar income				
Interest payable and similar charges	6		_____	_____
Profit on ordinary activities before taxation[3]	7			
Tax on profit on ordinary activities[3]	8		_____	_____
Minority interest			_____	_____

---

3   In circumstances where all profits are automatically divided before the year end this amount will be zero.

Consolidated income statement for the year ended 31 March 201X (*continued*)

	Notes	201X £'000	£'000	201Y £'000
Profit for the financial year before members' remuneration and profit shares				
Members' remuneration charged as an expense	4			
Retained profit for the financial year available for discretionary division among members[3]	4			

All of the group's operations are classed as continuing. [There were no gains or losses in either year other than those included in the above income statement].[4]

---

4 Disclosure required where there are no recognised gains and losses other than the profit or loss for the year and no statement of changes in equity is presented.

Consolidated statement of comprehensive income for the year ended 31 March 201X

	201X £'000	201Y £'000
Retained profit for the financial year available for discretionary division among members		
Currency translation differences on net investment in group undertakings		
[Actuarial gain in respect of defined benefit pension schemes]		
	——	——
Total comprehensive income for the year		
	═══	═══

Registered number OC354321

Consolidated statement of financial position as at 31 March 201X

	Notes	201X £'000	201Y £'000
Fixed assets			
Intangible assets	10		
Tangible assets	11		
Investments	12		
Current assets			
Work in progress	13		
Debtors	14		
Cash at bank and in hand			
Creditors: amounts falling due within one year	15		
Net current assets/(liabilities)			
Total assets less current liabilities			
Creditors: amounts falling due after more than one year	16		
Provisions for liabilities	18		
Net assets attributable to members before pension fund surplus/(deficit)[5]			
[Pension fund surplus/(deficit)][6]	20		
Minority interest			
NET ASSETS ATTRIBUTABLE TO MEMBERS			

---

5   Position of net pension fund surplus/(deficit) where the LLP has a defined benefit pension scheme.

6   In this example members' capital is returned on retirement and is therefore a liability.

Consolidated statement of financial position as at 31 March 201X (*continued*)

	Notes	201X £'000	201Y £'000
REPRESENTED BY			
Loans and other debts due to members within one year			
Members' capital classified as a liability[3]	19		
Other amounts	19		
Equity			
Members' other interests – other reserves classified as equity[7]	19		
Revaluation reserve	19		
Total members' interests			
Amounts due from members			
Loans and other debts due to members			
Members' other interests			

The financial statements were approved by the members on [   ] and were signed on its behalf by:

A Designate

Designated member

---

7   Profits which are only divided after the year end would be included within this balance.

Statement of financial position as at 31 March 201X

	Notes	**201X** **£'000**	**201Y** **£'000**
Fixed assets			
Intangible assets	10		
Tangible assets	11		
Investments	12		
Current assets			
Work in progress	13		
Debtors	14		
Cash at bank and in hand			
Creditors: amounts falling due within one year	15		
Net current assets/(liabilities)			
Total assets less current liabilities			
Creditors: amounts falling due after more than one year	16		
Provisions for liabilities	18		
Net assets attributable to members before pension fund surplus/(deficit)			
Pension fund surplus/(deficit)	20		
NET ASSETS ATTRIBUTABLE TO MEMBERS			

Statement of financial position as at 31 March 201X (*continued*)

	Notes	201X £'000	201Y £'000
REPRESENTED BY			
Loans and other debts due to members within one year			
Members' capital classified as a liability	19		
Other amounts	19		
Equity			
Members' other interests – other reserves classified as equity	19		
Revaluation reserve	19		
Total members' interests			
Amounts due from members			
Loans and other debts due to members			
Members' other interests			

The financial statements were approved by the members on [   ] and were signed on its behalf by:

A Designate

Designated member

Consolidated statement of cash flows for the year ended 31 March 201X

	Notes	201X £'000	201Y £'000
Net cash inflow/(outflow) from operating activities	a		
Cash flows from investing activities			
Interest received			
Purchase of intangible assets			
Purchase of property, plant and equipment			
Proceeds from sale of property, plant and equipment			
Purchase of subsidiary undertaking			
Net cash/(overdraft) acquired with subsidiary			
Purchase of interest in associate			
Net cash inflow/(outflow) from investing activities			
Transactions with members and former members			
Drawings and distributions to members			
Payments to former members			
Capital contributions by members			
Capital repayments to members			
Net cash inflow/(outflow) from transactions with members and former members			

Consolidated statement of cash flows for the year ended 31 March 201X (*continued*)

	Notes	**201X** **£'000**	**201Y** **£'000**
Cash flows from financing activities			
New long-term loans			
Repayment of long-term loans			
Repayment of capital element of finance lease rentals			
Net cash inflow/(outflow) from financing activiites			
Increase/(decrease) in cash in the year	b		

Notes to the statement of cash flows

a	Reconciliation of operating profit/(loss) to net cash inflow/(outflow) from operating activities	201X £'000	201Y £'000
	Operating profit/(loss)		
	Depreciation		
	Amortisation of intangible assets		
	Loss/(profit) on sale of tangible fixed assets		
	Decrease/(increase) in work in progress		
	Decrease/(increase) in debtors		
	Increase/(decrease) in creditors		
	Increase/(decrease) in provisions		
	Interest paid		
	Net cash inflow/(outflow) from operating activities		

b   Cash and cash equivalents

Cash at bank and in hand
Less: bank overdraft

Notes to the financial statements for the year ended 31 March 201X

1   **Accounting policies[8]**

The financial statements have been prepared in accordance with FRS 102 *The Financial Reporting Standard applicable in the UK and Republic of Ireland* and the requirements of the Statement of Recommended Practice 'Accounting by Limited Liability Partnerships'. A summary of the significant accounting policies adopted are described below.

Basis of accounting

The financial statements have been prepared under the historical cost convention.

[Where relevant the members should include appropriate disclosure about their reasons for adopting the going concern basis and any material uncertainties that cast significant doubt over the LLP's ability to continue as a going concern]

Basis of consolidation

The financial statements consolidate the results and the assets and liabilities of the LLP and its subsidiaries. The results of subsidiaries acquired or disposed of during the year are included in the consolidated income statement from the effective date of the business combination or up to the effective date of disposal, where appropriate.

Where necessary, adjustments are made to the financial statements of subsidiaries to bring the accounting policies used in line with those used by the Group.

All intra-group transactions, balances, income and expenses are eliminated on consolidation.

Business combinations

Business combinations during the year have been accounted for in accordance with Section 19 *Business Combinations and Goodwill* of FRS 102 and the LLP has applied the purchase method of accounting for the business combination.

On the acquisition of a business, fair values are attributed to the groups' share of net separable assets acquired. Where the cost of the business combination exceeds the fair values attributable to such net assets, the difference is treated as goodwill and capitalised in the consolidated statement of financial position in the year of the business combination. The results and cash flows relating to an acquired business are included in the consolidated income statement and statement of cash flows from the date of acquisition.

---

8   The accounting policies shown here are illustrative and the policies disclosed should be those that are specific to the LLP.

Notes to the financial statements for the year ended 31 March 201X (*continued*)

Goodwill and other intangible assets

Goodwill arising in a business combination is the difference between the fair value of the consideration given and the fair value of the net assets acquired. It is included on the consolidated statement of financial position and is being amortised over a period of ten years. The members have been able to reliably estimate the useful economic life of this goodwill by reference to the product lifecycles of the business and the stability of the acquired business.

Trademarks are included at cost of acquisition and are depreciated over their estimated useful life of three years.

Share of profits and losses of associated undertakings

Undertakings, other than subsidiary undertakings, over which the LLP exerts significant influence, are treated as associated undertakings and are accounted for under the equity method. Under the equity method of accounting, the consolidated income statement includes the LLP's share of the associate's results. For operating profit, this is disclosed separately. For items below operating profit, the LLP's share of the relevant amounts for associates is included within the amounts for the group. In the statement of financial position, the LLP's share of the net assets of the associate is included within investments.

Fixed assets

Depreciation is provided on cost or revalued amounts in equal annual instalments over the estimated useful lives of the assets concerned. The following annual rates are used.

Freehold land and buildings –	in respect of buildings only, in equal instalments over 50 years
Short leasehold improvements –	in equal instalments over the shorter of the term to lease expiry or to the date of the next break clause
Fixtures and fittings –	15% reducing balance
Office equipment–	20% reducing balance
Motor vehicles–	25% reducing balance

Provisions for the estimated dilapidation costs at the end of a lease are built up over the final five years of a lease or to the date of the next break clause.

The LLP adopts the use of the cost model for its tangible fixed assets.

Investments

Investments are included at cost less any provision for impairment.

Notes to the financial statements for the year ended 31 March 201X (*continued*)

Professional indemnity insurance

Professional indemnity insurance premiums are charged as incurred and expensed to the income statement over the period of cover. Provision is made in respect of any uninsured excess that the group considers likely to be payable.

Taxation

The taxation payable on the profits of the limited liability partnership is the liability of the individual members. An amount is retained from each member to cover the members' estimated liability for income tax and social security contributions on their profit share. The amounts retained from allocated profits are included within 'loans and other debts due to members'.

Corporate subsidiaries of the LLP included within these consolidated financial statements are subject to UK corporation tax based on the profits of the accounting period which remains a liability of the company to which it relates (as opposed to the members). This tax charge is recorded in the profit and loss account under the heading 'tax on profit on ordinary activities' and any related liability is included as a creditor in the statement of financial position.

Deferred taxation

Deferred tax in respect of corporate subsidiaries of the LLP is provided for on a full provision basis on all timing differences which have arisen but not reversed at the reporting date. A deferred tax asset is not recognised to the extent that the transfer of economic benefit in the future is uncertain.

Members' remuneration[9]

Profits attributable to members are determined, allocated and divided between members after the year end and until that time are included as equity within members' other interests. Any drawings paid in respect of those profits are included as 'amounts due from members' within debtors.

The terms of the members' agreement require that capital be returned to a member on his or her retirement. Capital is accordingly accounted for as a liability of the LLP.

Pensions and other post retirement benefits

The defined benefit pension scheme is accounted for in accordance with Section 28 *Employee Benefits*. The scheme is funded with the assets of the scheme held separately from those of the group in separate trustee administered funds. The scheme is closed to new members.

---

9 The accounting policy reflects the particular profit sharing and capital arrangements of the LLP in this example.

Notes to the financial statements for the year ended 31 March 201X (*continued*)

Current service costs and curtailment gains are recognised in arriving at operating profit. The interest cost in respect of scheme liabilities, net of the expected return on scheme assets, is included in either 'interest receivable' or 'interest payable and similar charges'. Differences between amounts charged to the income statement and amounts funded are shown in either provisions or prepayments in the statement of financial position.

Scheme assets are measured at fair value and scheme liabilities are measured on an actuarial basis and discounted at a rate equivalent to a high quality Sterling bond with a term equivalent to the scheme liabilities. Changes in the scheme deficit arising from actuarial gains and losses are recognised immediately in other comprehensive income.

Contributions to defined contribution schemes are charged to the income statement as they become payable in accordance with the rules of the scheme.

Under the terms of the members' agreement, former members are entitled to an annuity payment based on a formula directly linked to the profits of the LLP. Provision is made in the accounts for the estimated present value of the expected future payments to that member. Amounts in respect of current members are included within 'members' remuneration charged as an expense', and amounts with respect to former members are included within 'staff costs'. The liability with respect to current members is included within 'loans and other amounts due to members' and the liability to former members is included within 'provisions for liabilities'.

Leases

Assets held under finance leases are included in fixed assets and the capital element of the related lease commitment is shown within creditors as 'obligations under finance leases'. The lease rentals are treated as consisting of capital and interest elements. The capital element is applied to reduce the outstanding obligations and the interest element is charged against profit using the effective interest method. The finance charge is allocated to each period during the term of the lease so as to produce a constant periodic rate of interest on the remaining balance of the liability.

Rental costs under operating leases are charged to the income settlement on a straight-line basis over the lease term.

Notes to the financial statements for the year ended 31 March 201X (*continued*)

Foreign currencies

Transactions denominated in a foreign currency are translated into Sterling at the rate of exchange ruling at the date of the transaction. At the reporting date, monetary assets and liabilities denominated in foreign currency are translated at the rate ruling at that date. Resulting exchange differences are dealt with in the income statement.

The income statements of overseas subsidiaries are translated at average rates of exchange for the financial year.

Exchange differences arising from the retranslation at the closing rate of the opening net investment in overseas subsidiaries and of their results for the year are taken to other comprehensive income and accumulated in equity.

Work in progress

Where work has been performed in relation to which revenue will be recognised in a later period, work in progress is recognised at the lower of cost and estimated selling price less costs to complete.

Cost comprises direct staff costs and a share of overhead appropriate to the relevant state of completion of the related project. The relevant proportion of the salaried remuneration of members is included within cost. Members' profit allocations are excluded.

Revenue recognition

Turnover represents the value of fees and commissions earned in the period, net of VAT.

Where fees for professional work have been unconditionally earned but not invoiced at the period end, these amounts are included within accrued income.

Revenue in respect of professional services is recognised by reference to the fair value of the services provided at the reporting date as a proportion of the total value of the engagement. Unbilled revenue is included within debtors as accrued income.

2   **Business combination**

On [ ], the LLP acquired the entire share capital of ABC Limited for cash consideration of £[   ]. In addition, the former shareholders of ABC Limited have been offered an enhanced allocation of profits in addition to that available to all members, which is calculated by reference to a formula linked to the financial performance of ABC Limited. An amount of £[   ], being the current best estimate of the amounts payable, is included in 'members' other interests' within loans and other debts due to members. The business combination has been accounted for using the purchase method of accounting. The amount of goodwill arising as a result of the acquisition is £[   ].

Notes to the financial statements for the year ended 31 March 201X (*continued*)

2   **Business combination** (*continued*)

The income statement of ABC Limited for the period from 1 April 201Y to the date of acquisition and for the previous financial year were as follows[10]

	1 April 201Y to date of acquisition £'000	Preceding financial year ended 31 March 201Y £'000
Turnover		
Operating profit		
Profit before tax		
Taxation		
Profit after tax		

The following table summarises the adjustments made to the book value of the major categories of assets and liabilities acquired to arrive at the fair values included in the consolidated financial statements at the date of acquisition.

	Book value £'000	Fair value adjustments £'000	Fair value £'000
Tangible fixed assets			
Current assets			
Creditors			
	———	———	———
	═══	═══	═══
Consideration			
Cash (including acquisition costs of £[ ])			
Contingent consideration		———	———
Goodwill			═══

The fair value adjustments comprise [   ]

---

10   This example assumes that the acquisition is significant to the group.

Notes to the financial statements for the year ended 31 March 201X (*continued*)

3   Turnover[11]

	201X £'000	201Y £'000
United Kingdom		
Rest of the World		
	———	———
	≡≡≡	≡≡≡

4   **Information in relation to members**

	201X Number	201Y Number
The average number of members during the year was		
	≡≡≡	≡≡≡

	£'000	£'000
[*The average members' remuneration during the year was*[12]]		
	≡≡≡	≡≡≡

	£'000	£'000
Salaried remuneration of members		
Paid under employment contract		
Paid under the terms of the LLP agreement	———	———
	≡≡≡	≡≡≡
The amount of profit attributable to the member with the largest entitlement was		
	≡≡≡	≡≡≡

Profit attributable to the member with the largest entitlement is determined by reference to [   ]

---

11 Analysis only required where there is more than one class of business or geographic segment.
12 This disclosure is optional.

Notes to the financial statements for the year ended 31 March 201X (*continued*)

5   **Employee information and staff costs**

The average number of persons (including members with contracts of employment) employed by the LLP during the year was:

	201X Number	201Y Number
Selling and distribution		
Administration		
	————	————
	════	════

	£'000	£'000
Staff costs for the above persons were:		
Wages and salaries		
Social security costs		
Pension costs		
	————	————

6   **Interest payable and similar charges**

	201X £'000	201Y £'000
Bank loans and overdrafts		
Finance leases		
Net return on pension and other retirement schemes		
	————	————
	════	════

Notes to the financial statements for the year ended 31 March 201X (*continued*)

7 Profit on ordinary activities before taxation

	201X £'000	201Y £'000
Profit on ordinary activities before taxation is stated after charging/(crediting):		
Depreciation		
– owned assets		
– assets held under finance leases		
Goodwill amortisation		
Amortisation of intangible assets		
Operating leases – property		
– other		

The analysis of auditors' remuneration is as follows:	201X £'000	201Y £'000
Fees payable to the LLP's auditors for the audit of the LLP's annual accounts		
Fees payable to the LLP's auditors and their associates for other services to the group		
Fees payable in respect of the audit of the LLP's subsidiaries pursuant to legislation		
Total audit fees		
Tax services		
Corporate finance services		
Other services		
Total non-audit fees		
Fess payable to the LLP's auditors in respect of associated pension schemes		
Audit		

Notes to the financial statements for the year ended 31 March 201X (*continued*)

8 **Tax on profit on ordinary activities**

	£	£
UK corporation tax at [ ]%		
Under/(over) provision in respect of prior years		
Deferred tax		
Share of associated undertakings tax charge		
Tax charge for the year		

The standard rate of tax for the year, based on the UK standard rate of corporation tax is [   ]%. The actual tax charge for the current and previous year is less than the standard rate for the reasons set out in the following reconciliation:

	201X £	201Y £
Profit on ordinary activities before tax		
Tax on profit on ordinary activities at the standard rate		
Factors affecting charge for the period:		
Profits of LLP not chargeable to corporation tax		
Capital allowances for period in excess of depreciation		
Expenses not allowable for tax purposes		
Other timing differences		
Adjustments to tax charge in respect of prior periods		

Notes to the financial statements for the year ended 31 March 201X (*continued*)

9   Profit of the LLP

As permitted by section 408 of the Companies Act 2006 as applied to LLPs, the LLP is exempt from presenting its own profit and loss account. The profit of the LLP for the financial year amounted to £[   ] (201Y: £[   ]).

10   Intangible fixed assets

Group

	Goodwill £'000	Trademarks £'000	Total £'000
Cost			
At 1 April 201Y			
Additions			
At 31 March 201X			
Amortisation			
At 1 April 201Y			
Charge for year			
At 31 March 201X			
Net book value			
At 31 March 201X			
At 31 March 201Y			

Notes to the financial statements for the year ended 31 March 201X (*continued*)

10 Intangible fixed assets (*continued*)

LLP

	Trademarks £'000
Cost	
At 1 April 201Y	
Additions	
	————
At 31 March 201X	
	════
Amortisation	
At 1 April 201Y	
Charge for the year	
	————
At 31 March 201X	
	════
Net book value	
At 31 March 201X	
	════
At 31 March 201Y	
	════

Notes to the financial statements for the year ended 31 March 201X (*continued*)

11   Tangible fixed assets

Group	Freehold land and buildings £'000	Short leasehold improvements £'000	Office fixtures and fittings £'000	Motor vehicles £'000	Total £'000
Cost or valuation					
At 1 April 201Y					
Additions					
Acquired with subsidiary					
Disposals					
At 31 March 201X					
Depreciation					
At 1 April 201Y					
Charge for the year					
Disposals					
At 31 March 201X					
Net book value					
At 31 March 201X					
At 31 March 201Y					

The net book value of the group's office fixtures and fittings includes £[   ] (201Y: £[   ]) in respect of assets held under finance leases.

Notes to the financial statements for the year ended 31 March 201X (*continued*)

11   Tangible fixed assets (*continued*)

LLP	Freehold land and buildings £'000	Short leasehold improvements £'000	Office fixtures and fittings £'000	Motor vehicles £'000	Total £'000
Cost or valuation					
At 1 April 201Y					
Additions					
Disposals					
At 31 March 201Y					
Depreciation					
At 1 April 201Y					
Charge for the year					
Disposals					
At 31 March 201Y					
Net book value					
At 31 March 201Y					
At 31 March 201Y					

The net book value of the LLP's office fixtures and fittings includes £[   ] (201Y: £[   ]) in respect of assets held under finance leases.

Notes to the financial statements for the year ended 31 March 201X (*continued*)

12 **Investments**

Group

	Interest in associated undertakings £'000
At 1 April 201Y	
Group share of result for the period	————
At 31 March 201X	════

LLP

	Investment in associated undertakings £'000	Investment in subsidiary undertakings £'000	Total £'000
At 1 April 201Y			
Additions			
Disposals	————	————	————
At 31 March 201X	════	════	════

The principal undertakings in which the group's interest in the ordinary share capital at the year end is more than 20% are as follows:

Subsidiary undertakings	Country of registration	Activity	Portion of ordinary shares held
ABC Limited	[ ]	[ ]	[ ]
XYZ Limited	[ ]	[ ]	[ ]
Associated undertakings			
123 Limited	[ ]	[ ]	[ ]

Notes to the financial statements for the year ended 31 March 201X (*continued*)

13 Work in progress

	Group		LLP	
	201X	201Y	201X	201Y
	£'000	£'000	£'000	£'000
Work in progress				

14 Debtors

	Group		LLP	
	201X	201Y	201X	201Y
	£'000	£'000	£'000	£'000
Trade debtors				
Amounts owed by subsidiary undertakings				
Amounts owed by associates				
Amounts due from members				
Other debtors				
Prepayments and accrued income				

15 Creditors: amounts falling due within one year

	Group		LLP	
	201X	201Y	201X	201Y
	£'000	£'000	£'000	£'000
Bank loans and overdrafts				
Obligations under finance leases				
Trade creditors				
Amounts owed to subsidiary undertakings				
Corporation tax				
Other taxation and social security				
[Retirement benefits due to former members][13]				
Other creditors				
Accruals and deferred income				

---

13 Where the amount of retirement benefits to former members is fixed it should be included within creditors (split between due within and due after one year) rather than be included within provisions.

Notes to the financial statements for the year ended 31 March 201X (*continued*)

16 **Creditors:** amounts falling due after more than one year

	Group		LLP	
	201X	201Y	201X	201Y
	£	£	£	£
Bank loans and overdrafts				
Obligations under finance leases				
Retirement benefits due to former members	_____	_____	_____	_____
	======	======	======	======

17 **Borrowings**

	Group		LLP	
	201X	201Y	201X	201Y
	£	£	£	£
Bank overdraft				
Bank loan				
(secured [ ]% above LIBOR)	_____	_____	_____	_____
Obligations under finance leases	_____	_____	_____	_____
	======	======	======	======
Due within one year				
Due after one year	_____	_____	_____	_____
	======	======	======	======
Maturity analysis				
Within one year or on demand				
More than one year but less than two years				
More than two years but not less than five years				
More than five years	_____	_____	_____	_____
	======	======	======	======

[Bank loans and overdrafts are secured by fixed and floating charges over the assets of the LLP and its subsidiary undertakings].

Notes to the financial statements for the year ended 31 March 201X (*continued*)

18 **Provisions for liabilities**

Group and LLP

	Post-retirement payments to former members £'000	Provisions for dilapidations £'000	Total £'000
At 1 April 201Y			
Subsidiary acquired			
Income statement charge			
Amounts utilised			
	———	———	———
At 31 March 201X			
	═══	═══	═══

Notes to the financial statements for the year ended 31 March 201X *(continued)*

19 Reconciliation of members' interests – Group

	EQUITY Members' Other interests				DEBT Loans and other debts due to members less any amounts due from members in debtors			TOTAL MEMBERS' INTERESTS
	Members' capital (classified as equity) £'000	Revaluation reserve £'000	Other reserves £'000	Total £'000	Members' capital (classified as debt) £'000	Other amounts £'000	Total £'000	Total £'000
Amounts due to members								
Amounts due from members								
Members' interests at 1 April 201Y								
Members' remuneration charged as an expense								
Profit for the financial year available for discretionary division among members								
Members' interests after profit for the year								
Other divisions of profits/losses								
Exchange movements								
Surplus arising on revaluation of fixed assets								
Introduced by members								
Repayments of capital								
Repayment of debt								
Drawings								
Other movements								
Amounts due to members								
Amounts due from members								
Members' interests at 31 March 201X								

Amounts due to members will rank pari pasu with other unsecured creditors in the event of a winding up. In such a circumstance, the members have subordinated their rights to payments of amounts owed to them in preference to external creditors.

Notes to the financial statements for the year ended 31 March 201X (continued)

19 Reconciliation of members' interests – LLP

| | DEBT | | | | EQUITY | | | TOTAL |
| | Members' other interests | | | | | Loans and other debts due to members less any amounts due from members in debtors | | |
	Members' capital (classified as equity) £'000	Revaluation reserve £'000	Other reserves £'000	Total £'000	Members' capital (classified as debt) £'000	Other amounts £'000	Total £'000	MEMBERS' INTERESTS Total £'000
Amounts due to members								
Amounts due from members								
Members' interests at 1 April 201Y								
Members' remuneration charged as an expense								
Profit for the financial year available for discretionary division among members								
Members' interests after profit for the year								
Other divisions of profits/losses								
Surplus arising on revaluation of fixed assets								
Introduced by members								
Repayments of capital								
Repayment of debt								
Drawings								
Other movements								
Amounts due to members								
Amounts due from members								
Members' interests at 31 March 201X								

Notes to the financial statements for the year ended 31 March 201X (*continued*)

20 Pension costs

Section 28 requires considerable disclosures with respect to pension costs relating to defined benefit schemes. Where relevant, reference should be had to the standard.

21 Operating lease commitments

At 31 March 201X the LLP had annual commitments under non-cancellable operating leases as follows:

	201X	201Y	201X	201Y
	Property £'000	Property £'000	Other £'000	Other £'000
For leases expiring:				
Within one year				
Between two and five years				
In excess of five years				

22 Capital commitments

	201X £	201Y £
Contracted but not provided for		

23 Contingent liabilities

The LLP has guaranteed the borrowings of individual members taken out in order to fund their capital interests in the LLP. At 31 March 201X the total amount guaranteed was £[   ]. 201Y £[   ].

24 Related party transactions

The LLP has taken advantage of the exemption in Section 33 *Related Party Disclosures* from reporting related party transactions with its wholly-owned subsidiaries.

[Related party transactions of the group and the parent (except for those with its wholly-owned subsidiary) should be disclosed here]

Notes to the financial statements for the year ended 31 March 201X (*continued*)

25 **Controlling party**

In the opinion of the members there is no controlling party.

26 **Events after the reporting date**

[Material non-adjusting events after the reporting date should be disclosed in accordance with Section 32 *Events after the End of the Reporting Period.*]

LLP pro forma financial statements – single LLP

XYZ LLP

REPORT AND FINANCIAL STATEMENTS

FOR THE YEAR ENDED

31 MARCH 201X

NOTE – in this example all profits require the approval of members before they are divided and division occurs after the year end. Capital is returned to members on their retirement.

These illustrative financial statements use the terminology found in FRS 102 (eg 'statement of financial position' instead of 'balance sheet'). Alternative titles can be used for the financial statements according to paragraph 3.22 of FRS 102 provided they are not misleading, hence the term 'balance sheet' and 'profit and loss account' may still be used.

Contents

Designated members and advisers

Designated members
A Designate
B Smith
C Jones

Registered office
1 The Long Street
Longtown
Longshire
LL1 1XY

Bankers
Big Bank plc
85 The Long Street
Longtown
Longshire
LL1 1YZ

Auditors
Stuart & Wilson LLP
5 The Short Street
Longtown
Longshire
LL2 1AB

Solicitors
Wright & Prentice LLP
25 The Short Street
Longtown
Longshire
LL2 1BC

Members' report

The members present their report and the financial statements for the year ended 31 March 201X.

Activities

The principal activity of the LLP continues to be [   ].

Review of business

[The SORP requires disclosure of the principal activities of the LLP and its subsidiary undertakings, indicating any significant changes during the year. Whilst there are no statutory requirements with respect to additional information that might be included here, the members may wish to include further information about the performance of the LLP in support of the financial disclosures.]

Designated members

The following were designated members during the year:

A Designate

B Smith

C Jones

Members' drawings and the subscription and repayment of members' capital

During the year members receive monthly drawings representing payments on account of profits which may be allocated to them. The amount of such drawings is set at the beginning of each financial year, taking into account the anticipated cash needs of the LLP and may be reclaimed from members until such time as profits have been allocated to them.

Profits are determined, allocated and divided between members after the finalisation of the accounts. Prior to the allocation of profits and their division between members, drawings are included as 'amounts due from members' within debtors. Unallocated profits are included within equity as 'members' other interests'.

Capital requirements are determined by the designated members and are reviewed at least annually. All members are required to subscribe a proportion of that capital, with the amounts being determined by reference to experience.

On retirement, capital is repaid to members.

Auditors

[A resolution to reappoint Stuart & Wilson LLP as auditors will be proposed at the next members' meeting.] Or [Stuart & Wilson LLP have indicated their willingness to be reappointed and the members have made appropriate arrangements for them to be deemed reappointed as auditors].

Approved by the members

and signed on their behalf

A Designate

Designated member

Statement of members' responsibilities in respect of the financial statements[1]

The members are responsible for preparing the Annual Report and the financial statements in accordance with applicable law and regulations.

The Limited Liability Partnerships Regulations 2008 requires the members to prepare financial statements for each financial year which give a true and fair view of the state of affairs of the LLP and of the profit or loss of the LLP for that period in accordance with United Kingdom Generally Accepted Accounting Practice. In preparing these financial statements, the members are required to:

- select suitable accounting policies and then apply them consistently;

- make judgements and estimates that are reasonable and prudent;

- state whether applicable UK Accounting Standards have been followed, subject to any material departure disclosed and explained in the financial statements;

- prepare the accounts on the going concern basis unless it is inappropriate to presume that the LLP will continue in business.

The members are responsible for keeping adequate accounting records which disclose with reasonable accuracy at any time the financial position of the LLP and to enable them to ensure that the accounts comply with the Limited Liability Partnerships Regulations. They are also responsible for safeguarding the assets of the LLP and thence for taking reasonable steps for the prevention and detection of fraud and other irregularities.

These responsibilities are exercised by the designated members on behalf of the members.

Disclosure of information to the auditor

Each of the persons who is a member at the date of approval of this report confirms that:

- so far as the member is aware, there is no relevant audit information of which the auditor is unaware; and

- the member has taken all the steps that he/she ought to have taken as a member in order to make himself/herself aware of any relevant audit information and to establish that the auditor is aware of that information.

The following is an illustrative unqualified audit report

---

1 This statement can alternatively be included within the members' report and is only required where the LLP is subject to audit.

Independent auditors' report to the members of XYZ LLP

We have audited the financial statements of XYZ LLP (the 'LLP') for the year-ended 31 March 201X which comprise the income statement, statement of financial position, statement of cash flows and related notes. The financial reporting framework that has been applied in their preparation is applicable law and United Kingdom Accounting Standards (United Kingdom Generally Accepted Accounting Practice).

This report is made solely to the LLP's members, as a body, in accordance with Chapter 3 of Part 16 of the Companies Act 2006, as applied to limited liability partnerships by the Limited Liability Partnerships (Accounts and Audit) (Application of Companies Act 2006) Regulations 2008. Our audit work has been undertaken so that we might state to the LLP's members those matters we are required to state to them in an auditor's report and for no other purpose. To the fullest extent permitted by law, we do not accept or assume responsibility to anyone other than the LLP and the LLP's members as a body, for our audit work, for this report, or for the opinions we have formed.

Respective responsibilities of members and auditor

As explained more fully in the Members' Responsibilities Statement, the members are responsible for the preparation of the financial statements and for being satisfied that they give a true and fair view. Our responsibility is to audit and express an opinion on the financial statements in accordance with applicable law and International Standards on Auditing (UK and Ireland). Those standards require us to comply with the Auditing Practices Board's Ethical Standards for Auditors.[2]

Scope of the audit of the financial statements

An audit involves obtaining evidence about the amounts and disclosures in the financial statements sufficient to give reasonable assurance that the financial statements are free from material misstatement, whether caused by fraud or error. This includes an assessment of: whether the accounting policies are appropriate to the LLP and have been consistently applied and adequately disclosed; the reasonableness of significant accounting estimates made by the members; and the overall presentation of the financial statements. In addition, we read all the financial and non-financial information in the annual report to identify material inconsistencies with the audited financial statements. If we become aware of any apparent material misstatements or inconsistencies we consider the implications for our report.

---

2 The Auditing Practices Board is no longer in existence and some firms refer to the Financial Reporting Council (FRC). It is preferable to follow the guidance in the relevant guidance issued by the FRC on the wording in the audit report.

Opinion on financial statements

In our opinion the financial statements:

- give a true and fair view of the state of the LLP's affairs as at 31 March 201X and of its profit for the year then ended;

- have been properly prepared in accordance with United Kingdom Generally Accepted Accounting Practice; and

- have been prepared in accordance with the requirements of the Companies Act 2006 as applied to limited liability partnerships.

Matters on which we are required to report by exception

We have nothing to report in respect of the following matters where the Companies Act 2006 as applied to limited liability partnerships requires us to report to you if, in our opinion:

- adequate accounting records have not been kept by the LLP, or returns adequate for our audit have not been received from branches not visited by us; or

- the LLPs financial statements are not in agreement with the accounting records and returns; or

- we have not received all the information and explanations we require for our audit.

J J Smith (Senior Statutory Auditor)

For and on behalf of Stuart & Wilson LLP
5 The Short Street
Longtown
Longshire
LL2 1AB

[Insert date of report]

Income statement for the year ended 31 March 201X

	Notes	201X		201Y
		£'000	£'000	£'000
Turnover	2			
Operating costs				
Staff costs	4			
Depreciation and other amounts written off tangible fixed assets				
Other operating charges				
Other operating income				
Operating profit				
Interest receivable and similar income				
Interest payable and similar charges	5			
Profit for the financial year before members' remuneration and profit shares	6			
Members' remuneration charged as an expense	3			
Retained profit for the financial year available for discretionary division among members[3]	3			

All of the LLP's operations are classed as continuing. There were no gains or losses in either year other than those included in the above income statement.

---

3   In circumstances where all profits are automatically divided before the year end this amount will be zero.

Registered number OC354321

Statement of financial position as at 31 March 201X

	Notes	201X £'000	201Y £'000
Fixed assets			
Intangible assets	7		
Tangible assets	8		
Current assets			
Work in progress	9		
Debtors	10		
Cash at bank and in hand			
Creditors: amounts falling due within one year	11		
Net current assets/(liabilities)			
Total assets less current liabilities			
Creditors: amounts falling due after more than one year	12		
Provisions for liabilities	14		
NET ASSETS ATTRIBUTABLE TO MEMBERS			

Statement of financial position as at 31 March 201X (*continued*)

	Notes	201X £'000	201Y £'000
REPRESENTED BY			
Loans and other debts due to members within one year			
Members' capital classified as a liability			
Other amounts		___	___
		___	___
Equity			
Members' other interests – other reserves classified as equity			
		___	___
		___	___
Total members' interests		___	___
Amounts due from members			
Loans and other debts due to members			
Members' other interests			
		___	___
		___	___

The financial statements were approved by the members on [   ] and were signed on its behalf by:

A Designate

Designated member

Statement of cash flows for the year ended 31 March 201X

	Notes	201X £'000	201Y £'000
Net cash inflow/(outflow) from operating activities	a		
		———	———
Cash flows from investing activities			
Interest received			
Purchase of intangible assets			
Purchase of property, plant and equipment			
Proceeds from sale of property, plant and equipment		———	———
Net cash inflow/(outflow) from investing activities			
		———	———
Transactions with members and former members			
Drawings and distributions to members			
Payments to former members			
Capital contributions by members			
Capital repayments to members		———	———
Net cash inflow/(outflow) from transactions with members and former members			
		———	———

268

Statement of cash flows for the year ended 31 March 201X (*continued*)

	Notes	201X £'000	201Y £'000
Cash flows from financing activities			
New long-term loans			
Repayment of long-term loans			
Repayment of capital element of finance lease rentals			
Net cash inflow/(outflow) from financing activities			
Increase/(decrease) in cash in the year	b		

Notes to the statement of cash flows

a	Reconciliation of operating profit/(loss) to net cash inflow/(outflow) from operating activities	201X £'000	201Y £'000
	Operating profit/(loss)		
	Depreciation		
	Amortisation of intangible assets		
	Loss/(profit) on sale of tangible fixed assets		
	Decrease/(increase) in work in progress		
	Decrease/(increase) in debtors		
	Increase/(decrease) in creditors		
	Increase/(decrease) in provisions		
	Interest paid		
	Net cash inflow/(outflow) from operating activities		

b Cash and cash equivalents

Cash at bank and in hand
Less bank overdraft

Notes to the financial statements for the year ended 31 March 201X

1   **Accounting policies[4]**

The accounts have been prepared in accordance with FRS 102 *The Financial Reporting Standard applicable in the UK and Republic of Ireland* and the requirements of the Statement of Recommended Practice 'Accounting by Limited Liability Partnerships'. A summary of the significant accounting policies adopted are described below.

Basis of accounting

The accounts have been prepared under the historical cost convention [Where relevant the members should include appropriate disclosure about their reasons for adopting the going concern basis and any material uncertainties that cast significant doubt over the LLP's ability to continue as a going concern]

Intangible assets

Trademarks are included at cost of acquisition and are depreciated over their estimated useful life of three years.

Fixed assets

Depreciation is provided on cost in equal annual instalments over the estimated useful lives of the assets concerned. The following annual rates are used.

Freehold land and buildings –	in respect of buildings only, in equal instalments over 50 years
Short leasehold improvements –	in equal instalments over the shorter of the term to lease expiry or to the date of the next break clause
Fixtures and fittings –	15% reducing balance
Office equipment –	20% reducing balance
Motor vehicles –	25% reducing balance

Provisions for the estimated dilapidation costs at the end of a lease are built up over the final five years of a lease or to the date of the next break clause.

The LLP adopts the use of the cost model for all its tangible fixed assets.

Investments

Investments are included at cost less any provision for impairment

---

4   The accounting policies shown here are illustrative and the policies disclosed should be those that are specific to the LLP.

Notes to the financial statements for the year ended 31 March 201X (*continued*)

Professional indemnity insurance

Professional indemnity insurance premiums are charged as incurred and expensed to the income statement over the period of cover. Provision is made in respect of any uninsured excess that the LLP considers likely to be payable.

Taxation

The taxation payable on the profits of the limited liability partnership is the liability of the individual members. An amount is retained from each member to cover the members' estimated liability for income tax and social security contributions on their profit share. The amounts retained from allocated profits are included within 'loans and other debts due to members'.

Members' remuneration[5]

Profits attributable to members are determined, allocated and divided between members after the year end and until that time are included as equity within members' other interests. Any drawings paid in respect of those profits are included as 'amounts due from members' within debtors.

The terms of the members' agreement require that capital be returned to a member on his or her retirement. Capital is accordingly accounted for as a liability of the LLP.

Pensions and other post-retirement benefits

Contributions to defined contribution schemes are charged to the income statement as they become payable in accordance with the rules of the scheme.

Under the terms of the members' agreement, former members are entitled to an annuity payment based on a formula directly linked to the profits of the LLP. Provision is made in the financial statements for the estimated present value of the expected future payments to that member. Amounts in respect of current members are included within 'members' remuneration charged as an expense', and amounts with respect to former members are included within 'staff costs'. The liability with respect to current members is included within 'loans and other amounts due to members' and the liability to former members is included within 'provisions for liabilities'.

---

5 The accounting policy reflects the particular profit sharing and capital arrangements of the LLP in this example.

Notes to the financial statements for the year ended 31 March 201X (*continued*)

Leases

Assets held under finance leases are included in fixed assets and the capital element of the related lease commitment is shown within creditors as 'obligations under finance leases'. The lease rentals are treated as consisting of capital and interest elements. The capital element is applied to reduce the outstanding obligations and the interest element is charged against profit using the effective interest method. The finance charge is allocated to each period during the term of the lease so as to produce a constant periodic rate of interest on the remaining balance of the liability.

Rental costs under operating leases are charged to the income statement on a straight-line basis over the lease term.

Foreign currencies

Transactions denominated in a foreign currency are translated into Sterling at the rate of exchange ruling at the date of the transaction. At the reporting date, monetary assets and liabilities denominated in foreign currency are translated at the rate ruling at that date. Resulting exchange differences are dealt with in the income statement.

Work in progress

Where work has been performed in relation to which revenue will be recognised in a later period, work in progress is recognised at the lower of cost and estimated selling price less costs to complete.

Cost comprises direct staff costs and a share of overhead appropriate to the relevant state of completion of the related project. The relevant proportion of the salaried remuneration of members is included within cost. Members' profit allocations are excluded.

Revenue recognition

Turnover represents the value of fees and commissions earned in the period, net of VAT.

Where fees for professional work have been unconditionally earned but not invoiced at the reporting date, these amounts are included within accrued income.

Revenue in respect of professional services is recognised by reference to the fair value of the services provided at the reporting date as a proportion of the total value of the engagement. Unbilled revenue is included within debtors as accrued income.

Notes to the financial statements for the year ended 31 March 201X (*continued*)

2   **Turnover**[6]

	201X £'000	201Y £'000
United Kingdom		
Rest of the World		

3   **Information in relation to members**

	201X Number	201Y Number
The average number of members during the year was		

	£'000	£'000
[*The average members' remuneration during the year was*[7]]		

	£'000	£'000
Salaried remuneration of members		
Paid under employment contract		
Paid under the terms of the LLP agreement		

The amount of profit attributable to the member with the largest entitlement was

Profit attributable to the member with the largest entitlement is determined by reference to [   ]

---

6   Analysis only required where there is more than one class of business or geographic segment. Small LLPs are required only to disclose the percentage overseas turnover comprises to total turnover

7   This disclosure is optional.

Notes to the financial statements for the year ended 31 March 201X (*continued*)

4   **Employee information and staff costs**

The average number of persons (including members with contracts of employment) employed by the LLP during the year was:

	201X Number	201Y Number
Selling and distribution		
Administration		

	£'000	£'000
Staff costs for the above persons were:		
Wages and salaries		
Social security costs		
Pension costs		

5   **Interest payable and similar charges**

	201X £'000	201Y £'000
Bank loans and overdrafts		
Finance leases		

Notes to the financial statements for the year ended 31 March 201X (*continued*)

6   **Profit for the financial year before members' remuneration and profit shares**

	£'000	£'000
Profit for the financial year before members' remuneration and profit shares is stated after charging/(crediting):		
Depreciation		
– owned assets		
– assets held under finance leases		
Amortisation of intangible assets		
Operating leases – property		
– other		

The analysis of auditors' remuneration is as follows:	201X	201Y
	£'000	£'000
Fees payable to the LLP's auditors for the audit of the LLP's annual accounts		
Fees payable to the LLP's auditors and their associates for other services to the LLP		
Total audit fees		
Tax services		
Corporate finance services		
Other services		
Total non-audit fees		

Notes to the financial statements for the year ended 31 March 201X (*continued*)

7 **Intangible fixed assets**

	Trademarks £'000
Cost	
At 1 April 201Y	
Additions	
	————
At 31 March 201X	
	════
Amortisation	
At 1 April 201Y	
Charge for the year	
	————
At 31 March 201X	
	════
Net book value	
At 31 March 201X	
	════
At 31 March 201Y	
	════

Notes to the financial statements for the year ended 31 March 201X (*continued*)

8   **Tangible fixed assets**

	Freehold land and buildings £'000	Short leasehold improvements £'000	Office fixtures and fittings £'000	Motor vehicles £'000	Total £'000
Cost or valuation					
At 1 April 201Y					
Additions					
Disposals					
At 31 March 201X					
Depreciation					
At 1 April 200Y					
Charge for the year					
Disposals					
At 31 March 201X					
Net book value					
At 31 March 201X					
At 31 March 201Y					

The net book value of the LLP's office fixtures and fittings includes £[   ] (201Y: £[   ]) in respect of assets held under finance leases.

Notes to the financial statements for the year ended 31 March 201X (*continued*)

9   Work in progress

	201X £'000	201Y £'000
Work in progress		
	══════	══════

10   Debtors

	201X £'000	201Y £'000
Trade debtors		
Amounts due from members		
Other debtors		
Prepayments and accrued income		
	──────	──────
	══════	══════

11   Creditors: amounts falling due within one year

	201X £'000	201Y £'000
Bank loans and overdrafts		
Obligations under finance leases		
Trade creditors		
Other taxation and social security		
[Retirement benefits due to former members][8]		
Other creditors		
Accruals and deferred income		
	──────	──────
	══════	══════

---

[8]   Where the amount of retirement benefits to former members is fixed it should be included within creditors (split between due within and due after one year) rather than provisions

Notes to the financial statements for the year ended 31 March 201X (*continued*)

12   **Creditors:** amounts falling due after more than one year

	LLP	
	201X	201Y
	£	£
Bank loans and overdrafts		
Obligations under finance leases		
[Retirement benefits due to former members][8]		

13   **Borrowings**

	201X	201Y
	£	£
Bank overdraft		
Bank loan		
(secured [ ]% above LIBOR)		
Obligations under finance leases		
Due within one year		
Due after one year		
Maturity analysis		
Within one year or on demand		
More than one year but less than two years		
More than two years but not less than five years		
More than five years		

[Bank loans and overdrafts are secured by fixed and floating charges over the assets of the LLP].

Notes to the financial statements for the year ended 31 March 201X (*continued*)

14 Provisions for liabilities

	Post-retirement payments to former members £'000	Provisions for dilapidations £'000	Total £'000
At 1 April 201Y			
Profit and loss account charge			
Amounts utilised			
At 31 March 201X			

Notes to the financial statements for the year ended 31 March 201X (*continued*)

15 Reconciliation of members' interests

	EQUITY Members' other interests			DEBT Loans and other debts due to members less any amounts due from members in debtors			TOTAL MEMBERS' INTERESTS
	Members' capital (classified as equity) £'000	Other reserves £'000	Total £'000	Members' capital (classified as debt) £'000	Other amounts £'000	Total £'000	Total £'000
Amounts due to members							
Amounts due from members							
Members' interests at 1 April 201Y							
Members' remuneration charged as an expense							
Profit for the financial year available for discretionary division among members							
Members' interests after profit for the year							
Other divisions of profits/losses							
Introduced by members							
Repayments of capital							
Repayment of debt							
Drawings							
Other movements							
Amounts due to members							
Amounts due from members							
Members' interests at 31 March 201X							

Notes to the financial statements for the year ended 31 March 201X (*continued*)

16   **Operating lease commitments**

At 31 March 201X the LLP had annual commitments under non-cancellable operating leases as follows:

	201X Property £'000	201Y Property £'000	201X Other £'000	201Y Other £'000
For leases expiring:				
Within one year				
Between two and five years				
In excess of five years				

17   **Capital commitments**

	201X £	201Y £
Contracted but not provided for		

18   **Contingent liabilities**

The LLP has guaranteed the borrowings of individual members taken out in order to fund their capital interests in the LLP. At 31 March 201X the total amount guaranteed was £[   ]. 201Y £[   ].

19   **Related party transactions**

There were no related party transactions as defined by Section 33 *Related Party Disclosures* during the year.

20   **Controlling party**

In the opinion of the members there is no controlling party.

21   **Events after the reporting date**

[Material non-adjusting events after the reporting date should be disclosed in accordance with Section 32 *Events after the Reporting Period*].

Index

[All references are to paragraph number and appendices]

Accounts and Audit of Limited Liability Partnerships

Accounts and Audit of Limited Liability Partnerships

Fourth edition

Steve Collings FMAAT FCCA

Bloomsbury Professional

Published by
Bloomsbury Professional Ltd, Maxwelton House, 41–43 Boltro Road,
Haywards Heath, West Sussex, RH16 1BJ

© Bloomsbury Professional Ltd 2014

Bloomsbury Professional is an imprint of Bloomsbury Publishing Plc

British Library Cataloguing-in-Publication Data.
A catalogue record for this book is available from the British Library.

ISBN 978 1 84766 991 9

Typeset by Phoenix Photosetting, Chatham, Kent
Printed and bound in Great Britain by CPI Group (UK) Ltd, Croydon, CR0 4YY

Preface

The number of Limited Liability Partnerships (LLPs) that have emerged since the Limited Liability Partnerships Act 2000 came into force in 2001 has increased significantly over the years. This is testament to the flexibility which is offered by the structure of LLPs by maintaining a traditional partnership existence in the ways that profits are shared among members but also offering members the concept of *Limited Liability* which is traditionally afforded to Limited companies; the price to be paid, of course, for such a privilege is the requirement to file, on public record, the LLPs financial statements at Companies House.

Accounting in the United Kingdom and Republic of Ireland is changing extensively – in fact the most significant change in a generation is set to affect the ways in which LLPs will report financial information. The changes come in the form of FRS 102 *The Financial Reporting Standard applicable in the UK and Republic of Ireland* which is mandatory for accounting periods commencing on or after 1 January 2015, although earlier adoption of the standard is permissible.

As a direct consequence of the introduction of FRS 102, the Statement of Recommended Practice (SORP) relating to LLPs *Accounting for Limited Liability Partnerships* had to be revised and this was issued on 15 July 2014. The impact of FRS 102 on all companies and LLPs that fall under its scope can, in certain situations, be fairly significant, affecting many accounting policies and recognition and measurement issues for the financial statements.

It was not surprising that the UK and Republic of Ireland were to experience such a wholesale change in Generally Accepted Accounting Practice (GAAP) – such a project was initiated by the previously known Accounting Standards Board (ASB) several years ago with the intention that the UK and Republic of Ireland would always report under an international-based financial reporting framework. This was evidenced by the ASB's constant efforts to converge UK GAAP to international equivalents and the LLP SORP was amended in May 2006 to reflect changes in GAAP in respect of financial instruments.

In this fourth edition, I have incorporated the specific accounting issues brought about by FRS 102 and included practical examples where considered appropriate to 'bring to life' the theory inherent in accounting standards. FRS 102 essentially modernises the way in which all entities under its scope will account for items, although many of the 'traditional' accounting practices which have been established in the UK and Republic of Ireland for several years have also been carried over into the new UK GAAP (for example valuation of assets under the revaluation model and the option to capitalise borrowing costs). This fourth edition also incorporates new 'Signposts' at the start of each chapter so as to direct users to the relevant sections of the chapter that they need for easier navigation.

Special thanks go to Sarah Laing CTA and David Whiscombe who wrote the chapter on taxation.

I sincerely hope that this book will prove to be a useful reference guide to those dealing with the accounting and auditing issues relating to LLPs and feedback is welcomed via the publishers for future editions of this book.

Steve Collings, FMAAT FCCA
Audit and Technical Director
Leavitt Walmsley Associates Ltd

August 2014

Contents

Contents

Abbreviations and definitions

ASB	=	Accounting Standards Board
CA 06	=	Companies Act 2006
CCAB	=	Consultative Committee of Accountancy Bodies
EEA	=	European Economic Area
EU	=	European Union
FRC	=	Financial Reporting Council
FRS	=	Financial Reporting Standard (issued by the ASB)
FRSSE	=	Financial Reporting Standard for Smaller Entities
HMRC	=	HM Revenue & Customs
IFRS	=	International Financial Reporting Standard
IGU	=	Income-generating unit
LLP	=	Limited liability partnership
LLPA	=	Limited Liability Partnerships Act 2000
LLPAAR 2008	=	Limited Liability Partnerships (Accounts and Audit) (Application of Companies Act 2006) Regulations 2008
LLP 2001	=	Limited Liability Partnerships Regulations 2001
LMLLPR 2008	=	Large and Medium-sized Limited Liability Partnerships (Accounts) Regulations 2008
SLLPR 2008	=	Small Limited Liability Partnerships (Accounts) Regulations 2008
SORP	=	Statement of Recommended Practice Accounting by Limited Liability Partnerships
SSAP	=	Statement of Standard Accounting Practice (issued by the predecessor body to the ASB)
STRGL	=	Statement of total recognised gains and losses
UITF	=	Urgent Issues Task Force (assists the ASB in providing guidance on specific accounting areas; produces UITF Abstracts)

Table of Statutes

Table of Statutory Instruments